用英语说中国
INTRODUCE CHINA IN ENGLISH

Scenic Spots

主编	龚卫红	浩 瀚		
编委	齐 齐	宋美盈	王亚彬	李 硕
	李庆磊	刘雷雷	马 兰	蔡 丹
	姚 青	李林德	潘永亮	王应铜
	赵秀丽	尹晓洁	韩 磊	刘梓红
	徐 萍	马 迅	徐光伟	赵修臣
	李明亚	陈伟华	李 红	
策划	北京浩瀚英语研究所			

科学技术文献出版社

Scientific and Technical Documents Publishing House

北 京

(京)新登字 130 号

内 容 简 介

  中国是屹立于世界东方的文明古国,拥有十分丰厚的文化遗产和壮丽多姿的自然风光。仅世界遗产,中国就有 29 处,占世界第三位。本书按中国的地域特点选材,精心挑选了风采各异的 300 多处景区,着重介绍华夏大地著名景点、名胜。全书共分为北京六大景点和东北、华北、西北、西南、华东、华中、华南、港澳台地区九大部分。无论是名山大川、历史古迹,还是人文景观都有系统介绍。全面深入地展现了中华名胜的自然之美、文化之美和自然与文化结合之美。

  科学技术文献出版社是国家科学技术部系统唯一一家中央级综合性科技出版机构,我们所有的努力都是为了使您增长知识和才干。

前言 Foreword

  中国疆域辽阔、地大物博、山河壮美,是一个旅游资源大国。随着国民经济的发展,我国的旅游业取得了辉煌的业绩。为了向世人更多地展现中华名胜的魅力,我们特别推出了《用英语说中国——旅游亮点》这本书。

  全书分为:

  北京六大景点、东北、华北、西北、西南、华东、华中、华南、港澳台地区九大部分。全方位地介绍中国各大名景,体现中国特色。

  本书内容的编排由:流畅精句、精彩片段、文化链接、妙词连珠四大部分组成,从单词到句子,从句子到对话,层层递进,逐步深入。

流畅精句:选择了贴切、简单实用的语句,采用英汉对照的形式,让你脱口而出。

精彩片段:采用典型的具有代表性文章段落,介绍详细具体,一目了然,可让读者获得英语学习和景点了解的双重丰收。

文化链接:与本单元相关的趣味性知识链接,让大家在学习中寻找快乐。

妙词连珠:鲜活、亮丽词汇,为大家脱口而出打下坚实基础。

  用英语说中国,不仅让中国走向世界,也让世界更多地了解中国。

目 录

Chapter 1   The Six Scenic Spots in Beijing   北京六大景点

Unit 1   Tian'anmen
           天安门 ··· [1]

Unit 2   The Palace Museum
           故宫 ··· [7]

Unit 3   The Great Wall
           长城 ··· [14]

Unit 4   The Summer Palace
           颐和园 ··· [22]

Unit 5   The Temple of Heaven
           天坛 ··· [29]

Unit 6   The Thirteen Ming Tombs
           十三陵 ··· [39]

Chapter 2   Northeast China   东北

Unit 1   Heilongjiang Province
           黑龙江省 ··· [46]

Unit 2   Jilin Province
           吉林省 ··· [52]

Unit 3   Liaoning Province
           辽宁省 ··· [58]

Chapter 3
North China 华北

Unit 1　Hebei Province
　　　　河北省 ················· [65]
Unit 2　Shanxi Province
　　　　山西省 ················· [74]
Unit 3　Inner Mongolia Autonomous
　　　　Region
　　　　内蒙古自治区 ·········· [86]
Unit 4　Tianjin Municipality
　　　　天津市 ················· [91]

Chapter 4
Northwest China 西北

Unit 1　Shaanxi Province
　　　　陕西省 ················· [97]
Unit 2　Qinghai Province
　　　　青海省 ················· [105]
Unit 3　Gansu Province
　　　　甘肃省 ················· [110]
Unit 4　Ningxia Hui Autonomous
　　　　Region
　　　　宁夏回族自治区 ········ [119]
Unit 5　Xinjiang Uygur Autonomous
　　　　Region
　　　　新疆维吾尔族自治区 ···· [124]

Chapter 5　Southwest China　西南

Unit 1	Sichuan Province 四川省	[131]
Unit 2	Guizhou Province 贵州省	[141]
Unit 3	Yunnan Province 云南省	[148]
Unit 4	Tibet Autonomous Region 西藏自治区	[156]
Unit 5	Chongqing Municipality 重庆市	[166]

Chapter 6　East Chna　华东

Unit 1	Shandong Province 山东省	[173]
Unit 2	Jiangsu Province 江苏省	[180]
Unit 3	Zhejiang Province 浙江省	[187]
Unit 4	Anhui Province 安徽省	[194]
Unit 5	Fujian Province 福建省	[200]
Unit 6	Jiangxi Province 江西省	[206]
Unit 7	Shanghai Municipality 上海市	[212]

用英语说中国——旅游亮点
Introduce China in English—Scenic Spots

Chapter 7
Central China 华中

Unit 1 Henan Province
        河南省 ·· [218]
Unit 2 Hubei Province
        湖北省 ·· [226]
Unit 3 Hunan Province
        湖南省 ·· [234]

Chapter 8
South China 华南

Unit 1 Guangdong Province
        广东省 ·· [242]
Unit 2 Guangxi Zhuang Autonomous
        Region
        广西壮族自治区 ·· [251]
Unit 3 Hainan Province
        海南省 ·· [259]

Chapter 9
Hong Kong, Macao and Taiwan Province 港澳台地区

Unit 1 Hong Kong SAR
        香港特别行政区 ·· [264]
Unit 2 Macao SAR
        澳门特别行政区 ·· [272]
Unit 3 Taiwan Province
        台湾省 ·· [279]

1 北京六大景点
The Six Scenic Spots in Beijing

Unit 1 天安门 Tian'anmen

Key Sentences 流畅精句

1. Tian'anmen in English means the Gate of Heavenly Peace. It was first built in 1417 in the Ming Dynasty (1368-1644). It served as an entrance to the Imperial Palace.
   天安门的含义是"天上平安之门"。它始建于明朝（1368-1644）时的1417年。它是皇宫的入口处。
2. Tian'anmen is in the centre of Beijing.
   天安门位于北京的中心。
3. Tian'anmen Square is large enough to hold one million people for assembly or celebration, so it is the largest city-centre square in the world.
   天安门广场，能容纳百万人举行集会和庆典，它是世界上最大的城市中心广场。
4. Tian'anmen Square has witnessed many important historical events, such as the May 4th Movement, the ceremony of the founding of the People's Republic of China.

天安门广场经历了许多重大的历史事件,如五四运动和中华人民共和国成立的庆典。

5. There are three main sections inside the Memorial Hall. The marble statue of Chairman Mao is placed on a platform in the front lobby.
纪念堂由三个部分组成。毛主席的大理石塑像立在前厅平台上。

6. Here is the Monument to the People's Heroes. The monument was built in memory of thousands of martyrs who died for the revolutionary cause of the Chinese people.
这里是人民英雄纪念碑。此纪念碑是为纪念成千上万为中国人民革命事业献身的烈士而建的。

7. On the front side of the monument is an engraved inscription in Chinese, written by Chairman Mao which reads: "Eternal Glory to the People's Heroes!"
纪念碑的正面雕刻着毛主席亲笔题写的碑文:"人民英雄永垂不朽"。

8. At the base of the monument are eight marble reliefs, depicting the Chinese history since 1840.
在纪念碑的基座上有8块大理石浮雕,描绘着自1840年以来中国的历史进程。

9. On the east side of the square are the National Museum of China.
广场的东侧是中国国家博物馆。

10. Here is Tian'anmen Gate. Two stone lions stand by the gate, like sentries guarding the gate.
这里是天安门城门。城门前有两座石狮,像卫兵一样守护着大门。

11. The national emblem is a pattern of Tian'anmen Rostrum encircled by ears of wheat and gear wheel.
国徽图案是被麦穗和齿轮环绕的天安门城楼。

12. On the east side is the Working People's Cultural Palace. Its original name was the Supreme Ancestral Temple for storing the tablets of the deceased emperors of the Ming and Qing dynasties.
东侧是劳动人民文化宫,原名"太庙",在明、清时是供奉先帝灵牌的地方。

Wonderful Paragraph
精彩片段

Paragraph 1

天安门
Tian'anmen

Tian'anmen is situated on the north-south axle in central Beijing. With Chang'an Boulevard an Boulevard running across its front, Tian'anmen Gate is not only connected with, but also stays aloof from other architecture on the square. As the main gate of the imperial palace of the Ming and Qing Dynasties, and symbol of Beijing and China today, Tian'anmen has experienced the vicissitudes of history. On visiting Beijing, every tourist, from either home or abroad, cannot help being greatly impressed by the magnificence of Tian'anmen gate and the imposing atmosphere of the entire square.

As Beijing's famous scenic spot, Tian' anmen gate, Tian'anmen Square and all other architectures there are viewed as messengers of Chinese culture by a growing number of Chinese and foreign tourists.

Paragraph 2

天安门广场
Tian'anmen Square

Like the Red Square in Moscow, the Arc De Triomphe in Paris and the Washington Monument, Tian'anmen Square is the symbolic architecture of Beijing. It was named ."the largest public square in the world" evaluated at the "World Top Tourism in Beijing" in 1992. Millions of tourists are attracted to the square by its long history and splendid appearance, and it has become the very image of Beijing's charm to its many visitors.

Located on the central axle of Beijing, Tian'anmen Square begins from the northern red wall, reaches Zhengyangmen Gate Tower, or Front Gate, in the south and the Great Hall of the People in the west, and includes the Museum of Chinese History and the Museum of Chinese Revolution in the east.

It is 880 meters from north to south, and 500 meters from east to west, and has a total area of 440 000 square meters. As many as one million people can gather here at one time. It has witnessed the magnificent sight of the founding ceremony of the PRC and National Day military parades, and is the witness of every great leap forward by the country.

Paragraph 3

F升降旗仪式
lag-Raising and Flag-Lowering Ceremonies

Since May 1, 1991, regulations issued by the Beijing municipality began to be enforced. They stipulate that on the first, 11th and 21st day of each month and on important national festivals (such as New Year's Day, Spring Festival, International Labor Day, the founding day of the Party, Army Day and National Day), flag-raising and flag-lowering ceremonies are to be held and the national anthem be played by the military band. On other days, ceremonies shall also take place and a recording of the national anthem is to be payed. Since then, the flag-raising and flag-lowering ceremony has become a favorite event for both domestic and foreign tourists.

Paragraph 4

M人民英雄纪念碑
onument to the People's Heroes

Located to the south of the five-star red flag of Tian'anmen Square, the monument was erected in memory of the people's heroes who sacrificed their lives for the revolution between 1840 and 1949. Designed by Liang Sicheng, construction began August 1 1952, and it was completed in April 1958. Made from 17 000 pieces of granites and white marble, it is 37.94 meters in height and covers an area of 3 000 sq meters. Constructed from a complete piece of granite, the main part of the monument is 14.7 meters long, 2.9 meters wide, one meter thick and weighs 103 tons. Standing upright and stately at the center of the square, it is situated 440 meters away from the wall base of the square. Directly facing Tian'anmen Gate, eight gilded characters written by the late Chairman Mao are inscribed at the center of the tablet, stating Immortality to the People's Heroes.

Paragraph 5

Memorial Hall of Chairman Mao
毛主席纪念堂

The great leader Chairman Mao passed away on Sept. 9, 1976. The central government determined to build a memorial hall to preserve Chairman Mao's body. Located between the Monument to the People's Heroes and Zhengyangmen Gate, the memorial hall faces north, opposite Tian'anmen Gate. The foundations was laid on Nov. 24 1976 and the hall completed the following May. Covering an area of 28 000 sq meters, the hall is supported by 44 octagonal granite pillars. Two groups of 8.7-meter-high carvings have been erected in the courtyard. The grand architecture embodies the greatness of Chairman Mao.

Cultural Links
文化链接

华表上的"望天犼"

华表上面,是一圆盘,称为承露盘,承露盘上蹲立一怪兽"望天犼"。盘下,横插有两块云板。中间的石柱上,缠绕一四足五爪的游龙,翻腾于祥云之间。华表下面是一八角形的须弥基座,底部是一方形石栏,四角有柱,每一柱上蹲有一只小石狮。华表与须弥座一起,高达9.57米。关于华表上方的怪兽"望天犼",还流传着这样的说法:望天犼高高蹲立在华表上,时刻注视着帝王的一切行动。当帝王外出巡幸或私访久久不归时,望天犼会告诫皇帝赶紧归来,处理朝内事务。这指的是天安门外的两只头向南方的望天犼,称为"望君归"。相应的,天安门的两只望天犼则被称为"望君出",头向北方紫禁城的方向,注视着后宫,劝诫皇帝不要只顾沉溺于宫中的生活,应该出来到民间走一走,以体察民间的疾苦。

用英语说中国——旅游亮点
Introduce China in English—Scenic Spots

Vocabulary
妙词连珠

rostrum 城楼,检阅台
hectare 公顷
assembly 集会
historical 历史的
event 事件,大事
ceremony 典礼,仪式
statue 雕像,塑像
platform 台,平台
monument 纪念碑
martyr 烈士
granite 花岗岩
inscribe 雕刻,题赠
inlay 镶嵌
inscription 碑文
engrave 雕刻上
relief 浮雕
auditoria 礼堂
anthem 赞歌,国歌
column 圆柱
slogan 口号,标语
emblem 标志,象征
Chairman Mao Memorial Hall 毛主席纪念堂

the Monument to the People's Heroes 人民英雄纪念碑
flagpole of the National Flag 国旗旗杆
Outer Golden Water River Bridge 外金水桥
Marble Column 华表
historical events 历史事件
national anthem 国歌
national badge 国徽
portrait 肖像
gateway 门洞
arc 弧线
railing 栏杆
lotus 莲花
main gate 正门
take shape 成形
founding ceremony 开国大典
National Day 国庆节
military parades 阅兵
Tian'anman Gate Tower 天安门城楼

Unit 2　The Palace Museum　故宫

Key Sentences 流畅精句

1. The Palace Museum was also known as the Forbidden City. It was the imperial palace of the Ming and Qing dynasties.
   故宫亦叫"紫禁城",是明、清两朝的皇宫。

2. Fourteen emperors of the Ming Dynasty and ten emperors of the Qing Dynasty lived and ruled China in this palace for as long as 490 years from 1421 to 1911.
   从1421年至1911年,有14位明朝皇帝、10位清朝皇帝曾在这里生活、执政长达490年。

3. The 1911 Revolution overthrew the Qing Dynasty. In 1924, the last emperor Pu Yi was driven out of the palace. After that, the Forbidden City was converted into the Palace Museum and has been open to the public since then.
   1911年的辛亥革命推翻了清王朝。1924年,末代皇帝溥仪被赶出皇宫,从此紫禁城转变成故宫博物院并对外开放。

4. In the Outer Court, there are three main halls. The halls were built on an 8-metre-high marble terrace with three tiers.
   外朝有三大殿,这三大殿建在一个三层、8米高的大理石石台上。

5. At the back of the Hall of Preserving Harmony there is a marble carving named the Marble Ramp with cloud and dragon designs.
   在保和殿的后面有一块大理石雕,叫"云龙阶石"。

6. The second hall on the terrace is the Hall of Complete Harmony. This is a square building with a single pyramid roof.
   石台上的第二大殿是中和殿。这是一座攒尖顶的方形大殿。

7. The Hall of Mental Cultivation was the place where the emperor granted audience to officials and summoned his ministers for consultations.
养心殿是皇帝会见大臣商议政务的地方。
8. The west chamber was the place where the emperor read report, signed documents and discussed military and political affairs with his officials.
西殿是皇帝批阅公文及与官员们商议军政大事的地方。
9. On the north side of the Inner Court is the Imperial Garden. It is 90 metres from north to south and 130 metres from east to west.
内朝的北面是御花园,南北宽90米,东西长130米。
10. Near the north gate of the Imperial Garden there is a group of man-made rockeries called the Hill of Collecting Elegance.
御花园北门附近有一片假山,叫堆秀山。
11. The Palace Museum is listed by the Chinese Government as one of the important historical relics under special preservation.
故宫被中国政府列为重点历史文物,受到特殊的保护。
12. Now the Forbidden City is not forbidden any more, but welcomes visitors from all over the world.
紫禁城不再警戒森严,而是对来自世界各地的游客开放。
13. The Forbidden City was listed by the United Nation's Educational, Scientific and Cultural Organization (UNESCO) as one of the World Cultural Heritage sites in 1987.
紫禁城于1987年被联合国教科文组织(UNESCO)列为世界文化遗产。

The Six Scenic Spots in Beijing

Wonderful Paragraph
精彩片段

Paragraph 1

紫禁城
Forbidden City

The former Imperial Palace, known to Westerners as the Forbidden City, rectangular in shape and 720 thousand square meters in size, is surrounded by walls ten meters high and a moat 52 meters wide. The buildings with some nine thousand rooms are more than 560 years old and constitute the largest and most complete existing ensemble of traditional Chinese architecture.

Construction of the palace begins in 1406 during the reign of the third emperor of the Ming Dynasty, Yongle. It was finally completed in 1420. The Imperial Palace is composed of the outer palace, where the emperors held official audiences. and the inner palace, which served as the living quarters for the imperial family. This harmonious assemblage of buildings displays the best characteristics of ancient Chinese architecture—majestic style, flawless construction, and fine coordination of the while and the parts. Now, the Forbidden City, the Palace Museum, is a treasure house of cultural relics, and a place that attracts approximately ten thousand visitors each day with its magnificent architecture and precious collections of cultural and art objects.

Paragraph 2

外朝
The Outer Court

The Imperial Palace grounds are divided into the Outer Court and the Inner Court by the Gate of Heavenly Purity. The main structures of the Outer Court are the Hall of Supreme Harmony Taihedian, the Hall of Central Harmony Zhonghedian and the Hall of Preserving Harmony Baohedian. They were where the emperor held official audiences, award ceremonies, weddings, birth celebrations and official banquets. The emperor received greetings from attending officials and foreign envoys in the Hall of Supreme Harmony.

Paragraph 3

太和殿
Hall of Supreme Harmony

Hall of Supreme Harmony Taihedian Commonly known as the Hall of Gold Throne, the magnificent structure was built in 1406 and renovated in 1695. It is 35.5 meters high and has a floor space of 2 300 square meters with 182 beams and 84 pillars. It is the largest wood structure extant in China. During the Ming and Qing dynasties grand ceremonies such as the enthronement of the emperor, New Year's Day, proclamation of imperial edicts, receiving successful candidates of imperial examination, appointment of commander-in-chief of expedition troops were held here.

Inside the Hall of Supreme Harmony The interior of the Gold Throne Hall is preserved as in ancient times. On the raised platform is the gilded imperial throne placed on a dais two meters high. Behind the throne is a carved screen. On either side of the throne are a crane-shaped candlestick, an elephant-shaped in-cense burner and a column shaped incense burner with a pagoda on top which are all cloisonne wares.

Throne The painted golden throne with a splendid screen behind it stands on a two-me-ter high dais in the center of the Hall of Supreme Harmony. Its back and the lower part are covered with coiled dragons. This is the most magnificent of all the thrones in the palace.

Paragraph 4

后三宫
The Inner Court

Behind the three great halls of the Outer Court is a long open ground running from east to west, which serves as a demarcation line between the

Outer Court and the Inner Court. The emperor lived in the Inner Court with his empress and scores of concubines, served by thousands of palace maids and eunuchs. The buildings in the Inner Court, like those in the Outer Court, are arranged along three lines.

Paragraph 5

养心殿和后六宫
The Hall of Mental Cultivation and The Six Western Palaces

The Hall of Mental Cultivation (Yangxindian) stands in a large compound south of the Six Western Palaces. During the Qing Dynasty it was the second most important place in the Imperial Palace, only next to the Hall of Supreme Harmony. The front part of the hall was used as the office and the rear part as the bedroom of the emperor. The officials who were to be promoted, transfered was to expire were presented to the emperor by the Minister of Interior in this hall.

The West Warm Chamber and East Warm Chamber of the Hall of Mental Cultivation were where the emperor read official reports and met high-ranking officials. During the Qing Dynasty memorials to the throne from various offices were first sent to two collecting points and then brought to the emperor by special eunuch messengers.

The Six Western Palaces are located north of the Hall of Mental Cultivation. They are the Palace of Eternal Longevity Yongshougone, the Palace of Assisting the Empress Yukungong, the Palace of Gathering Elegance Chuxiugong, the Hall of Evolution Taijidian, the Palace of Eternal Spring Changchungong, and the Palace of Cultivating Happiness Xianfugong. During the Ming Dynasty they were the residence of imperial concubines. In the Qing Dynasty some empresses lived here too.

Paragraph 6

御花园
Imperial Garden

The Imperial Garden, built in 1417, is the oldest garden in Beijing. It occupies an area of 1.3 hectares at the northern end of the central axis of the former Imperial Palace. During the Qing Dynasty the emperor, empress and imperial concubines came to the garden to worship the Cowherd Star and the Girl Weaver Star on the 7th day of the 7th lunar month. On the Mid-Autumn Festival they came here to offer a sacrifice to the moon, and on the double-Ninth Festival the 9th day of the 9th lunar month they came here to ascend the Hill of Collecting Excellence in the garden and enjoy scenic beauty within and outside the Imperial Palace.

The main scenic spot it the northeastern part is the Hill of Collecting Excellence. The Pavilion of Imperial Landscape stands on the hill. In front of Li Zao Hall by the hill is a small pond of clear water. The main scenic spot in the northwestern part is the Pavilion of Lasting Splendor. In front of the pavilion there are some ancient cypress trees over 400 years old.

Cultural Links
文化链接

紫禁城内共有多少个房间

民间传说称：故宫内有房九千九百九十九间半，并说天上玉帝的皇宫里有房一万间，地下的皇帝不敢超越，故少半间。那么，这半间房在那里呢？即指文渊阁楼下西头的那一小间。事实上，紫禁城内有房屋九千余间，而所谓的半间不过是一种牵强附会的造作而已。文渊阁西边的那一间，其面积虽小，仅能容得一楼梯，但仍是一个整间。因为文渊阁是储藏中国第一部《四库全书》的所在，为了取"天一生水，地六成之，以水克火"之意，故文渊阁的房间数便一反紫禁城内房屋均以奇数为间的惯例，采用了不讲对称的偶数——六间。然而，为了布局上的美观，只得把西头的一间造得格外小一些。

Vocabulary
妙词连珠

forbidden 被禁止的	divine 神圣的
imperial 帝国的,皇家的	the Outer Eastern Palace 外东宫
emperor 皇帝	Nine-Dragon Screen 九龙壁
court 宫廷,朝廷	Meridian Gate 午门
moat 护城河	the Gate of Divine Prowess 神武门
magnificent 宏大的,庄严的	The Throne Hall 金銮殿
meridian 子午线	audience chamber 会客厅
symbolize 装在……上	imperial seal 御玺
staircase 台阶	five virtues 五德
throne 宝座,王位	be open and aboveboard 正大光明
plaque 匾	over step 逾越
aboveboard 光明正大的	ledge 屋檐
conferment 授予	moat 护城河
summon 召集,传唤	solemnity 庄严,隆重
precious 珍贵的	the Qing government 清政府
compound 院子	Gate of supreme Harmony 太和门
enclose 包围,围住	Gate of Heavenly Purity 乾清门
elegance 优雅	Palace of Eternal Spring 长春宫
treasure 财宝,珍品	the Hall of Union and Palace 交泰殿

Unit 3　The Great Wall
长城

Key Sentences
流畅精句

1. Construction of the Great Wall lasted for more than two thousand years, It extends over 6 700 kilometres, so it is the longest defensive engineering project in ancient times in the world.
   长城的建造持续了两千多年,它绵延6 700公里,是古代世界上最长的防御工事。
2. Construction of the Great Wall started from seven century BC. It began from the Warring States Period.
   长城的修建始于公元前7世纪,从战国时期开始。
3. Badaling is the best-preserved part of the Great Wall and is 75 kilometres northwest of Beijing.
   八达岭长城是长城保存得最好的一段,在京城西北75公里处。
4. You can see the pass tower—the Juyong Pass. Above the gate there is a plague, which reads: "the First Magnificent Pass Under Heaven."
   你可以看见关城城楼——居庸关,城门上有一块匾,上面写着"天下第一雄关"。
5. In the centre of the Juyong Pass, there is a massive marble terrace called "The Cloud Terrace," which was built in the Yuan Dynasty.
   在居庸关的中心有一个巨大的石台叫云台,建于元朝。
6. There is also a Great Wall Museum nearby.
   附近还有一个长城博物馆。
7. It was extremely difficult to build the wall along the high mountains and the deep valleys.
   沿着高山和深谷修建长城是极其困难的。

8. But now the Great Wall has lost its military importance. It has become a famous scenic spot in the world, attracting millions of visitors each year from all over the world.

   但是现在,长城已经失去了军事上的意义。它成为世界上一个著名景点,每年吸引成千上万来自世界各地的游客。

9. From visiting the Great Wall we can see the wisdom and strength of the Chinese people. How Chinese labouring people in ancient times suffered tremendous hardship for building the Great Wall!

   通过游览长城,我们可以看到中国人民的智慧和力量。为了修建长城,古代的中国人民承受了何等巨大的苦难!

10. The Great Wall is listed as one of an important historical monument under special preservation by the Chinese Government.

    长城被列为国家重要的历史文物,受到中国政府的特殊保护。

Wonderful Paragraph
精彩片段

Paragraph 1

长城——人类史上的奇迹
The Great Wall: A Wonder in Human History

Its construction began at 7th or 8th centuries BC, and continued now and then for over 2 000 years. The wall stretches across the vast area of north and central China, with a total length of more than 50 000km (100 000 li), reputed as "Enlivened for 2 000 years and Maneuvering for 100 000 li".

Historical records show that since the Warring States Period, more than 20 lord states and imperial dynasties launched construction of defense walls, and the length would exceed 100 000 li (50 000 km). In other words, the bricks, stones, and earth are excessive for a modern highway of 10 m wide and 0.5 m thick to go around the planet for 10 circles. That is amazingly great indeed, well worth its fame as one of the seven wonders in human history.

The Great Wall boasts serene scenery and historical value. Much of the Great Wall we see today was constructed in Ming Dynasty. After careful renovation, representative sections, such as Shanhai Pass, Juyong Pass, Badaling Section, Simatai Section, Mutianyu Section, Jiayu Pass, Gubeikou Pass and Jinshanling Section, has already become the world-renowned tourist attractions. Among them, Badaling Section, Juyong Pass, Simatai Section, Jinshanling and Mutianyu Section are the most famous sections of the Great Wall.

Paragraph 2

B八达岭长城
adaling Section

Construction of Badaling in Yanqing County, Beijing, started in the Ming Dynasty (1368-1644) and underwent 18 rebuilt from the Hongwu to the Wanli reign (1368-1620). Badaling leads to Beijing in the south, Yanqing in the north, Xuanhua and Datong in the west. Hence the name Bade means reaching out in all directions. The wall, built with huge stone slabs on the outside, is 7.8 meters high on the average and 5.8~6.5 meters wide. The crenellated wall has parapets; and watchtowers and fighting platforms are built at 250~500 meters intervals. The castle was built in 1505 (the 18th year of the Ming Hongzhi reign). The best preserved section of the Great Wall, Badaling locates at a very important position and has a beautiful surrounding scenery and its structures show a special grandeur.

Paragraph 3

M慕田峪长城
utianyu Section

Lies in Huairou County, Mutianyu Section is 73 kilometers away from Beijing City. It links with Juyong Section in Changping County in the west and Gubeikou Section in Miyun County in the east. Commanding the strategic importance, Mutianyu Section is called as the Majestic Pass on Precipitous Mountains. It is integrated with Juyong Section and Frontier Fort, and consti-

北京六大景点
The Six Scenic Spots in Beijing

tutes a complete defensive system. It is one of the best-preserved parts of the Great Wall.

Due to its relatively gentle terrain, watchtowers of Mutianyu Section were built in large numbers to strengthen its defensive functions. The closest watchtowers spaced less than 50 meters apart. Both arms of Mutianyu Section stretch upwards along the ridges of continuous mountains. Mainly built on precipitous mountains and 5—7 meters high, the Mutianyu Section we see today is expanded on the foundation of Ming Wall. It is characterized with a thick cluster of watchtowers atop, strategic passes, majestic vigor and unique structrue. The gate tower is the most unique building of Mutianyu Section.

Paragraph 4

司马台长城
Simatai Section

Located on the boundary of Gubeikou Town, Miyun County, Beijing, and Luanping County, Hebei Province, the 19 kilometer Simatai began in the first year of the Ming Hong Wu reign. The design and construction of this section of the Great Wall are exquisite and striking. Every one of the 35 watchtowers is original and different. The Tower for Viewing the Capital, 986 meters above sea level, is constructed on sheer precipices, commanding a panoramic view of "snow-capped Wuling" in the east, rolling mountains like "crouching tigers and coiling dragons" in the west, a "mirror-like reservoir" in the south and "verdurous Yanshan Mountain" in the north. Just as outstanding are the natural sceneries at Heavenly Ladder, Fairy Bridge, Heavenly Pool and the Spring of Mandarin Duck and Drake which compliment the scenes of the man-made Great Wall.

Paragraph 5

居庸关
Juyongguan

Juyongguan lies to the northwest of Changping County, Beijing. The term juyong, appearing first in The Spring and Autumn Annals of Mr Lu of the Warring States Period, was attached to this pass during Qin Shi Huang's time. In the Han Dynasty it was called Juyongguan, in the Three Kingdom's period the West Pass, in Northern Qi, the Tax Pass, in the Tang Dynasty Juyongguan Pass, Jimen Pass or Jundu Pall. All through Liao, Kin, Yuan, Ming and Qing dynasties to the present day it has been called Juyongguan.

The castle of this important pass of the Great Wall was built in 1368 (the beginning of the Ming Hong Wu reign) by Xu Da, one of the military commanders who assisted Emperor Hong Wu (named Zhu Yuanzhang) to found the Ming Dynasty. It has been renovated many times afterwards.

Paragraph 6

水关长城 Shuiguan great wall

Shui Guan (Water Pass), which was first built in the Ming Dynasty (1368-1644), was an indispensable part of the defense system of Badaling Great Wall. The pass mainly functioned to defend against invaders by the force of torrential water flowing through between the two mountains. It is one of the best preserved sections of the Great Wall of China, which stretches about one thousand meters (0.62 miles). It also has seven enemy towers and an arrow tower which is 15 meters (50 feet) in height and 12 meters (40 feet) in width. Looking out from the arrow tower, you can imagine an ancient battle fields and see the importance of the wall as a defence against invaders.

Paragraph 7

古北口长城 Gubeikou Section

This section is located in Gubeikou Township, Miyun County, Beijing. Very dangerous in geological sense, it controls the important passage from Beijing to frontier plateaus. Its wall links up Mt Dragon and Mt Tiger into a powerful defense. The section was the wall of State of Yan in Warring States

Period, and many well known battles fought here. In 1379, General Xu Da of Ming Dynasty rebuilt the section and named it Ying City, but only some remains of it are still there now. On the south slop of Gubeikou is a shrine for the well respected General Yang Ye of Song Dynasty.

八达岭的由来

八达岭长城是北京最著名的景观之一，关于"八达岭"这一地名的由来，历来说法不一，主要有五种：

一、八达岭由"八大岭"谐音而得名。因这一带山峦层叠，地势险峻，据说所建的长城在这里要转八道弯，越过八座大的山岭，所以当年兴建这段长城很艰难，建筑材料难以运送到山上，工期迟迟完不成，曾先后有八个监工为其而死。最后通过仙人的点化，采取"修城八法"，即"虎带笼头羊背鞍，燕子衔泥猴搭肩，龟驮石条兔引路，喜鹊搭桥冰铺栈"，才把建筑材料运送到山上，所以人们就把这段长城称为"八大岭长城"，后来地名就谐音成"八达岭"。

二、八达岭由"巴达岭"谐音而得名。相传元代有一位叫"巴达黎黎"的皇帝到此，见这里关山险峻，崇峦叠翠，于是龙颜大悦，给此处赐名"巴达岭"，后讹传为"八达岭"。此说不实，因查阅《历代帝王录》、《中国皇帝大事年表》和《中国历代帝王年号手册》等史料，均查不出元代有过叫"巴达黎黎"的皇帝。但却有一位叫爱育黎拔力八达的，他就是元代第四位皇帝仁宗。据传他出生在八达岭所在的延庆县内，其名字中确含有"八达"二字，也许"巴达黎黎"是一种误传。若联想到元朝时皇帝每年要从北京到上京（在今天的内蒙古巴林左旗南部）往来一次，而处于必经之地的八达岭，被这位皇帝乘兴赐名"八达岭"也是有一定可能的。

三、八达岭由"把鞑靼"谐音而得名。据传明代的时候，八达岭一带曾一度成为防守满族军队的前沿阵地，因明时汉人把东北方的满族人称为"鞑靼"，所以有人认为八达岭是"把鞑靼"（意为把守鞑靼之岭）的谐音，这种说法似乎也没有什么道理。因为满族人多生活在今天的辽宁、吉林大部分地区，离这里还很远，不是在居庸关外，而是在山海关外，而离这里较近的应是蒙古人。

四、八达岭由"八道岭"谐音而得名。传说明末李自成率起义大军征战到此,由于关城易守难攻,起义大军受阻于长城之外,数日不进,李自成不由得心急如焚。这时探马来报,说前方还有八道险关。李自成听罢长叹一声:"这里的八道岭实在是难以越过,看来强攻是不行!"于是命令起义大军改道而去,后来这里被称为"八道岭",时间一长就被谐音成"八达岭"。

五、以上四种说法多是传说,没有确切的文字记载,难以考证。其实最可信的说法,应是《长安客话》中的解释:"路从此分,四通八达。"因为八达岭是居庸关的外口,北往延庆、赤城、蒙古,西去张家口、怀来、宣化、大同,东到永宁、四海,南去昌平、北京等地区,可谓是交通四通八达,所以它是古代一条重要的交通要道和防卫前哨,素有"京北第一屏障"之称。

Vocabulary 妙词连珠

extend 伸展	invade 侵略
fortress 要塞	forestall 预先;抢先在……前面行动
strategic 战略的	signal 信号
battlement 城垛	transmit 传递
warn 警告,警戒	foundation 建立,创立,创办
miracle patriotic 奇迹	feeling 感觉
steep 陡峭的	heritage 遗址
beacon 烽火台	protection 保护
Badaling Pass 八达岭城关	the Pyramid in Egypt 埃及的金字塔
Juyong Pass 居庸关	one of the seven wonders 七大奇迹之一
the Cloud Terrace 云台	
a strategic point 战略要地	the Jiayu Pass 嘉峪关
protective screen 保护屏障	the Shanhai Pass 山海关
defensive engineering 国防工程	artificial constructions 人工建筑
total 总数	the Spring-Autumn and Warring States 春秋战国
artificial 人工的	

北京六大景点
The Six Scenic Spots in Beijing

the Ming Dynasty 明朝
cable car 缆车
watch towers 敌楼
good-neighbour policy 睦邻政策
Mongolian nationality 蒙古族
at the top 在顶部

a world cultural heritage protection site 世界文化遗产保护区
at the foot of the wall 在长城脚下
hot springs 温泉
Badaling Expressway 八达岭高速公路

Unit 4　The Summer Palace
颐和园

Key Sentences
流畅精句

1. The Summer Palace is the most beautiful and the largest imperial garden existing in China.
   颐和园是中国现存最美最大的皇家园林。
2. The Summer Palace consists of two parts, the Longevity Hill and the Kunming Lake. The lake occupies three quarters of the whole area.
   颐和园包括万寿山和昆明湖两部分，湖面占整个面积的四分之三。
3. The East Palace Gate is the main entrance to the Summer Palace.
   东宫门是颐和园的正门。
4. The Hall of Jade Ripples used to be the place where Qing Emperor Qianlong spent his leisure hours with his ministers and friends.
   玉澜堂曾是清朝乾隆皇帝和他的大臣、朋友们消遣娱乐的地方。
5. The Hall of Happiness and Longevity was the residence of Empress Dowager Cixi during her stay in the Summer Palace.
   乐寿堂是慈禧太后住在颐和园时的寝宫。
6. The Gate of Dispelling Cloud is at the centre of the Long Corridor.
   排云门位于长廊的中央。
7. The Tower of Buddhist Incense is a 3-storey octagonal wooden tower.
   佛香阁是一座三层、八角形木楼。
8. To the west of the Tower of Buddhist Incense is the Pavilion of Precious Clouds.
   佛香阁的西面是宝云阁。
9. The Hall for Listening to Orioles used to be a theatre with a two storey stage.

北京六大景点
The Six Scenic Spots in Beijing

听鹂馆以前曾是有一个两层舞台的戏楼。

10. The West Dike spans from northwest to south on the Kunming Lake, dividing the lake into two parts.

    西堤从西北到南部横跨昆明湖,把湖面分为两半。

11. The Shopping Street is in the middle section of the back lake. It stretches 300 metres along the bank of the Back Lake with 64 shops and 8 small bridges.

    苏州街在后湖的中部。它沿着后湖的湖岸延伸300米,有64个店铺和8座小桥。

12. The Four Great Regions is a massive complex of religious buildings of Tibetan style, and it's on the northern slops of the Longevity Hill.

    四大部洲是西藏风格的巨大的宗教建筑群,它位于万寿山的北坡。

Wonderful Paragraph 精彩片段

Paragraph 1

皇家园林博物馆
Museum of Imperial Garden

Summer Palace is at the northwest suburb of Beijing, about 15dm from the capital proper. Originally it was the Garden of Clear Ripples, built in 1750. Later in 1860 it was burnt down by Anglo-French allied forces. Qing govenment rebuilt it in 1888 with fund set aside for China's navy, as a place of leisure for Empress Dowager to enjoy her senior years, and accordingly named it with the implication of peaceful and harmonious life.

The palace occupies about 293 hectares, made up of mainly Longevity Hill and Kunming Lake, with the lake takes up about three fourths of the whole garden. The primary buildings of the palace center on Tower of Buddhist Incense, with over 3 000 towers, pavilions, halls, or houses. The general design follows the tradition of Chinese landscape construction, and the buildings are arranged in harmony with the natural landform. It also borrowed the poetic and other techniques of garden construction in southern China, therefore the palace is not only imperial and grand but also elegant and rich with variation. It is a perfect combination of the natural landscape and human features full of artistic impact.

The palace is highly valued not only in the sense of its landscape art but also its role in science and history, which ranks it among the most world famous resorts of tourists. In 1998 World Heritage Committee of UNESCO inscribed it in World Heritage List.

The palace is the largest royal garden in the world most perfectly preserved with the richest cultural connotation, hence honored as a museum of royal gardens. Its general layout makes full use of the hill and the lake, together with the borrowed views from the peaks of the west mountains, which brings about infinite scenery variations with exceeding beauty. The buildings in the palace are the architectural cream from all parts of China. The administrative and residential areas in the east of the palace are typical of the quadrangle in northern China, where the enclosed courtyards are connected by various roofed causeways. The lake area in its south, however, is an imitation of West Lake of Hangzhou, where a dyke divides the lake in two, thus giving it an obvious touch of southern China landscape. On the north side of Longevity Hill, the scene is that of Tibetan lamasery, where stand white pagodas and buildings like blockhouses. And in the north, the Suzhou Market Street, with all kinds of shops and its crisscrossing watercourses, is again in the style of the waterscape in southern China.

Paragraph 2

行政区
The Administrative Area

There are in all over 3 000 hall buildings in the Summer Palace. The varied style ancient architectures among the beautiful landscape of the lakes and hills may dazzle the tourists. Upon second observation, you can find that the overall arrangement is properly spaced.

In accordance to their functions, the Palace consists of three parts: the administrative area with the Hall of Benevolent Longevity, the imperial living area with the Hall of Joyful Longevity and the scenic area with Kunming Lake and Wanshou Hill. And the scenic area is divided into three parts due to their different geographical locations: the southern slope of the Wanshou Hill, the Kunming Lake and the rear hill and back lake.

Paragraph 3

帝后生活区
The Imperial Living Area

The Summer Palace served mainly as the temporary dwelling palace for Cixi at the end of the 19th century and the beginning of the 20th century. Thus, the living quarters of Cixi, Emperor Guangxu and the empress Longyu compose the main part of the imperial living area, the major part of the imperial living area, the major part for our tour. Located to the north of the eastern bank of Kunming Lake, the imperial living area comprises traditional single-story houses with rows of rooms around the four sides of a courtyard, all linked by verandas.

Paragraph 4

昆明湖景区
Kunming Lake Area

The lake takes up three fourths of the total area. Its front part in the south looks beautifully vast in a faint mist. To its west is the view of extending peaks, while to the north are towers and pavilions one group after another. Lying in the lake, the three isles are also built with various buildings in classic style, and the Seventeen-arch Bridge offers not only an access to the interior of the lake, but also another unforgettable scene with elegance of itself.

用英语说中国——旅游亮点
Introduce China in English—Scenic Spots

Paragraph 5

长廊
Long Corridor

There thronged various architectures on the southern slope of the Wanshou Hill, related and orderly. The Foxiang Pavilion compound stands in the middle, sided by pavilions and buildings of varied shapes. The 782-meter Long Corridor connects them with each other. In this way, the scenery appears more orderly.

The Long Corridor was firstly built in 1750, destroyed by the war of 1860 and then restored to the present state in the Emperor Guangxu's reign. It originally functioned as the shelter for the empress and concubines when appreciating the beauty of Kunming Lake on rainy and snowy days. The longest corridor in China now, the Long Corridor starts from the Yaoyue Gate and reaches the Shizhang Pavilion, equal to length of 273 rooms. Taking the shape of soaring bat, the Long Corridor composes the traditional Chinese picture offering birthday felicitations, coupled with the peach-like Kunming Lake.

Paragraph 6

佛香阁
Foxiang Pavilion

When the Qingyi Garden was built in 1749, Emperor Qianlong originally had a nine-story pagoda built here as part of the grand Baoen Yanshou Temple. But he changed his mind when eight stories had been completed, and ordered to build a three-story octagonal pavilion with four eaves. Unfortunately, the war of 1860 reduced all wooden architectures to ashes, including the original Foxiang Pavilion. Only the stone base was left. Then, it was restored to the present state in 1891, the 17th year of the Emperor Guangxu's reign. The restoration project consumed over 780 000 liang of silver, the largest one of the construction of the Summer Palace.

Built on a 20-meter-high stone base, the Foxiang Pavilion was sustained by eight iron pillars. The 41-meter-high pavilion is rather complicated considering the overall structure. Thanks to its grandeur, elaborate pattern and the location on top of the Wanshou Hill, it has long been counted as the central architecture of the Summer Palace. Amitabha was worshipped in the pavilion. On every first and 15th days of te lunar month, the Empress Dowager would burn joss sticks and prayed for auspices.

Tourists can have a bird's-eye view of Kunming Lake, the Yuquan Hill in the west and the lovely pagoda. So the Foxiang Pavilion has been considered the perfect place for sightseeing and photography.

Paragraph 7

S苏州街
uzhou Market Street

The street refers to the shopping area built along Suzhou River (or Rear Lake) in the style of the waterscape of southern China. In the time of Garden of Clear Ripples the riverbanks were lined up with shops of jades and antiques, silk, cakes, tea, and jewelry.

When the emperor and empress or other imperial nobles came to visit, the street would begin its business, with eunuchs and palace maids acting as shop assistants and customers to produce a prosperous scene in the street. In 1860 it was burnt off by the foreign powers, and the present street is the restoration in 1986.

Cultural Links
文化链接

颐和园谐趣园的趣味究竟在何处

声趣：有山泉数股注入荷塘。该山泉的水源,来自昆明湖后湖的东端。谐趣园之所以取如此低洼的地势,主要是为了形成这道水泉,这样便可使谐趣园的水面与湖面形成一米到两米的落差,而在这一米到两米的落差之中,又运用山石的堆砌,分成了九个层次,川流不息的水声发出高低抑扬,优雅悦耳的琴韵,故在横卧于泉边的一块巨石上,游客可见刻有"玉琴峡"三字。

楼趣:在玉琴峡西侧有座瞩新楼,这座楼从内侧看是两层,可从外侧看却是一层。

桥趣:谐趣园中共有桥五座,其中以知鱼桥最为著称。它之所以取名为知鱼桥,这里引用了一个典故。战国时代,庄子和惠子在"秋水濠丘"有过一次关于知不知鱼乐的快乐对话:一个说鱼真快乐;另一个反驳道,你不是鱼,怎么能知道鱼快乐;另一个又反驳道,你不是我,怎么能知道我不知道鱼快乐。这就是以其人之道还治其人之身,用古人的故事为来访的游人增添了许多乐趣。

Vocabulary 妙词连珠

jar 坛子,罐,瓮
ripple 波纹,涟漪
gallery 美术馆,游廊
ox 公牛
dike 堤
causeway 堤道
veranda 走廊,阳台,游廊
the Longevity Hill 万寿山
the Kunming Lake 昆明湖
Jar Hill 瓮山
imperial garden 皇家园林
the Garden of Clear Ripples 清漪园
the East Palace Gate 东宫门
the Hall of Benevolence and Longevity 仁寿殿
the Garden of Virtuous Harmony 德和园
the Great Theatre Building 大戏楼
the Hall of Pleasure Smile 颐乐堂
the Hall of Happiness and Longevity 乐寿堂
Long Corridor 长廊
the Hall of Buddhist Incense 佛香阁
The Hall of the Sea of Wisdom 智慧海
the Pavilion of Precious Clouds 宝云阁
the Hall for Listening to Orioles 听鹂馆
Marble Boat 石舫
West Dike 西堤
the Gilded Bronze Ox 铜牛
Garden of Harmonious Interest 谐趣园
Shopping Street 苏州街
the Four Great Regions 四大部洲
the Hall of Jade Ripples 玉澜堂

Unit 5　The Temple of Heaven

Key Sentences
流畅精句

1. The Temple of Heaven is situated in the southern part of Beijing. It was first built in 1420 in the Ming Dynasty and encompass 273 hectares.
   天坛位于北京城南,最初建于明朝时期的 1420 年,占地 273 公顷。
2. The Temple of Heaven was the place where the emperors of the Ming and Qing dynasties came to worship to the God of Heaven and pray for good harvests.
   天坛是明、清两朝皇帝祭天、祈祷五谷丰登的地方。
3. The architecture of the Temple of Heaven is distinctive, the 6-me-tre-high wall surrounding the temple takes a square shape in the south and a semi-circular shape in the north.
   天坛的建筑很独特,6 米的高墙环绕着整个建筑。高墙的外形南部为方形,北部为半圆形。
4. The three main buildings in the Temple of Heaven are the Circular Mound Altar, the Imperial Vault of Heaven and the Hall of Prayer for Good Harvests.
   天坛的一个主要建筑为圜丘坛,皇穹宇和祈年殿。
5. The altar was for the ceremonies held on the day of winter solstice.
   圜丘坛是在冬至举行大典的地方。
6. Totally there are 3 402 pieces of stone on the three terraces and this number is multiple of nine. Nine was considered the supreme odd numbers, so the whole design of the altar makes people feel closer to the heaven.

总共有 3 402 块石板铺在圜坛的三层石台上。这个数字是 9 的倍数，9 被认为是最高的奇数数字。大坛的整个设计使人们感到与天更近了。

7. The Imperial Vault of Heaven was a circular structure, covered with blue glazed tiles and topped by a gilded ball.

皇穹宇是一个圆形的建筑，顶上被蓝色的琉璃瓦覆盖，顶端有一个镀金的球。

8. The Red Stairway Bridge is a 360-metre-long road. The road symbolizes the distance between the heaven and the human world.

丹陛大道是一条 360 米长的路。这段路象征着从天上到人间的距离。

9. The Hall of Prayer for Good Harvests was the place where emperors of the Ming and Qing dynasties came to pray good harvests on the 15th day of the first lunar month every year.

祈年殿是明、清两代皇帝每年正月十五祭天、祈求五谷丰登的地方。

10. The Hall of Abstinence is a group of buildings located on the west side of the temple. Before the emperor worshipped the God of Heaven the emperor had a three-day fast in this palace.

斋宫是位于天坛西侧的一组建筑。皇帝祭天之前要在这里斋戒三天。

11. Close to the eastern gate of the Temple of Heaven, there stand seven pieces of massive rock. Those were believed to be the Dippers from the sky.

天坛的东门内有七块巨石，这些石头被认为是从天上掉下来的陨石。

12. The Temple of Heaven was listed as an important historical monument by the government and also inscribed in the World Heritage list by UNESCO.

天坛被政府列为重点历史文物，同时也被联合国教科文组织列为"世界文化遗产"。

北京六大景点
The Six Scenic Spots in Beijing

Wonderful Paragraph
精彩片段

Paragraph 1

G概况 eneral

The Temple of Heaven is situated in the southern part of Beijing, about 6 Km away from the center of the city. Traditionally, this temple was for imperial use only. It was built in 1420, covering an area of 273 hectares, it is the one of the largest parks in Beijing. The Temple of Heaven was the place where the emperors of the Ming and Qing dynasties worshipped heaven and prayed for good harvests. The emperors visited the temple three times a year: on the 8th day of the first lunar month to pray for a good harvest; during the Summer Solstice to pray for rain; and during Winter Solstice to give thanks for a good harvest. During each ceremony, the emperors worshipped heaven and prayed for a good harvest. In addition, the emperors also worshipped their ancestors and other natural phenomena such as the Cloud God, Rain God and Wind God.

It is among the first key cultural sites under state protection, and in December 1998 the UNESCO incribed it on the World Heritages List.

Paragraph 2

C圜丘坛 ircular Mound Altar

The altar seats inside the South Gate. Constructed in 1530, it is a circular stone platform of 3 tiers, 5m high, guarded with stone slabs between balustrades, encircled by a low wall of round inside but square outside as a reference to "round sky and square land". Four groups of Lingxing gates, three in a unit, stand in the four directions outside the inner and outer walls of the temple, but the Circular Mound Altar is double walled and has two rings of the gates, to form a 3-dimensional geometry that is grand and great.

Circular Mound Altar is long known as a holy, a sacred site for offering worship sacrifice. It is truly the heavenly a altar, also popularly referred to as the Altar, Altar to Worship Heaven, or Altar of Obeisance for Heaven.

Paragraph 3

D天库 ivine Court

This refers to the part storing the tablets of Supreme Ruler of Heaven and other gods, which are to be escorted to Circular Mound only for major ceremonies. The court, to the south of Circular Mound Altar inside Gaze Gate, includes mainly the Echo Wall, Imperial Vault of Heaven, east and west side halls.

Glaze Gate: It is the entrance of Divine Court, so called for its glaze brackets, the only prototype found in China, and for the glaze tiles of sky blue on its wall of finely laid bricks.

Paragraph 4

T皇穹宇 he Imperial Vault of Heaven

North of the Circular Mound Altar is the Imperial Vault of Heaven, which was originally built in 1530 and rebuilt 1752. Its structure is made from wood and brick with a blue tiled roof that is top with a gilded ball. It is 19.5 meters high and 15.6 meters in diameter. From a distance, the Imperial Vault of Heaven looks like a small version of the Hall of Prayer for Good Harvest.

As you can see, the building does not have any horizontal beams as support. The entire building is supported by 8 pillars and a span work of bars, laths and brackets, which is in complete conformity with the principles of dynamics. The decorative painted appear fresh because they were retouched in 1974.

In the center of the Imperial Vault of Heaven stands the shrine where the tablet of God of Heaven was placed. There are four stone platforms one each side where the tablets of the emperor s eight ancestors were kept. During each winter solstice, these tablets were placed in a small pavilion-like cage and removed to the Circular Mound for the Worshipping Heaven ceremony. After the ceremony, the tablets were returned to the stone platforms.

Two chambers located at the front of the Imperial Vault of Heaven contained different tablets used for worship. The left chamber contained tablets of the gods of basic elements including gold, wood, water, fire and earth. The right chamber contained tablets of gods of natural phenomena including wind, rain, thunder, lightning and so on.

Paragraph 5

E东西配殿
East and West Side Halls

The side halls, delicate with gray walls, blue tiles, and painted pillars, were for tablets of the subordinate gods.

In east side hall were the tablets of God of the Sun, Five stars of Venus, Jupiter, Mercury, Mars, and Saturn, as well as the Plough, the 28 stars on the moon's pat, etc.. Now the hall has newly added to itself the wax works of heaven worship.

In west side hall were the tablets of God of the Moon and gods of cloud, rain, and wind.

Paragraph 6

R丹陛桥
Red Stairway Bridge

The Red Stairway Bridge is a 360 meter passage that leads directly to the Gate of Prayer for Good Harvests. The bridge gradually increases in height from one end to the other. The southern end is about 1 meter high and the north end is about 4 meters high. It is 29.4 meters wide. The bridge represents the distance between the heaven and earth.

You can see three parallel paths on the bridge. Unlike other temples or the Forbidden City, the left path was reserved for the emperor. The central path was for the god of heaven while the right path was used by ministers.

The Red Stairway Bridge is called as such because there is a crossing under the bridge which was used by animals designated for sacrifice. Near the northern end of the bridge is a 150 square meter terrace which the emperor used to change his robes. A tent was set up to insure his privacy. Within the tent, a throne, incense burners and other necessities could be found.

Paragraph 7

The Hall of Prayer for Good Harvest

The highlight of the Temple of Heaven is the Hall of Prayer for Good Harvest. The hall was originally built in 1420 based on a model of the Temple of Heaven and Earth in Nanjing. At that time, it was called the Hall of Great Sacrifice. In 1530, the Temple of Earth was built in the northern part of Beijing, so only heaven was worshipped here. The hall was restored in 1751 and given its present name. In 1889, lightning caused extensive fire damage to the hall, but fortunately it was reconstructed.

The hall is a cone-shaped structure with triple eaves. Originally, the triple eaves were painted in different colors. The top was blue, which symbolized Heaven, the middle was yellow to symbolize the emperor and the bottom was green to represent commoners. During the Emperor Qianlong's reign (1736-1795), all the eaves were painted blue to follow the color of the sky.

A six meter high, triple-tiered circular stone terrace forms the base of the structure. The hall is 32 meters high and 30 meters in diameter. In the past, the hall was one of the highest buildings in Beijing. Despite its size, only 28 massive wooden pillars support the entire structure.

A number of wooden bars, laths and brackets join the entire structure together. Steel and cement were not used. The four large pillars in the center are known as the Dragon Well Pillars with each pillar representing one of the four seasons. The other 24 pillars are arranged in two circles surrounding the four central ones. The 12 inner pillars represent the 12 months of the year and the 12 outer pillars represent the divisions of day and night.

The ceiling framework is extremely intricate. The first or the lowest roof rests on a circular framework that is supported by the 24 outer pillars. The second roof partially rests on the 12 inner pillars and partially in the circle itself which is supported by crossbeams that are connected to the four Dragon Well Pillars. The third and highest roof rests on the four central pillars and on eight shorter pillars that are built on the same circular framework. A dragon is carved into the center of the ceiling and it represents supreme power and royalty.

A round marble stone called the dragon and Phoenix stone lies in the center of the room. Its name comes from pattern of the stone which resembles a dragon and phoenix.

The tablets of heaven and the tablets of dead emperor are found on the platforms. The tablets of heaven are in the center. Silk fabrics, jade carvings, fruit wines and other such items were placed in front of each tablet as an offering. Also, a pig, sheep or a cow was sacrificed at each ceremony.

Rectangular, blue-roofed buildings stood on either side of the courtyard. These buildings originally served as annexes; however, the west building is now a souvenir shop and the east one is an exhibition room for all the musical instruments used in the ceremony.

The Hall of Zenith is located on the lower level north of the Hall of Prayer for Good Harvest. The tablets for the ceremony of prayer were usually kept in the Hall of Zenith. There are many wax statutes that illustrate what an imperial ceremony was like.

用英语说中国——旅游亮点
Introduce China in English—Scenic Spots

Paragraph 8

Hall of Abstinence
皇乾殿

The Hall of Abstinence is located near the western entrance of the Temple of Heaven. It is encircled by two walls. The Inner wall is called Brick City, and the outer wall is called the Purple Wall. To further ensure the safety of the emperor, a moat was built to surround the Purple Wall. A bell tower, two stone pavilions and a beamless hall are the main structures here. The bell tower is in the northeast corner of the Hall of Abstinence. Before each ceremony. bells would be struck when the emperor left for the Circular Altar Mound and would not stop until the emperor arrived, After the ceremony, the bells would be struck again.

Of the two stone pavilions, the right pavilion kept time while the left one has a bronze plate with the word "fasting" engraved on it as a constant reminder to the emperor to observe fasting rules. The beamless hall was one of the most famous buildings in Beijing. A blue-tiled roof atop the hall symbolized that the emperor must always acknowledge the Supremacy of the Heavenly Emperor.

Paragraph 9

Double-Circle Longevity Pavilion
双环万寿亭

The pavilion is west of Hall of Prayer for Good Harvest. Its structure cleverly connects two round pavilions to form a unique masterpiece. It was originally built in 1714 by Emperor Qianlong for his mother's 50th birthday in the Imperial Palace, and in 1977 relocated here form Zhongnaihai. Nearby are Pavilion of All Flowers, Pavilion of Thousands Scenes, Sector Pavilion and so on.

古代郊祭与天坛建筑中的崇"九"文化

祭祀天地等活动是中国历代王朝的重要政治活动。帝王登基时必须效祀天地,以示"受命于天",承"天"之意来治理国家,而且每年的冬至日为祭天日已成为惯例。由于对天、地、日、月的祭祀活动多在郊外进行,因此对这类祭祀活动统称为郊祭。封建帝王对祭祀坛的建筑设计有着严格的思想要求,要求在形式上表现出天、地、日、月的崇高,神圣和皇帝与自然界的亲密关系。天坛内的建筑都完美地体现了这一设计内涵。

天坛里圜丘坛的台阶、栏杆、石块等,都和"九"这个数字密切相关。在中国传统文化里,认为一位数里最大的阳数是九,九也就意味着最大、无限、至极。中国过去皇帝称为"九五"之尊,中国古诗词中也有"九霄"、"九天"、"九重天"……其中的"九"都是这个意思。圜丘在建筑设计中多出现奇数,而且反复使用"九"的倍数,正是古代匠师对这一概念的运用和发挥,使"天"的观念能在祭祀建筑中更好地体现出来。

圜丘坛共有三层,每登上一层都要踏过九级台阶。顶层台面所辅的石板中心是"天心石",其外共环砌着九圈巨大的扇形石板。从中心向外第一圈是九块,第二圈是18块,以后每圈按九的倍数增加,直到最外的第九圈,恰好是81块。台面周围的护围石栏板,也自然地被四面台阶分为四部分,每部分都为九块;石台面的中层和下层石栏板也同样被分割为四部分。中层的圜丘坛三层的圆形石台,上层直径为九丈,中层直径为15丈,下层直径为21丈。不仅全为阳数,而且三层台面直径相加等于45丈,恰为"九五"之数,喻示皇帝乃"九五"之尊,也暗合《周易》中"九五,飞龙在天,利见大人"之说,大吉大利。

用英语说中国——旅游亮点
Introduce China in English—Scenic Spots

妙词连珠

worship 崇拜,(宗)礼拜	Red Stairway Bridge 丹陛桥
circular 圆形的	the Hall of Prayer for Good Harvests
semicircular 半圆形的	祈年殿
altar 圣坛,祭坛	Hall of Abstinence 斋宫
diameter 直径	Seven-Star Stone 七星石
abstinence 斋戒	winter solstice 冬至
ceremonial 礼仪的	worship the heaven 祭天
axis 轴线	pray for rainfall 求雨
ancestor 瓷砖,瓦	gathering place 集合地点
gilded 镀金的	fan-shape 扇形
entwine 缠绕,盘绕	concentric circle 同心圆
vault 拱顶	the chiming of bell 钟声
echo 回声	Heavenly Heart Stone 天心石
pray 祈求,祈祷	God of Heaven 天神
Circular Mound Altar 圜丘坛	Nine-Dragon Cypress 九龙柏
Imperial of Heaven 皇穹宇	the triple-layer eaves 三层檐
Echo Wall 回音壁	inner frame work 内部构架
Triple-sound Stone 三音石	Dragon Well Pillars 龙井柱

北京六大景点
The Six Scenic Spots in Beijing

Unit 6　十三陵　The Thirteen Ming Tombs

Key Sentences　流畅精句

1. The Ming Tombs are the burial ground of the Ming Dynasty emperors. Of the 16 Ming emperors, 13 were buried there, and so it's also known as the Thirteen Ming Tombs.
   明陵是明王朝的墓地。明朝有16位皇帝,其中13位埋在明陵,所以这里又称为"十三陵"。

2. This site of the Ming Tombs was chosen with special care, according to the geomancy (fengshui).
   十三陵的位置是按照中国的风水,精心选择的。

3. As a scenic area, there are three places we can visit. One is the Sacred Way. The second is Changling, the tomb of Emperor Yongle (1403-1424). The third one is Dingling, the tomb of Emperor Wanli (1573-1620) and his two empresses.
   作为旅游区十三陵有三个地方可以游览:第一是神路;第二是长陵,为永乐皇帝的墓地;第三是定陵,为万历皇帝和他的两个皇后的墓地。

4. At the end of the Sacred Way is the Dragon Phoenix Gate. The gate is also known as the Flame Gate, because of the flame carving on the top of the gate.
   神路的终点是龙凤门,此门也叫火焰门,因为大门的上方雕刻着火焰的图案而得名。

5. The third Emperor Yongle of the Ming Dynasty and his wife Empress Xu were buried in this tomb.
   明朝第三位永乐皇帝和他的皇后就埋在此陵。

6. The Changling Tomb is located at the foot of the Heavenly Longevity Mountain.

   长陵位于天寿山的山脚下。

7. Dingling is the only one of the 13 Ming tombs excavated so far.

   定陵是明十三陵中至今惟一挖掘出的陵墓。

8. The Soul Tower is also the mark of Dingling and is made of stone, but it is painted like a wooden structure.

   明楼也是定陵的标志,是由石头建成的,表面涂上了油漆像一个木质结构。

9. The Underground Palace. is 27 metres below the ground and composed of five chambers and covers an area of 1 195 square metres.

   地下宫殿在地下 27 米处,由五个殿组成,占地 1 195 平方米。

10. The five chambers include the antechamber, central chamber, left and right annex chambers and the rear chamber.

    这五殿包括前殿、中殿、左配殿、右配殿和后殿。

11. It was supposed to be an "everlasting lamp." The lamp was lit, when the emperor was buried. But after the tomb was closed the light naturally went out for lack of oxygen.

    这可能是一盏长明灯。皇帝死后被埋葬时灯点着,但当墓地关闭后长明灯由于缺少氧气而自然熄灭了。

12. The Ming Tombs have been listed by the Chinese Government as one of the important historical monuments under special preservation.

    十三陵被中国政府列为重点历史文物而受到特殊的保护。

Wonderful Paragraph
精彩片段

Paragraph 1

十三陵
The Ming Tombs

The Ming Tombs are located at the southern foot of Tianshou Mountain in Beijing's Changping District, occupying an area of over 40 square kilometers. The burial ground is so called because all thirteen ming emperors who ruled China after the Chinese capital was moved to Beijing were buried there. Construction of the Ming Tombs took over two centuries, starting from the building of Changling in the 7th year of the Ming Yong Le reign to the completion of Siling in the early years of the Qing Shun Zhi reign. The major attractions of the Ming Tombs are Shen Dao (the Sacred Way) and the ground and underground architecture of the bombs. Of the thirteen tombs, three are currently open to the public, namely, Changling, Dingling and Zhaoling. The tombs exhibit an elegant yet dignified architectural style. No other imperial mausoleums in the world are so well preserved and have entombed so many imperial bodies as the Ming Tombs.

According to the order of construction time, they ranked as followed: Changling Tomb, Xianling Tomb, Jingling Tomb, Yuling Tomb, Maoling Tomb, Tailing Tomb, Kangling Tomb, Yongling Tomb, Zhaoling Tomb, Dingling Tomb, Qingling Tomb, Deling Tomb and Siling Tomb. Only Changling Tomb, Zhaoling Tomb and Dingling Tomb open to tourists now.

Paragraph 2

十三陵总神道
Sacred Way

The sacred way (or the tomb passage) was originally designed for the Changling Tomb. Since the sacred way to other tombs originated from this one, it became the general sacred way for all. Along the 7.3-km-long sacred way stands the Stone Archway, the Great Red Gate, Cloud Pillar and Stele Pavilion and so on. demonstrating the inviolable imperial power. The construction of these architectures began in 1435, the 10th year of Ming Emperor Xuande's reign, and more structures were added in 1540. the 19th year of Ming Emperor Jiajing's reign. The present Museum of the Sacred Way displays the series of structures to tourists, from the Stele Pavilion to the Dragon and Phoenix Gate.

C长陵 hangling Tomb

The first built of the 13 tombs, the Changling Tomb buried the Ming Emperor Yongle and his empress Xu. It was the largest (occupying 10 hectares), most advanced and best preserved imperial mausoleum, using the best materials. Built in 1409, even the underground palace of the massive project took four years to complete. Having undergone the weathering of 600 years, the Changling Tomb remains intact and resplendent and magnificent.

Its design followed that of Xiao Mausoleum for Emperor Zhu Yuanzhang the dynasty founder: the front is a rectangular courtyard and the rear is the round Treasure Dome (tomb mound). led in by 15km Divine Avenue from south to north. The Divine Avenue extends from the stone archway at the mausoleum entrance straight forward to the gate of the mausoleum palace as the axis of the entire mausoleum and the symbol of the supreme majesty of the monarch. Northward from the stone archway along the Divine Avenue are arranged in order the Big Red Gate, Stele of Achievements and Virtues, Watch Post, and stone animals and figures, the line ending at an exquisite and unique Lingxing Gate, the entrance to the mausoleum proper.

D定陵 ingling Tomb

Dingling Tomb was the imperial mausoleum for Emperor Wanli and his two empresses and also the only excavated one. Its construction began in 1584 and completed in 1590, covering an area of 180 000 square meters. It took 8 million liang of silver, equivalent to two-year tax income during the mid-period of Emperor Wanli's reign. At present, only the Baocheng, Memorial Tower and the city wall, among the above-ground architectures, survived the past severe destruction.

This is the tomb of Zhu Yijun, the 13th emperor of Ming Dynasty, and his two empresses, located at the foot of Dayu Hill at the northwest of the Thirteen Mausoleums, occupying an area of about 18 hectares.

Zhu Yijun assumed the crown when only 10 years old, titled his reign as Wanli Period and ruled for 48 years, the longest among all the emperors of Ming Dynasty. Since the construction of his mausoleum began in his life time in 1584, he personally inspected the six-year construction for six times, thus the officials in charge dared no risk but deployed 20 to 30 thousand laborers each day and produced an extraordinarily exquisite and elegant tomb. It is said that the pavement brick would take 8 month to prepare its earthen base, the burning with selected tree branches would last for 136 days, and another 3 months were needed to soak the finished bricks in Tong oil, so that the bricks would be fine, smooth, and yellowish in color, thus called "golden brick". This might give some idea of their extravagant meticulosity about the building materials. The total expenditure on Ding Mausoleum amounts to about 8 million taels of silver, and the luxury reveals fully the political corruption and social extravagance in the middle and towards the end of Ming Dynasty.

The aboveground buildings of Ding Mausoleum imitate Chang Mausoleum in its layout: rectangular in shape, square in front and round in rear. In order on the axis are the similar buildings like mausoleum gate, Stele Pavilion, Gate of Prominent Favor, Mausokeum Tower, and Treasure City. Yet the craft is more meticulous everywhere, such as the three additional single arched stone bridges in front of the mausoleum gate, the Stele Pavilion behind the bridges in the style of double-eave between four ridges, and the stele carrier tortoise was carved with lively sea waves and coast cliffs, etc. No far away east of the stele pavilion, there was also the "Office for Ding Mausoleum" in charge of the daily management and maintenance, and the rooms provided for the office alone amounted to over 300.

Zhaoling Tomb
昭陵

Similarly structured with other mausoleums, the Zhaoling Tomb is noted for its unique grave mound. Earth was heaped over the grave mound from the drains inside Baocheng of the other six mausoleums including Xianling Tomb and Kangling Tomb. The grave mound of Zhaoling Tomb, however, was nearly equal in height to the city wall of Baocheng. On this account, special enclosed wall was built to protect the grave mound. Coupled with the city wall of Baocheng, the enclosed wall formed a closed courtyard, referred to as Mute Courtyard by later generations. The later-built Qingling Tomb, Deling Tomb and imperial mausoleums of Qing emperors followed this practice.

Cultural Links
文化链接

十三陵的"无字碑"

游览过北京十三陵的人都知道定陵矗立着一块"无字碑"。

定陵,是陵园中的第十三个陵墓,埋葬着明代后期的第 13 个神宗皇帝——朱翊钧(年号"万历")和他的两个皇后孝端、孝靖。这个皇帝昏聩残暴,颇有点自命不凡。在万历 11 年(公元 1583 年),他趁祭陵之便,带领文武官员、术士、钦天监等,不但在京西天寿山亲自选定陵地,确定建陵规划,而且还对所立石碑煞费了一番苦心。

这是座无字碑,它巍峨壮观,雕饰精美。碑座是一昂首远眺的蠵龟,环周衬以波涌浪迭,急流飞泻;那雕饰的鱼、虾、蟹、鳖,似凌波而起,蠵龟则宛如浮游于惊涛骇浪中。顶端六龙交盘,似在游水戏珠,栩栩如生。然而其碑身却并非是洁白无瑕的汉白玉,而是呈光泽清润的淡青色,在此底衬上,散布着浓浓相宜的斑纹,恰如高天徐徐飘动的云朵。更有趣的是在碑阴的右上方,闪映着一个如盘大小的圆斑,质地缜密,晶莹洁白,与环周的颜色

北京六大景点
The Six Scenic Spots in Beijing

若明若暗,氤氲朦胧,犹似夜空中形成的"月晕"。神宗皇帝或许是要显示他的"正大光明"吧,遂将其美曰"高悬的明月"。后人故有"月亮碑"之称。为之还有一个离奇的传说,说这座石碑中集聚了很多宝物:碑上"月亮"不但会闪闪发光,还会随天宇间的日、月、星辰不停地转动……后来陵园遭到失火,碑中宝物乃烧至殆尽,"月亮"也随之停止了转动。

多么优美的传说,殊不知这块碑石纯系大自然的造化。在岩石学上称其为"结晶灰岩",因其一经磨光,便酷似晒干的淡青色"艾叶",故又名"艾叶青",是属彩石的一种。此碑只是做了人为的附会和想像罢了。

Vocabulary 妙词连珠

tomb 坟	the Underground Palace 地下宫殿
burial 埋葬	the Funeral Chamber 埋葬殿
sacred 神圣的	Antechamber 前殿
mythical 神秘的	Central Chamber 中殿
eminent 著名的,突出的	Rear Chamber 后殿
sacrificial 献祭的	Annex Chambers 配殿
soul 灵魂	well-known 闻名的
wick 灯芯	inscribe 刻;雕;写
funeral 葬礼	empress 女皇;皇后
the Thirteen Ming Tombs 十三陵	layout 布局;设计
the Sacred Way 神路	superstitious 迷信的
Marble Archway 石牌坊	cite 引用;传讯
the Great Palace Gate 大宫门	coffin 棺材
tablet tower 碑亭	bier 棺材架;棺材;尸体架
Soul Tower 明楼	massive 大量的,巨大的
Dragon and Phoenix Gate 龙凤门	

2 东北
Northeast China

Unit 1　Heilongjiang Province
黑龙江省

Key Sentences
流畅精句

1. Located in the most northeastern part of China, Heilongjiang Province occupies the land along the northern and the eastern frontiers.
   黑龙江省位于中国最东北部,中国陆地国土的最北端与最东端均位于黑龙江省境内。

2. The land is fertile, and it is a well-known productive base of crops as well as of cows.
   这里土地肥沃,是全国著名的粮仓和养牛基地。

3. It was called Sushendi in ancient times, where the ancestors of the northern ethnic groups survived. On this land was Bohai Kingdom set up during the Tang Dynasty. It was once the cradle of the Northern Wei, Liao, Jin and Qing dynasties.
   古为肃慎地,从远古时代起便有北方少数民族的祖先在此生息、繁衍,唐代建立了封建政权——渤海国。是北魏和辽、金、清朝的发祥地。

4. Dwelling mainly in Tongjiang, Wuyuan and Raohe counties, the Hezhen is a unique nationality in Heilongjiang Province with the smallest population of 2 000 in China.

赫哲族是黑龙江省独有的民族，也是我国人口最少的民族之一。现有2 000多人，主要聚居在同江、抚远和饶河县境内。

5. Harbin's major tourist attraction is Ice Sculpture Festival.
   哈尔滨吸引旅游者的主要景致是冰雕节。
6. The annual Harbin Summer Music Festival is held in July.
   每年一度的哈尔滨夏季音乐节在7月举行。
7. The Sun Island is an ideal place for summer holiday.
   太阳岛是夏日度假的理想去处。
8. Dream World is a great place to swim all year round.
   梦世界是常年可游泳的好地方。
9. There are many Russian churches and synagogues in Harbin.
   哈尔滨有许多俄式教堂和犹太教堂。
10. You can see a lot of Russian and Japanese architecture and cobble-stone street in Harbin.
    在哈尔滨你可看到许多俄式和日式建筑以及鹅卵石街道。

Wonderful Paragraph 精彩片段

Paragraph 1

Wudalian Lakes 五大连池

Situated on the southwest slope of Mt. Xiaoxing'anling in the northwest of Heilongjiang Province, Wudalianchi City is surrounded with 14 volcanoes and a dozen mineral springs, forming a unique and typical as well a volcanic spectacle, hence the name of the Park of Volcanoes. It is a popular volcanic resort in China.

用英语说中国——旅游亮点
Introduce China in English—Scenic Spots

Jingpo Lake

Jingpo Lake Lying in Ning'an and 110 kilometers from Mudanjiang City, the 95-square-kilometer Jingpo Lake is one of the largest alpine lakes in China, at an altitude of 350 meters above sea level. Embraced by rolling mountain, the lake is famous for beautiful scenery. The Diaoshuilou Waterfalls, located in northern part of the lake, rushes down with a height of 25 meters, forming a spectacular scene.

Dragon Tower

The Dragon Tower in Harbin, Heilongjiang Province, the highest steel structure tower in Asia, makes icon of the nation's leading scenic spots in terms of infrastructure and service quality. The first steel tower of Asia is 336 meters high, like a dazzling jewel inlaid on the earth of Longjiang.

The dragon collects many kinds of comprehensive functions, including the transmission of television of radio in the tower, go sightseeing, in a body advertisement propagate, food and beverage amusement, scientific and technological paradise, wireless communication, environmental meteorological observation and monitoring, etc., and become new significant view of Harbin, well-known city of northern part of the country, that has enjoyed the reputation of "eastern Moscow" and even Heilongjiang Province. Scientific and technological paradise behaviour area is located in tower flat basement and tower 2, roam leisurely on Hi-Tech and front line science world with glamour space limitless, let you enjoy oneself so much as to forget to go home; MTV photography recording canopy will help you to realize the colored star's dream; Ten thousands of square meters share space, reach richly spacious and lightly, transparent and make eyes comfortable; the transparent lift on tower turns on the domestic beginning; Arrive 181-

metre-high visit layer, gaze far into the distance everything, step on transparent glass fibre reinforced plastic floor just like strolling among the clouds; 185-meter-high revolving restaurant, adopts the domestic first getting straggly platform, view and food &beverage melting each other, bring up the new concept of food and beverage of port of Harbin; Dragon advertising exhibition locating inside and outside of the tower, show corporate image, " gold stage" of enterprise promoting product sales. In addition, the Dragon Tower is the best place that travel and shopping, recreation getting happy, the recreation square of the Dragon Tower is the new developing pleasant world in the city.

Paragraph 4

圣·索菲亚教堂
St. Sophia Church

St. Sophia Church, first built in 1907, 53.35 meters in height and 720 square meters in area, is the largest Eastern Orthodox Church in the Far East. The splendid and elegant structure of bricks and wood shows a strong influence of the Byzantine style of architecture.

Paragraph 5

太阳岛
Sun Island

Facing the downtown area across the Songhua River, Sun Island is a 38-square-km sand bar lapped by the waters of the river. In summer, leafy trees and carpet-like lawns can make visitors feel so comfortable they are often reluctant to leave. In winter, the island has become the venue of international ice sculpture competition.

Paragraph 6

哈尔滨冰雪节
Ice and Snow Festival in Harbin

Harbin Ice and Snow Festival, held on January 5 every year, reflects the city's economic development and its unique culture. The festival is a unique event celebrated by the Harbin people. Each year, many tourists from home and abroad, especially those who have never seen ice and snow, will come to the event to enjoy the magic ice sculptures made by the Harbin people. Various splendid ice lanterns will be shown in the Harbin Ice Lantern Park and snow sculptures will be on display at the Sun Island in the city. Besides the ice art exhibition, a series of activities will be held, including winter swimming, ice hockey, skiing and trade fairs. The festival, which has been held every year since 1985, is expected to attract foreigners to invest in the city once they have seen its beauty.

Cultural Links
文化链接

药泉的传说

  五大连池的矿泉水能够治疗许多疾病,故称"药泉"。药泉的功能是如何发现的?民间有一段美丽的传说。

  相传在很久以前,五大连池附近有一对给牧主当奴隶的青年恋人。小伙子叫嘎拉桑白音,姑娘叫阿美其格。有一次,嘎拉桑白音被牧主吊在马棚里拷打至昏,恋人阿美其格就牵出一匹快马,驮着嘎拉桑白音逃出了牧主的围子。牧主发现后骑马追赶,并用毒箭射中了阿美其格的左腿。这对恋人快马加鞭甩掉了牧主,最后摔下马来,阿美其格昏迷过去。嘎拉桑白音为恋人拔毒箭、吮毒血,却不见恋人苏醒。就在这时,他发现一只右腿血淋淋的小鹿,一瘸一拐走进相距不远的一个水坑里洗起来,然后健步跑到另一个泉边喝了一阵水,便蹦蹦跳跳地离去了。嘎拉桑白音连忙将阿美其格抱到水坑边,为她清洗伤口,阿美其格很快苏醒过来,伤口也立时长好了。他喜出望外,自己也跳到水坑里洗起来,鞭伤也马上痊愈了。接着俩人到另一泉边喝了泉水,浑身立刻有了力气。

  他们发现这个药泉后,就堆起了一堆石头作为记号。后来,他俩告诉附近的牧民都来泉边治病,牧民们非常感激。

  由于发现药泉水的这一天是端午节,所以就形成了后来的五月初五的"药泉会"。

东北 Northeast China

Vocabulary 妙词连珠

northermost 最北部的	link up with 连接
Ice Sculpture 冰雕	in the old days 古时候
amazing 吸引人的	as many as 多达
symbol 象征	endangered spicy animals 濒危动物
figure 造型	mink 貂
winter 冬天	muskrat 麝鼠
exquisite 精致的,高雅的	straw patchwork 草编装饰物
lotus 莲	horn carving 角雕
line 排列	Sun Island Park 太阳岛公园
willow 柳树	Oilfield 油田
seclusion 隐蔽,僻静	Jingpo Lake 镜泊湖
asstume 呈现	Harbin 哈尔滨
slink 轻手轻脚、偷偷摸摸地走动	

Unit 2　Jilin Province
吉林省

Key Sentences
流畅精句

1. Jilin Province sits in the middle of Northeast China.
   吉林省位于东北中部。
2. Jilin Province was named after Jilin General, who ruled over this land in the later Qing Dynasty.
   吉林以清末于吉林将军辖境建省得名。
3. Changchun is noted for a city of forests.
   长春素有"森林之城"的美称。
4. The province of Jilin borders on Korea and Russia.
   吉林省与朝鲜和俄罗斯接壤。
5. Jilin's 27 million people include, Han, Korean, Manchu, Hui, Mongol and Xibo.
   吉林有2 700万人口,包括汉族、朝鲜族、满族、回族、蒙古族和锡伯族。
6. The Songhua River runs through the Jilin city.
   松花江穿吉林市而过。
7. The famous Crater Lake in Changbai Mountains is beautiful Heaven Lake.
   长白山区最著名的火山口湖是美丽的天池。
8. The famous 900-kilometer-long Songhua River rises from the Heaven Lake on the White-Headed Mountain.
   著名的松花江全长900公里,发源于白头山天池。
9. Yalu and Tumen rivers, both rising from the Changbai Mountain, are the boundary rivers between China and Korea.
   鸭绿江和图们江发源于长白山脉,是中朝两国的界河。

东北
Northeast China

10. Major cities of Jilin include "the Auto City"—Changchun, the famous historical and cultural cities of Jilin and Jian, and Yanji, capital of Yanbian Korean Autonomous Prefecture.
吉林省的重要城市有省会"汽车城"长春,历史文化名城吉林、集安、延边朝鲜族自治州首府延吉等。

11. Main tourist spots in Jilin province are Changbai Mountain, Heaven Lake, Songhua Lake, Jingyue Pool, Puppet State's Imperial Palace, Motion Picture City, and so on.
吉林名胜有长白山、天池、松花湖、净月潭风景区、长春电影城、伪皇宫等。

Wonderful Paragraph 精彩片段

Paragraph 1

长白山自然保护区
Changbai Mountain Nature Reserve

Changbaishan means eternally white mountains and is located in the southeast of Jilin near the Korean border. It is China's largest nature reserve and is home to the rare Manchurian tiger, snow leopards and wild ginseng.

Covering a total area of 2 000 square km, Changbai Mountains Nature Reserve is, as a mammoth natural zoo and botanical garden, part of the UNESCO'S Man and Biosphere Program.

The most famous scenic area in Changbaishan is Baitoushan (White Head Mountain) and Tianchi (Lake of Heaven), a 2 million year old volcanic crate lake at the mountain summit. Tianchi has a circumference of 13km and has an average depth of 204 meters. Surrounded by beautiful mountains, hot springs and waterfalls this area is considered sacred by both Koreans and Manchus.

用英语说中国——旅游亮点
Introduce China in English—Scenic Spots

Paragraph 2

Tianchi Lake 天池

The volcanic Tianchi (Heavenly) Lake, 10 square km in area and 204 meters in average depth (373 meters at the deepest), marks the boundary of China and Korea on the top of Baitou Mountain, the main peak of Changbei Mountains. Skirted on all sides by mountains, the lake is known for its sublime natural beauty.

Paragraph 3

Rimed Trees in Jilin 吉林雾凇

Rimed Trees in Jilin The rimed trees of Jilin are extolled as one of four major and natural wonders of China along withe the landscape of Guilin, the Stone Forest of Yunan, and the Three Gorges of the Yangtze River. In winter the Songhua River keeps flowing through Jilin despite the subfreezing temperature, and the vapour rising from the surface of the river freezes when it meets the branches of pines and willows ashore. Thus encrusted with layers upon layers of ice, the tree branches and twigs look transparent and form a spectacular crystal world.

Paragraph 4

Songhua Lake 松花湖

Spreading out in the middle part, southeast of Jilin City and among the Yongji City, Jiaohe City and Huadian County, Songhua Lake encompasses 425 square kilometres. The surface of the lake is at an elevation of 266.5 metres, with the deepest of the lake being 77.5 metres. It has water storage of 10.8 billion cubic metres. It is the man-made lake on the upper reaches of Songhua River. At the estuary of the lake is the Fengman Hydropower

东北
Northeast China

Station. The scenery of the lake is fantastic and charming, famous for soft rime (or hoar frost). Points of interest include Aohua Platform (鳌花台), Stone Dragon Wall (Screen) (石龙壁), Camel Summit (骆驼峰), Five-Tiger Isle (五虎岛), and Reclining (or Recumbent) Dragon Pool (卧龙潭). It is a key national scenic spot.

Paragraph 5

净月潭公园
Jingyue Pool Park

Jingyue (Clear Moon) Pool Park 15 kilometers southeast from Changchun downtown and 150 square kilometers in area, it is one of the largest artificial forests in Asia and a national forest park where the ecological system is well protected. The place, with a total of 86 peaks, has become a scenic resort where holiday makers go for sightseeing, recuperating, recreation, and other purposes. The 4.3-square-kilometer Jingyue Pool is regard as a "sister" to Taiwan's Riyue (Sun and Moon) Pool.

Paragraph 6

中国高句丽王城、王陵及贵族墓葬
Capital Cities and Tomes of China's Ancient Koguryo Kingdom

Capital cities and tombs of China's ancient Koguryo Kingdom were inscribed on the World Heritage List on July 2, 2004 by the 28th Session of the World Heritage Committee Convention in Suzhou, East China's Jiangsu Province. The ruins are scattered in Ji'an City of Northeast China's Jilin Province and Huanren Manchu Autonomous County of the neighbouring Liaoning Province. They include remains of three cities and 40 tombs, Wunu Mountain City, Guonei City and Wandu Mountain City, with 14 tombs of imperial families and 26 of nobles. They all belong to the Koguryo culture, named after the dynasty that ruled over parts of northern China and the northern half of the Korean Peninsula from 37 BC to AD 668.

The selection committee also agreed to put the Complex of the Koguryo

Tombs, which is inside the Democratic People's Republic of Korea (DPRK) on the heritage list in 2004.

Cultural Links
文化链接

天池的传说

古时候,东海龙王出宫巡游。这一天,龙王巡游到圆心湖,发现湖边有许多闪闪放光的水珠,龙王就让随从捧起来,放在手心里,这水珠就像珍珠一般。龙王喜爱地看了又看,尝了又尝,这水珠甜丝丝的,清香可口。从此,龙王就管这水珠叫珍珠水。

龙王回到龙宫,一心要寻找这种珍珠水源,就下了一道命令,让鱼兵虾将到四海去寻找。鱼兵虾将跑遍了五湖四海,也没找到,就回报了龙王。但龙王还是不甘心,又下了一道命令,让鱼兵虾将继续寻找。

龙王的鱼兵虾将终于在东北角的偏僻地方,找到了一座高高的大山——长白山。从远处望,高山顶上有一池清清的水。珍珠水就是从这座深山大谷里淌出来的。

龙王知道了珍珠水打哪儿来,就上书给玉皇大帝。玉皇大帝十分高兴,把长白山顶上的这个池封为天池。天池里有珍珠水的喜讯很快就在天宫里传开了。

这一天早晨,南天门"哗啦"一声开了,从门里出来七个穿着彩衣的仙女。她们驾着彩云来到了长白山的天池。

湛蓝湛蓝的天池水面上,印出了七个美丽俊俏的仙女。她们观看了天池四周的美丽景致,就脱去了彩衣,下到天池里去洗澡。仙女在天池里游来游去。突然,有个仙女一不小心喝进了一口天池水,觉得这水真是香甜清爽。她想:如果让这水流下山去,让世上的人都喝到天池水,那有多好!她向姐妹们说明了想法,大家都很赞同。于是,七个美丽的仙女就用七把木勺舀起天池水,往北边一泼,这勺水经过龙门直流下山崖,变成瀑布,曲曲弯弯地流进了松林。春天松树花飘落到水面,飘飘荡荡顺水流下山去,后来人们给它起名叫松花江。仙女们又舀水往东边一泼,水刚刚流下就被耸立的山峰挡住了去路,这股水就调头顺着石缝流下去,流啊流啊,流了很长一段路,才从山谷里涌出地面,继续向东流去,人们给这条江起名为图们江。仙女们又舀水向西南泼去,一直流到大海里,人们给它起名为鸭绿江。

从那时起,长白山天池孕育了三条大江——松花江、图们江和鸭绿江。这三条大江浩浩荡荡地向北、东、西三个方向流淌,多少年来,一直滋润着肥沃的土地,也哺育了这块土地上成千上万的人们。

Vocabulary 妙词连珠

tractor 拖拉机	Songhua River 松花江
ski 滑冰	climate 气候
sea cucumber 海参	topography 地形
Arladi Village 阿拉迪村	trading caravans 商旅队
winter sports 滑雪运动	highlight 亮点,最吸引人之处
hot spring 温泉	traditional 传统的
bank 岸	charm 魅力
Rime Festival 雾凇节	implication 含蓄
Songhua Lake 松花湖	classical 经典的
Tianchi Lake 天池	Physiongnomy 地貌
rimed trees 雾凇	exotic 奇异的、充满异国情调的
nature reserve 自然保护区	layout 布局
Manchu 满族	grandeur 壮观
scenic spots 景点	aesthetic 审美的
ancient 古代的	

Unit 3　Liaoning Province
辽宁省

Key Sentences
流畅精句

1. Liaoning Province lies in the valley of the Liaohe River, with the vast plain in the middle and the adulating hills on the both east and west sides. Originating from Mt. Changbai, the Yalu River meanders through between China and Northern Korea.
   辽宁省位于辽河流域,境内的中朝界河鸭绿江源于长白山,注入黄海。东、西两侧为低山丘陵,中部为广阔的平原。

2. Most part of Liaodong Peninsula is hilly with zigzag coastal lines and lots of excellent ports.
   辽东半岛大部分为低丘,海岸曲折多良港。

3. Shengyang Palace of the Qing Dynasty Before the Manchurian came to Central China, their royal palace was located in Shengyang City, which was built by the first and second emperors of the Qing Dynasty as their palace.
   清代入关前,其皇宫设在沈阳,沈阳故宫是清太祖努尔哈赤、清太宗皇太极营建和使用的宫殿。

4. Dalian's Seaside—Lushunkou: As the most beautiful place, Dalian's Seaside lies on the coast in the south of Dalian, between Dalian Bay and Lushunkou.
   大连海滨——旅顺口,在大连南部沿海,介于大连湾到旅顺口之间,这是大连风景最为优美的地方。

5. Liaoning borders on the Democratic People's Republic of Korea.
   辽宁与朝鲜民主主义共和国接壤。

6. Shengyang today is an industrial and cultural center.
   沈阳如今是个工业和文化中心。
7. Dalian is a beautiful and well-organized city.
   大连漂亮美丽，规划齐整。
8. You can enjoy scuba diving, fishing, and mountaineering in Dalian.
   你可在大连享受潜水、垂钓、登山之乐。
9. The Jade Buddha in Anshan was carved ou of one piece of huge stone.
   鞍山的玉佛是由一块巨石雕刻而成的。
10. The jade market in Anshan is said to be the largest such market in China.
    鞍山的玉石市场据说是全国最大的。
11. Fushun is known for the War Criminal Prison Museum.
    抚顺因有战犯监狱博物馆而闻名。

Wonderful Paragraph 精彩片段

Paragraph 1

沈阳故宫
Shenyang Imperial Palace

The Shenyang Imperial Palace, located at No. 171, Shenyang Road, Shenhe District in Shenyang City, is the only existing royal palace in China outside of the Forbidden City in Beijing. The main structure of the palace was built in 1625 when Nurhachi was in power. It was finished in 1636 by his son Abahai (Huangtaiji). Nurhachi and Abahai were both founding emperors of the Qing Dynasty.

Covering an area of more than 60 000 square meters (about 71 760 square yards), the Shenyang Imperial Palace is one twelfth the size of the Forbidden City in Beijing. The palace consists of more than 300 rooms, formed around 20 courtyards.

The palace can be divided into three sections-the eastern section, the middle section and the western section. Each section boasts of unique characteristics.

The eastern section contains the very impressive Hall of Great Affairs (Da Zheng Dian). Here emperors ascended the throne, enacted imperial edicts, and welcomed victorious generals and soldiers. A group of pavilions, known as the Ten Kings Pavilion, stand to its east and west. They formerly served as the place where emperors and leaders from the eight banners (Ba Qi) settled national affairs. This architectural style of Shenyang Imperial Palace is unique. The style of the buildings, which displays an amalgamation of Han, Manchu and Mongolian cultures, all originated from the shape of a nomadic tent. The eastern section of the palace is representative of the whole palace.

The middle section starts from the Da Qing Gate, with Chong Zheng Dian (Jin Luan Dian), the Phoenix Tower and Qingning Palace arranged on a central axis from south to north. Chong Zheng Dian is the place where Abahai held court. It is the most important building in the Shenyang Imperial Palace. The Phoenix Tower, a three-storied building, was the highest structure in the whole city at that time. Qingning Palace was the bedchamber for Abahai and his concubines.

The western section was constructed by order of Emperor Qianlong (1711-1799). Its main structure is the Wen Su Pavilion. In front of this, there are the Opera Stage and Jiayin Hall and behind it is the Yang Xi Room. The Wen Su Pavilion, which contains the Complete Collection of Four Treasures, has a black roof because black was considered to represent water which could be used to extinguish a fire to protect the priceless books contained inside.

The Shenyang Imperial Palace houses many ancient cultural relics, such as Nurhachi's sword and Abahai's broadsword. There are also many artworks displayed here, such as paintings, calligraphy, pottery, sculptures and lacquer ware.

Besides the Forbidden City in Beijing, the Shenyang Imperial Palace is

东北
Northeast China

the only other existing palace complex in China. Within its walls much is revealed about the early Qing Dynasty. It was listed by UNESCO as a World Cultural Heritage Site in 2004 as an extension of the Forbidden City and is now the most popular and renowned tourist attraction in Shenyang.

Paragraph 2

D 大连金石滩
Dalian Golden Pebble Beach Resort

Dalian Golden Pebble Beach National Resort, one of the 12 national resorts firstly approved by the State Council in 1992, mainly aims at receiving foreign guests. It's the tourism functional zone of the four open-up pioneering zones of Dalian City.

Dalian Golden Pebble Beach has been developed and constructed since 1985. In 1988, the State Council approved Golden Pebble Beach as the state key scenic resort, and approved to construct national resort on December 4th, 1992. Dalian Golden Pebble Beach National resort Administrative Committee, assigned by Dalian Municipal Government, is responsible for local development.

Paragraph 3

B 北陵（又称昭陵）
Beiling Park (also known as Zhaoling)

Encompassing 180 000 square metres, Beiling (North Tomb), also known as Zhaoling, which was the resting place of Huangtaiji (1592-1643), founder of the Qing Dynasty. Workers have demolished different structures including hotels, restaurants, markets and parking lots. The surrounding area has been redesigned and the park has been restored to its original royal flavour. Restoring Beiling Park to its original look has been part of Shenyang's efforts to protect the city's cultural and historical relics. A new storehouse has been built in a corner of the palace grounds to house and preserve the large number of ancient works of calligraphy, paintings, porcelains, sculptures, enamel ware, jewels and stone vessels from the palace.

Paragraph 4

Tiger Beach 老虎滩

There is a touching folklore about Tiger Beach. It is a love story about a hunter and a beautiful girl. They fell in love at first sight. A tiger demon lusted after the charming of the girl and possessed her. The hunter vowed to take his lover back. After a fierce battle, the hunter killed the tiger, but he lost his fair lady forever. Now in Tiger Beach Park, people still could find tiger cave and sharply-cut rocks.

Paragraph 5

Qianshan Mountain 千山

Qianshan Mountain Also called "A-Thousand-Lotus-Flower Mountain", it is located southeast of Anshan, 20 kilometer from city proper. The mountain is densely wooded, and abounds in flora and fauna, and is a national scenic resort. Among its scenic spots is a new discovery—a nature statue of the Buddha forming by peak, which stands 70 meters high. The place has since become a holy land of Buddhism in northeast China. And many sacrificial utensils of the Ming and Qing dynasties were discovered at the foot of the peak.

Paragraph 6

The Jade Buddha Garden 玉佛园

Located in the suburb of Anshan, the Jade Buddha Garden covers 220 000 square metres, the city shelters a Guinness-Record-Winning Buddha carved Iram jade. The world's biggest jade Buddha (Jade King), 7.95 metres high, 6.88 metres wide, 4.1 metres thick, was carved in 1995 from a stone weighing 261 tons. The splendid sculpture, merging seven colours together—three shades of green, yellow, white, black and blue—(the Buddha is bright and dazzling) is an eye-catching artistic wonder produced by 120 jade sculptors in 27 months. It has been listed in the Guinness Book of Records as the world's largest jade Buddha. The stone came from Anshan's Xiuyan County (the hometown of jade), which has proven jade deposits of 3 million tons. The huge jade weighing 60 000 tons were also discovered there. Jade artifacts are the best souvenirs for tourists. Due to its unique geological structure, Aashan is rich in geothermal resources. A natural Buddha formed by a whole hill made Mount Qianshan a holy land for Buddhists in Northeast China.

Paragraph 7

冰峪沟
Ice Valley

Ice Valley attract visitors with its unique landscape. The charming scenes are as intriguing as the famous Stone Forest and as delicate as Guilin Scenery with hills and waters. Legend tells Li Shimin, a Tang Dynasty emperor, led his expedition and stopped in the valley in spring time. He was surprised to see that outside the valley was a world of green woods and colorful flowers whereas inside the valley was a space of ice and snow. The emperor named the place of wonder "Ice Valley".

"老虎滩"的由来

关于老虎滩名字的由来，说法很多。有人说从前这里很荒凉，山上有老虎，也有人说靠海的山洞叫老虎洞，每到夜半涨潮时，海浪袭来，会发出虎啸一样的回声。

另有一民间传说，流传很广，说这山上经常有一只猛虎下山伤人畜，有

用英语说中国——旅游亮点
Introduce China in English—Scenic Spots

一天,龙王的女儿在山坡上采花,被恶虎叼跑,有一个叫石槽的青年听到救命声,挥剑追赶,迫使恶虎丢下龙女逃跑。为了报答石槽救命之恩,龙女便与他结为夫妇。石槽想恶虎不除,百姓一天不得安宁,于是婚后第一天便要上山除虎。龙女告诉他,这恶虎是天上黑虎星下凡,只有用龙宫里的宝剑才能制服它。龙女回宫借宝剑。

不想,在龙女离开当天恶虎又下山伤人,石槽等不及宝剑,便与恶虎搏斗,挥剑砍飞虎牙,落到海里,成了虎牙礁;又一把拽住老虎尾巴,甩到旅顺港湾,成了老虎尾;最后砍去半个虎头成了半拉山;虎身瘫在海边,成了虎滩。石槽伤累而死,变成礁石。龙女借剑回来,见夫已死,痛不欲生,卧在夫身边,化成美人礁。

Vocabulary 妙词连珠

East Tomb 东陵	Dalian Golden Pebble Beach Resort 大连金石滩
Phoenix Tower 凤凰塔	Mount Qianshan in Anshan 鞍山千山
Palace of Pure Tranquility 清宁宫	The Jade Buddha Garden 玉佛园
Laohutan Park 老虎滩公园	Shenyang Imperial Palace 沈阳故宫
Museum of Natural History 自然博物馆	the Phoenix Tower 凤凰楼
Dragon Spring Temple 龙泉寺	the Palace of celestial Peace 清宁宫
Thousand Lotuses Hill 千莲山	Jade Buddha 玉佛
black beans 黑豆	The yalu River 鸭绿江
Shenyang Imperial Palace 沈阳故宫	beach 海滨
Beiling Park, also known as Zhaoling 北陵,又称昭陵	Star Sea square 星海广场
	Heavenly Bridge 天桥
Former Residence of Zhang Xueliang 张学良故居	Hushan Section of the Great Wall 虎山长城

3 华北
North China

Unit 1 河北省 Hebei Province

Key Sentences 流畅精句

1. Facing the Bohai Bay and situated in the Great Plain in Northern China, Hebei was named so for its location on the northern side of the lower reaches of the Yellow River.
   河北省地处华北平原,渤海之滨,因位于黄河下游以北而得名。
2. Heibei called Jizhou in history and much later in 1928 named Hebei Province, Hebei simply refers to as Ji nowadays.
   河北古为冀州地,简称冀,1928 年始称河北省。
3. Chengde Royal Summer Garden & Waibamiao Temples are located in the northern of Chengde City.
   避暑山庄和外八庙坐落在承德市区北半部。
4. Shijiazhang is about 175 miles southwest of Beijing.
   石家庄位于北京西南部,大约 175 英里处。
5. The historic mountain resort of Chengde is in Hebei province, 250km northeast of Beijing.
   具有历史意义的承德避暑山庄在河北省,位于北京的东北方向 250 公里处。

6. Qinhuangdao is one of China's busiest harbors, with an urban population of about 448 000, it is one of the 14 Open Coastal Cities.

   秦皇岛是中国最繁忙的港口之一,也是14个沿海开放城市之一。拥有城市人口大约44.8万。

7. Dong Shan is where the Qin emperor searched for the pills of longevity and boarded his ships. There's a good view of the sea and the sunrise.

   东山是一个观海和看日出的好地方,秦始皇曾遣人在此泊船求取长生不老之药。

8. Shanhaiguan in northeastern Hebei province is an important pass in the Great Wall.

   河北省东北部的山海关是长城的一个重要关隘。

9. Temple of Universal Joy was built in 1766 and covers an area of 24 000 square meters, facing west, Xuguangge (Pavilion of the Rising Sun), its principle structure, 23 meters in height and 21.68 meters in diameter, is a replica of the Hall of Prayer for Good Harvests in Beijing's Temple of Heaven.

   普乐寺建于清乾隆三十一年(公元1766年),坐东朝西,占地面积约2.4万平方米。主殿旭光阁,高23米,直径21.68米,为仿照北京天坛祈年殿而建。

Wonderful Paragraph
精彩片段

Paragraph 1

承德避暑山庄与外八庙
Chengde Mountain Resort and Outlying Temples

Chengde City is located in the northeast part of Hebei Province, 230km from Beijing. Announced among the first 24 historical and cultural cities of the nation, Chengde has the largest existing royal garden on his land: Mountain Resort and the outlying temples of various nationalities, which, in

December of 1994, were inscribed in World Heritage List by World Heritage Committee of UNESCO.

The resort is also called "Tour Palace at Rehe Hot River", first constructed in the 18th century during the reigns of Emperors Kangxi and Qianlong. It was a second political center apart from Beijing, for the emperor would stay here for about half a year to attend to political, military, ethnic, and foreign affairs.

The design of the resort takes advantage of the natural and wild scenes for the carefully constructed buildings of over 120 groups, which integrate the features of both the northern meadows and the southern waterscape, in a layout of lake in the southeast, mountain in the northwest, and plain in the northeast.

The 12 temples flanking the resort occupy an area of 472 000m^2. They are just like historical milestones to mark the unity of all ethnic groups of Qing Dynasty. Architecturally, they are in combined style of Han, Tibetan, and many other ethnic groups.

The Mountain Resort for Escaping the Heat and the temples around it are located in Chengde City, Hebei Province. Its construction lasted 89 years from 1703 (the 42nd year of the Qing Kangxi reign) to 1792 (the 57th year of the Qing Qianlong reign). The various buildings possess characteristics of the scenery of both north and south China—maiesty and elegance. Being but so kilometers from Beijing and that documents could arrive from one place to the other the same day, Kangxi, Qianlong and emperors after them would come here with their harem and ministers every year from the third day of the third lunar month to the ninth day of the ninth month. The emperors continued to discuss court affairs and received the nobility of China's various nationalities and foreign envoys here and it became the second political center of the Qing Dynasty. The main hall called Danpojingcheng built entirely of a fine-grained hardwood—nanmu—is austere and unadorned. Wenjin Pavilion is built to house the "Complete Works of the Four Treasures" compiled in the Qing Dynasty. This copy is now in the collection of the National Library of China. Also in the grounds are Jinshan

Temple, Temple of Smoke and Rain and Ruyi Oasis.

Outside the enclosure of the Mountain Resort 12 lama temples dot the slopes in the north and in the east. They manifest the Qing policy of uniting the nationalities and befriending their nobility. The temples that remain to this day include Puning, Pule, Xumifushou, Putuzongsheng, Anyuan and Shuxiang.

Paragraph 2

清东陵
East Cemetery

East Cemetery situated at the foot of Mt Changrui, west of Malanyu, Zunhua City, Hebei Province, 125km from Beijing in the west, and 150km from Tianjin in the south. It is the largest of the three, surrounded by scenery hills around, 125km long from south to north, and 20km wide from west to east, occupying totally 2 500km^2.

The construction started in 1661 and ended 247 years later in 1908. Altogether 15 mausoleums were built here, 5 of emperors, 4 of empresses, 5 of concubines, and the one for a princess east of Malanyu. Their placement observed the principles: the emperor's as the center, the empresses' and the concubines' at the side in order of their ranks, 161 tombs in total.

East Cemetery is the largest of the existing imperial graveyards in China, harmonious and integrated with the natural environment to provide a beautiful scene for the world. But the most grandiose two, Yu Mausoleum and East Ding Mausoleum, were blasted open and seriously damaged by troops of warlord Sun Dian-ying in 1928.

Paragraph 3

清西陵
West Cemetery

The cemetery is at the foot of Mt Yongning, 15km west of Yixian County, Hebei Province. Surrounded by mountains and hills with thick woods, scenic and serene, it is an excellent site of geomancy. In the cemetery are

mausoleums of 4 emperors, 3 empresses, and 7 lords, princesses, or concubines, occupying 100km^2, with a total building floor of over 50 000m^2, and the wall around is as long as 21km. Altogether there are over 1 000 rooms of palaces and 100 or more stone works, all fairly well preserved.

Paragraph 4

J 金山岭长城
inshanling

The Jinshanling Great Wall is located on the boundary between Miyun County, Beijing and Luanping County, Hebei Province. Beijing a strategic point since ancient times, a pass and wall were built as early as the Northern Qi (550-577), the Five Dynasties (907-979), Liao (907-1125) and Kin (1115-1234) dynasties. In 1410 (the 8th year of the Ming Yongle reign) Jinshanling was built on the foundation of that old wall. Still too simple to be an effective defensive works, General Qi Jiguang, who was in command of the Jizhou garrison area, took charge to rebuild it in 1568 (the second year of the Ming Longqing reign). With his brother Qi Jimei succeeding him, construction went on for over a decade.

The Jinshanling Great Wall, 25 kilometers long, has over 150 watchtowers and battlemented platforms. They are designed in a great variety of shapes—square, circular, oval and multi-cornered. Their ceilings are also varied—flat, vaulted, domed, quadrangular or with an octagonal caisson. This is a very characteristic section of the Great Wall which displays a rich variety of architectural style.

Paragraph 5

S 山海关长城
hanhaiguan

Shanhaiguan became known as the First Pass Under Heaven since ancient times. It is situated in the east of Qinhuangdao City, Hebei Province, forming a pass of strategic importance at the eastern end of the Great Wall. It was set up by General Xu Da in 1381 (the 14th year of the Ming Hongwu reign) when a castle was erected here.

Shanhaiguan was shaped like an irregular trapezoid with a gate on each side, namely Zhendong, Yingen, Wangyang and Weiyuan. The south and north wings are fortifications where soldiers were stationed. Outside the east and west gates are outer walls to strengthen the defence of the castle. The average height of the Shanhaiguan Great Wall is 11.6 meters, its width over 10 meters. It is built of rammed earth faced with bricks. A horizontal board with the inscription for "First Pass Under Heaven" in the calligraphy of the Ming dynasty scholar Xiao Xian hangs on the second story of the gate-tower. There are two small fortifications, one in the south, the other in the north. They are the same shape and size. Together with towers at the northeast and southeast corner, they present a solemn majesty.

Five kilometers to the east of Shanhaiguan, the starting point of the Great Wall dips into the sea like a dragon's head. Piling 10 meters high and dipping 21 meters into the sea, the rocks churn the surging waves. Hence the name Old Dragon Head. It is a complex of a stone fortification, the Jinglu platform, the South sea pass, and the Chenghailou Tower and the Ninghai Castle.

Paragraph 6

安济桥 Anji Bridge

Anji Bridge Also called Zhaozhou Bridge, it is located in Zhaoxian County. The bridge spans the Jiao River, and has done for 1 300 years during the Sui Dynasty (581-618AD) by Li Chun, a famous artisan then. It is 50.82 meters long, 9.6 meters wide, with a span of 37 meters, and is believed as the oldest stone-arch bridge in China. The balustrades and railing boards are carved with dragons and mythical creatures, which reflect excellent stone-carving skills of the Sui Dynasty.

Paragraph 7

沧州铁狮子
Cangzhou Iron Lion

The iron lion is the oldest and largest iron-casting art piece still in existence in China, providing a high valuable material for the study of metallurgy, sculpture, and the history of Buddhism.

Paragraph 8

北戴河海滨
Beidaihe

Many residents in Beijing and Tianjin would like to go to Beidaihe, a seasider resort along the Bohai Sea some 300 kilometres northeast Beijing to escape the summer heat and damp nights of July and August. Since it has been used as a summer resort with 719 villas by the royal family of the Qing Dynasty and then, a century ago, by foreign communities in Beijing and Tianjin, Beidaihe has grown into a popular folks' destination to kill off the unbearable hot days. In fact, Beidaihe is so well known that many Chinese people think Qinhuangdao is a district of Beidaihe, not the other way round.

Paragraph 9

普乐寺
The Temple of Universal Happiness

Encompassing 24 000 square metres, the Temple of Universal Happiness (also known as Round Pavilion) was erected in 1766 when the upper strata personages from the Mongolian and the northwestern tribes came to pay respects to Qing emperor Qianlong for the stability and peace in northwestern region of China. The main building, the Pavilion of the Brilliance of the Rising Sun (旭光阁), is noted for its caisson ceiling and unique wooden mandala, the only one of its kind in China outside Tibet. The temple's outer walls were once topped by eight colourfully glazed-tile pagodas built on lotus flower pedestals, but nowadays only one of them still stands. Legend has it that they are said to symbolize the lotus flowers that appeared at every step taken by Sakyamuni, founder of Buddhism, when he was very young.

Cultural Links 文化链接

沧州铁狮子的传说

"沧州的狮子,定县的塔,正定府的大菩萨。"从这个广泛流传的民谣,可以看出沧州狮子是多么著名了。

据说,在很久很久以前,沧州这地方是一块风景幽美、土地肥沃的鱼米之乡。它一面临海,因而远远地望去,海碧天蓝。再加上气候温和,人又勤劳,家家户户的日子,过得都那么美好。所以就连飞禽、走兽,也都愿意到这里落脚。

有一年谷子黄梢,棒子苍皮的时候,海面上突然刮起一股黑风,卷着海浪,像虎叫狼嚎一样咆哮着直扑沧州城。眼看着船翻桅折,房倒屋塌,满洼的好庄稼被海水吞没。黑风恶浪来得急,老百姓来不及躲,人也淹死了不少。那情景是真叫惨啊!

这黑风恶浪怎么突然来得这么猛呢?原来是一条恶龙在兴妖作怪。它看着沧州这地方好,就一心想独吞这地方做它的龙宫。就在恶龙兴妖作怪、残害黎民百姓的时候,人们猛地听到一声像山崩地裂一样的怒吼。只见一头红黄色的雄狮,从海边一跃而起,像鹰抓兔子一样,嗖的一声,冲向大海,直取恶龙。海面上顿时水柱冲天,狂风大作,龙腾狮跃,雄狮和恶龙从天黑一直厮杀到黎明,恶龙招架不住,掉头就跑。它边跑边想:"我占不了这块地方,也叫这地方好不了。"于是它一边跑着一边吐着又苦又碱的白沫。雄狮在后面紧追不放,一直到东海深处,逼着恶龙收回了淹没沧州的海水,这才罢休。恶龙在逃跑的路上留下了一条深沟。传说,这条深沟就是现在的黑龙港河。现在沧州这地方,特别是黑龙港流域,那白花花的盐碱,据说就是那条恶龙吐出的白沫。

恶龙跑了,海水退了,沧州一带的老百姓,才避免了一场更大的灾难,又能安居乐业了。人们为了感谢为民除害的雄狮,就请一位叫李云的打铁

名匠,带领着九九八十一个手艺高超的徒弟,用了九九八十一吨钢铁,铸造了九九八十一天,终于在当年雄狮跃起的地方,铸成了这尊活灵活现非常雄伟的铁狮子。

那条恶龙虽然没死,可是它一望见这头铁狮子,就浑身发软,爪子发麻,再也不敢兴妖作怪了,所以,后来人们又把这尊铁狮子叫做镇海吼。

Mt. Yanshan 燕山	nobility 高贵;崇高;高位
Bohai Sea 渤海	envoy 使者;使节
Great Wall at Mt. Jinshan 金山岭长城	austere 严肃的;严厉的;朴素的
Baiyangdian lake 白洋淀	unadorned 未装饰的;朴素的
Shanhaiguan Pass 山海关	pavilion 大账篷;亭子;楼阁
North China Plain 华北平原	manifest 表明
Four Knowledge Study 四知书院	for the sake of 由于……的缘故
Golden Millet Dream Temple 黄粱梦	the frontier region 边疆
House of Mists and Residence 烟雨楼	the Main Hall 正宫
	the Pine and Crane Mansion 松鹤斋
The First Pass under Heaven 天下第一关	the Pine Valley Mansion 万鹤松风
stabilize 使安定;使稳固	the Eastern Hall 东宫
maintain 维护;坚持	jiaoshan 角山
unity 统一	Yansai Lake 燕塞湖
multi-nationality 多民族	The Eastern Qing Tombs 清东陵
landscape 风景	The Western Qing Tombs 清西陵
handle 处理	The Ancient Lotus Pond in Baoding 保定古莲花池
administrative 行政的;管理的	The Ancient City of Zhengding 正定古城
possess 拥有,占有	Cangzhou Iron Lion 沧州铁狮子
majesty 雄壮;威仪	Bashang Grassland 坝上草原

用英语说中国——旅游亮点
Introduce China in English—Scenic Spots

Unit 2　山西省 Shanxi Province

Key Sentences 流畅精句

1. Shanxi Province sits in the middle of the loess land and on the middle reaches of the Yellow River.
   山西省地处黄河中游东岸,黄土高原中部。
2. Shanxi is one of the cradles of Chinese civilization.
   山西是中华文明发祥地之一。
3. Pingyao Town dwells in the middle of Shanxi Province.
   平遥位于山西省中部。
4. Yungang Grottoes is situated on the southern side of Mt. Wuzhou, 16km to the south of Datong City.
   云冈石窟位于大同市西郊16千米处的武周山南麓,中国四大石窟之一。
5. Qiao's Courtyard Complex sits in Qiaojiabao Village in Qixian Country, which is 64 km away to the southwest of Taiyuan City.
   乔家大院在太原市西南60公里处的祁县乔家堡村,始建于清乾隆年间,是清代大户人家的典型宅院。
6. Taiyuan was founded in the Western Zhou, more than three thousand years ago.
   太原建于3 000多年前的西周。
7. The walls, shops and homes in Pingyao have untouched since Ming dynasty and Qing dynasty.
   平遥古城中的城墙、民居还保存着明清两代的原样。
8. Jinci Temple is 25km southwest of Taiyuan at the foot of Xuanweng Mountain.
   晋祠位于太原西南25公里处的悬翁山脚下。

北华
North China

9. Datong was a garrison town built between two sections of the Great Wall.
   大同是两段长城之间的一个驻防城市。
10. Mountain Wutai is one of the Four Great Buddhist Mountains of China.
    五台山是中国四大佛教名山之一。
11. Datong is basically a coal-mining town.
    大同基本上可以说是一个煤城。
12. Shanxi has an extremely large number of excavated tombs and neolithic sites.
    山西发掘出不计其数的坟墓和新石器遗址。
13. Huayan Monastry is one of the largest temples in China.
    华严寺是中国最大的寺院之一。

Wonderful Paragraph 精彩片段

Paragraph 1

云冈石窟
Yungang Grottoes

Yungang Grottoes was carved on the north cliff of Wuzhou Mountain, 16km west of Datong City, Shanxi Province. The caves were carved in the mid-5th century, North Wei Dynasty, stretching about 1km from east to west as one of the largest clusters of grottoes in China. With an enormous size and rich contents, Yungang Grottoes ranks side by side with Mogao Grottoes in Dunhuang of Gansu Province and Longmen Grottoes in Luoyang of Henan Province as the three great clusters of cave temples in China.

Of the three, Yungang Grottoes stands out for its rich contents and refined carving Preserved to the present in the Grottoes are 53 caves and over 51 000 statues. Li Daoyuan, a famous geologist of ancient China, described the Grottoes in his well reputed work "Annotated Book of Waters" that "cracked the rocks and hewed open the mountain, constructed with the topography: enormous, grandiose, and rare to find elsewhere: halls, temples, waters, and woods around the mountain rush in sight one after the other", which is indeed the true picture of the Grottoes of that time.

Yungang Grottoes consists of three sections, the east, the west, and the central, with caves of all sizes pleasantly scattered halfway on Yungang Mountain. Caves in the east section feature in pagodas, thus called pagoda caves. Those of the central section were all structured with a front and a rear chamber, with the Buddha in the center and relief carving all over the walls. Caves of the west section are mostly medium or small sized, or small niches added in later times, actually, in most cases, carved after the capital of North Wei Dynasty was moved from Datong to Luoyang. Statues in Yungang Grottoes model various religious figures with an image distinctive from each other. The technique not only inherited and developed the tradition from Qin and Han Dynasties, but also adopted much from Gandhara art, to create a unique style of Yungang Grottoes.

On the interior and exterior walls as well as the Buddha's halos and the caisson ceilings of the caves, there are vividly carved groups of apsaras to manliest the world of ultimate happiness pursued by Buddhists. All the statues are modeled with marvelous personification that gives the Buddha a human nature and expression as well as infinite vigor' as the ancient treasure of Chinese culture. In December of 2001, World Heritage Committee of UNESCO inscribed Yungang Grottoes in its World Heritage List.

Paragraph 2

平遥古城
The Ancient of Pingyao

This city with a history of over 2 700 years is located in middle of Shanxi Province, 90km from Taiyuan City, the provincial capital. Its origin says that this place was awarded to Emperor Yao, namely the Tao Tang family, thus it was called "ancient Tao's land". The city first appeared in 827-782 BC, militarily guarded by Yin Ji-fu, West Zhou Dynasty. Since the "Province and County System" by Emperor Qin in 221 BC, the city has been the county seat

in all the times. Despite so many events or incidents, it survived practically as it was in the 600 years or more since Ming and Qing Dynasties, and ranks as the only intact ancient city of Ming and Qing Dynasties well preserved in China.

The ancient city of Pingyao is known as "a treasure house of Chinese classic architecture" which has practically kept its original pattern of the 17-19th centuries, therefore enjoys the reputation of "museum of architecture in Ming and Qing Dynasties".

Paragraph 3

W 五台山
utai Mountain

Wutai Mountain, located at Wutai County, Shanxi Province, consists of five platform-shaped peaks as its name indicates. One of the four famous Buddhist shrines, the Wutai Mountain has a long history of Buddhism. Temples began to be built on the mountain in 68 (the 11th year of the Eastern Han Yong Ping reign). With construction going on all through the dynasties the Tang Dynasty, forming a treasure-trove of ancient Chinese architecture. These temples belong to the black and the yellow sect—representing the Han and the Tibetan Buddhism. They religion, culture and the arts. The mountain climate is cool and pleasant, therefore Wutai Mountain is also called thee Mountain of Coolness. The pleasant weather and the natural scenery make Wutai Mountain an ideal summer resort.

Paragraph 4

H 北岳恒山
engshan Mountain

Hengshan Mountain, the northern Sacred Mountain, rises 10 kilometers south of Hunyuan County, and is famed as "the famous mountain of the strategic importance". The mountain consists of two peaks: the Tianfengling on the east and the Cuipingfeng on the west. The two peaks stand facing each other, and form precipitous natural barrier, where was a place contested by all strategists. The terrain of the mountain is characterized by "parallel lines of mountains". The Hengshan Mountain Scenic Area was inscribed on the first list of major scenic areas and historical sites in the country proclaimed by the State Council. Major tourist attractions include the Midair Temple, Hall of Pure Trinity, Nine-Heaven Palace, Flying Stone Grottoes, and so on.

Paragraph 5

M恒山悬空寺
id-Air Temple at Mount Heng

Mid-Air Temple First built during the Northern Wei Dynasty, the Midair Temple is located at the cliff between the peaks of Tianfengling and the Cuipingfeng of the Hengshan Mountains. The whole temple was built on the rock face of a sheer cliff, and the highest place in the temple is about 50 meters above ground, like suspending on the cliff face. The temple has more than 40 halls and rooms, housing 78 bronzeiron, colored clay and stone statues.

Paragraph 6

J晋祠
in Shrine

The Jin Shrine stands at the foot of Xuanweng Mountain, 25 kilometers southwest of Taiyuan. It was built in memory of Shu Yu, the founding ruler of the State of Jin. The Jin Shrine is famous for it scenic beauty. All buildings in the shrine were laid out ingeniously and surrounded by ancient trees. In the Hall of Holy Mother are 43 statues of young maids sculptured in the Song Dynasty. The statues, the pines planted during the Zhou Dynasty and the Nanlao Spring are know as the three rarities of the Jin Shrine.

Paragraph 7

应县木塔
Yingxian Wooden Pagoda

Yingxian Wooden Pagoda—the world's oldest and tallest wooden pagoda was first built in 1056 in the Liao Dynasty (907-1125). It has become fragile after weathering climatic changes, numerous earthquakes and cannon attacks. Technicians repaired it. The elevated platform has been built for visitors to have a close look at the pagoda and the repair work. Towering 67.13 metres, the octagonal pagoda known as the Yingxian Wooden Pagoda is not only the tallest but also the oldest existing wooden pagoda in the world. It is one of the few surviving examples of a major Song-dynasty pagoda, rich in detail, dynamic in bracketing, and noble in proportion. The pagoda is 115 years older and 12.57 metres taller than the Leaning Tower of Pisa" in Italy (the Leaning Tower of Pisa stands 54.56 metres tall)." A panel of experts was sent to examine the pagoda in 2000. They said the building was on the verge of being destroyed by strong winds or an earthquake. The Chinese Government is determined to save the pagoda at all costs.

Paragraph 8

黄河壶口瀑布
Hukou Waterfalls of the Yellow River

The Hukou (Pot Spout) Waterfalls is situated at 25 kilometers west of Jixian County. When the Yellow River flows to the place, the water of the river is squeezed by mountains on both banks into a narrow gorge like the spout of pot and rush rapidly, forming the grand waterfalls with a height of 20 meters. The mountains echo with the deafening sound of the roaring water, which could be heard several kilometers away.

Paragraph 9

G鹳雀楼
uanque (Stork) Tower

Reconstruction of the main building of an ancient Guanque (Stork) Tower in Yongji City, North China's Shanxi Province, was completed in early 2001 after three years' work. Originally completed in 580, the building was one of the four noted ancient towers in China. The other three towers include the Yellow Crane Tower in Hubei Province, the Yueyang Tower in Hunan Province, and the Prince Teng Pavilion in Jiangxi Province, which have been revamped respectively.

Situated in the old town of Puzhou, the city of Yongji, Guanque Tower was first constructed in the Northern Zhou Dynasty (557-581) and was destroyed during wars in 1272.

Paragraph 10

Y雁门关
anmen Pass

This was also one of the key passes in Ming Dynasty, right on the entrance of Yanmen Gorge 20km northwest of Daixian County, Shanxi Province. Mountains after mountains surround the pass, with a road through the dark and chilling gorge to the pass city, which was always heavily guarded.

The present pass city was built in 1374. Remains of it are three gates, and the site of the shrine for Li Mu, an excellent general of State of Zhao in Warring States Period. On one of the survived steles is inscribed "Stele of Noble Wu An's Temple", a record of Li's serial victories over the Huns and of Yanmen Pass still as a key fort in the riot of Ming Dynasty.

Paragraph 11

N娘子关
iangzi Pass

This is the south one of the Inner Three Passes of Great Wall in Ming

North China

Dynasty, located northeast of present Pinding County, Shanxi Province, half way on Mt Mian west of Taihang Mountains. In Tang Dynasty, Princess Pingyang, 3rd daughter of Emperor Gaozu, once guarded here with her sister soldiers, and folks honored her troop as "Women" army, or Niangzi army in Chinese, hence the name for the pass.

The present pass city was built in 1542 with 2 gates. The outer gate is a brick arch, with a platform above for troop inspection and enemy watch. The lower part of the inner gate is also a brick arch, but above it is a tower, very solid in structure. Great Wall stretches out from both sides winding along with the mountain ridges as a natural safeguard of Shanxi and Hebei Provinces. Along with it at the mountain foot is the railway from Shijiazhuang to Taiyuan, and viewed from inside the train are the amazing scenes of lofty passes and towers as well as the cataract pouring its pearl like drops which is popularly praised as Cave of Water Curtain.

Paragraph 12

Huayan Temple

This temple is situated in the west suburb of Datong City, a large Buddhist temple built in Liao Dynasty. The buildings, statues, murals, and caisson ceilings, etc, are all well preserved and have a unique style and highly advanced artistry. Reputed as an "art museum of Liao and Jin Dynasties", the temple occupies an important position in the history of culture and architecture of China.

It is made up of an upper and a lower temple. The Grand Hall of Sakyamuni of the upper temple is the remain of Jin Dynasty, also the largest singular Buddhism hall of Jing Dynasty well preserved to the present in China. In the hall is modeled a golden and brilliant Buddha of Five Directions (east, west, south, north, and central) and all over the walls are painted huge murals.

The inscription on the door head of the main hall in the lower temple reads "Bhage Religious Depository", meaning "the storehouse of Buddhist sutras". In the central of the hall are three big statues, surrounded by the other 28 at the side. All of them beautiful in figure, plump in face, vivid in expression, with natural and floating drapery or ornaments. They are rare masterpiece sculptures of Liao Dynasty.

Paragraph 13

观音堂
Hall of Avalokitesvara

The hall stands on a little hill 7.5km west of Datong City. First constructed in Liao Dynasty, the present building is the restoration on the original site in 1651, the 8th year of Emperor Shunzhi's reign, Qing Dynasty. Its layout is compact, and on the axis are placed the theater tower, Hall of Avalokitesvara, Hall of Three Truths, and other towers or houses. The theater tower seats 8m above on a cavern, and below is the ancient passage for carts, cattle, and the folks. The main hall is 3-room wide and 2-room in depth, with an overhanging gable roof of glazed tiles. The interior of the hall is expanded with side chambers for larger Buddhist activities. Standing in the center of the hall is a 6m high stone statue of Avalokitesvara, wearing a crown touching the ceiling. Two statues of attendants stand on the left and right side. On the walls of the hall are 24 mural stories of Avalokitesvara saving the folks out of their miseries. The three-dragon glazed screen wall is built in Ming Dynasty. And research shows that the big Chinese character "Buddha" by contour drawing, about $3m^2$, carved on the cliff west of the temple, is the relic of Liao Dynasty.

Cultural Links
文化链接

西安下马陵的传说

在老西安,没有几个人能说清楚:南大街为什么短于其他三条大街。这里面有个传说。这个传说与下马陵有关,与汉儒董仲舒有关,甚至与传说里的董永有关；同时，在传说里也揭示了明洪武年间秦王朱樉"不喜儒生儒术"的荒唐行径。老西安民间的叙事体例里，往往在一个传说里兼收并蓄地讲叙几个朝代的人物故事，以历史典故相映相衬，逐渐逼近故事的核心，有些老西安民间传说甚至从神话讲起，然后自然通脱地扯出对历史人物本真本分的是非评判。下马陵的传说，在老西安民间流传了好几百年时间，但依稀保存着老西安口传叙述的特点。我很喜欢这种"叙事养题"的叙述方式，它有远通近控的妙用，也有触类旁通的功效，很合乎"讲故事"的传统叙述法则。在老西安民间，蕴藏着许许多多讲故事的能手，他们可以把平常人物的平常事件，讲叙出与神传仙话的自然联系。

传说西汉时期，书生董永因家贫卖身葬父，为财主当长工，苦度时日。董郎的正直与憨厚感动了天上的七仙女，遂私自下凡与他结成恩爱夫妻，并生下了一个聪明可爱的胖小子，起名董仲舒。后来天上的王母娘娘得知此事，盛怒之下，王母娘娘差遣天兵天将把七仙女强行押回天宫，留下董永父子在人间相依为命。董永由于思念妻子七仙女，再加上财主的盘剥与欺榨，身体日益衰弱，勉强把儿子董仲舒拉扯到十二岁，便一命身亡。无奈之下，幼小的董仲舒也以卖身葬父的形式，安葬了父亲。还好，收买董仲舒的是一户姓王的善良人家，王相公夫妇不但给他吃得饱、穿得暖，还供给他读书。王家没有儿子，就把董仲舒当亲儿子养育，还专门聘请关中鸿儒教授董仲舒诗文。董仲舒天资聪敏，因而学习起来长进很快，不几年就取得了功名。董仲舒对经书、史书颇有研究，22岁就撰写了研究《春秋公羊传》的儒学名篇。学成之后，董仲舒来到长安，深得汉景帝喜爱，被提拔为博士。但由于窦太后喜好妖言惑众之士，鄙薄儒术，因此董仲舒一直不被朝廷重用。

董仲舒为人刚正不阿，也不喜阿谀奉承，于是被奸邪小人所忌恨。但董仲舒深得城中学子敬重，因为他学识渊博，讲学时理路通明、阐释清晰，使学子一听就懂。由于董仲舒的人品学问皆高，所以汉代的儒林学士也把他当作可以推心置腹的朋友对待。不久，汉景帝驾崩，儿子刘彻继位。汉家江山进入了武帝时代。汉武帝听说董仲舒才德兼备，便升他为江都相，并采纳了"罢黜百家，独尊儒术"的治学治世思想。

次年，董仲舒以江山社稷为重，大胆揭露"富者田连阡陌，贫者无立锥之地"的社会现实，因此，彻底得罪了朝廷的大批贵族。他们借口董仲舒写的《灾异记》一书有影射朝廷之意，把董仲舒投进了大牢，判了死罪。临杀头的时候,汉武帝才下诏赦免了董仲舒。自此,由于朝廷群小的嫉妒和谗言,董仲舒再也没有被汉武帝重用。董仲舒退隐乡野、归志林泉,终日闭门著书,直到无疾而终。董仲舒自幼家贫,加上为官清廉,没有丝毫产业和积蓄。董仲舒死后,儒生们才发现,他穷得甚至连一口薄皮棺材都买不起。城里的汉儒及他的弟子们集资为董仲舒治丧。汉武帝得知此事后,备受感动,更有感于董仲舒"天人感应,君权神授"等主张,为汉家江山永固立下了"汗马功劳"。所以,汉武帝亲自为董仲舒踏勘墓地,选择了秦代遗留下的"宜春苑"作为董仲舒的墓地,并在这里为董仲舒举行了隆重的葬礼,还在董仲舒墓前依汉家江山的祖制修建了董子祠,并诏告天下,董仲舒享百代香火。

一天,汉武帝出城狩猎,路经董仲舒墓园时,出于对一代鸿儒的爱戴与尊敬,还离墓园有三十丈时,汉武帝就翻身下马,净心净手,步履而过。随行的大臣和护驾也都跟着汉武帝步行而过。从此,董仲舒墓园周围的这块土地,就被人们称作"下马陵"。并且形成了一种制度:凡过往的官员、儒生,一律在三十丈之外,下马步行而过。

隋文帝建大兴城和唐高祖建长安城时,都把"下马陵"留在了城内。可是到了明朝的时候,朱元璋定都南京,封他的次子朱樉为"秦王"治关中。秦王重建长安城,也就是现在的西安城。秦王推崇武治,不喜儒生,不尊儒术,所以下令缩短南城距离,把"下马陵"驱逐出城。秦王动用了数十万苦役修筑西安城,耗时整整十年的时间。谁知第二天秦王登城巡行,发现"下马陵"和陵前的祠堂又"跑"到了城里。秦王大怒,下令砍了南城监工,并传令拆了南城重筑,一定要把"下马陵"驱逐出城。于是工匠苦役们辛苦三年,总算把"下马陵"隔在了城外。可谁知,第二天"下马陵"又跑到了城里。秦王气得吹胡子瞪眼,遂令工匠推倒重筑。这回把"下马陵"抛出城数十丈之遥,而且隔了一道水深丈余的护城河。秦王看后不禁暗喜,心想:这下我看你怎么进城传播儒术?可第二天秦王登城一看,"下马陵"又进到了城里,光采依然,香火依然。秦王一气一惊,不久便一命身亡,奔了黄泉。

西安城的南大街由于接连被"斩"了三次,所以南大街远比东、西、北三条大街要短。虽然早已没有儒生去给董仲舒敬供香火,但下马陵依然还在城内,地名也依然叫"下马陵"。

North China

Vocabulary 妙词连珠

Temple of the Jin Minister Dou 窦大夫祠	The Yungang (Caves) Grottoes 云冈石窟
Monastery of Endless Happiness 多福寺	Mount Wutai 五台山
Nine Dragon Screen 九龙壁	Mid-Air Temple at Mount Heng 恒山悬空寺
Manshan Pavilion of Mt. Tianlong 天龙山漫山阁	Dazhai 大寨
	Huozhou 霍州
Suspending Temple 悬空寺	Hukou Waterfalls 壶口瀑布
Guandi Temple 关帝庙	Universal Salvation (Pujiu) Monastery 普救寺
Eternal Palace 永乐宫	
Dayu Ferry 大禹渡	Guanque (Stork) Tower 鹳鹊楼
Jin Memorial Temple 晋祠	Yingxian Wooden Pagoda 应县木塔
Huayan Temple 华严寺	Pingyao-An Ancient City 平遥古城

Unit 3 内蒙古自治区 Inner Mongolia Autonomous Region

Key Sentences
流畅精句

1. Inner Mongolia came into being in 1947.
   内蒙古自治区成立于1947年。
2. Inner Mongolia stretches through the widest longitudes in China, with vast outreaching grassland and deserts as well.
   内蒙古是我国跨经度最大的省份,境内同时并存有大面积的草原和沙漠。
3. The capital of Inner Mongolia Autonomous Region is Hohhot.
   内蒙古自治区的首府是呼和浩特。
4. Genghis Khan united the tribes living in Mongolian grasslands in 1206.
   1206年,成吉思汗统一了生活在内蒙古草原的部落。
5. The people are charming and wear their traditional costume during Nadamu Festival.
   在那达慕节日期间,人们穿着节日的盛装,满面笑容。
6. The Mongolian food might be fresh-killed mutton, boiled millet, and sesame pancake.
   蒙古饭食可以是新鲜羊肉、滚烫小米粥和芝麻大饼。
7. Wang Zhaojun was an imperial Han concubine more than 2 000 years ago.
   王昭君是2 000多年前汉王朝的一个妃子。
8. Baotou is a steel city of the grasslands.
   包头是草原钢城。
9. Hohhot means "Blue City" in Mongolian.
   呼和浩特在蒙古语中是"青色之城"的意思。

Wonderful Paragraph
精彩片段

Paragraph 1

成吉思汗陵
Genghis Khan Mausoleum

Mausoleum of Genghis Khan lies in Ejin Horo Qi, 180 km away from Baotou City in the north. It consists of the main Hall, Burial Hall, West and East Wings in Mongolian tent style. There are the saddle and rare things used by Genghis Khan himself, statue of Genghis Khan and wall paintings of his life stories. Outside there are Mongolian war chariots and weapons of all sorts exhibited.

Paragraph 2

成吉思汗庙
Genghis Khan Temple

The only temple in the world that commemorates the life of Chinese hero Genghis Khan, is the northern Inner Mongolia Autonomous Region, was expanded at a cost of 220 million Yuan (US $ 26.5 million) plan. The temple is located in the city of Ulan Hot, the Hong Kong-based World Chinese Advancement Association funded the project in accordance with a recently signed agreement between it and the city's government. Genghis Khan was born into an aristocratic family near the Onon River in Mongolia. In 1206 he unified the Mongol tribes and became Great Khan of the Mongol Empire. He was later conferred with the title of Genghis Khan, meaning "universal ruler" by the supreme assembly. One of his grandsons, Kublai Khan (1215-1294, ruled 1260-1294) later became the first emperor of China's Yuan Dynasty (1294-1368). Built in 1940, the Genghis Khan Temple features architectural styles of the Mongolian, Han and Tibetan nationalities. As a relic site with regional-level protection, the temple attracts more than 200 000 tourists annually. According to the expansion plan, a dozen scenic spots including a palace, an altar and an exhibition hall, will be constructed. The project will be completed within three to five years (2005-2007).

Paragraph 3

T昭君墓
omb of Princess Zhaojun

Tomb of Princess Zhaojun Located 9 kilometers to the south of Hohhot proper, the cemetery covers an area of 1.3 hectare. The tomb is 33 meters high. It was said that each year when it turned cold and grasses became yellow, only this tomb remained green, so it was also called "Qingzhong" (Green Tomb).

Wang Zhaojun, also named Wang Qiang, married Huhanye Chanyu, the emperor of Xiongnu, of her own free will during the reign period of Emperor Yuan of the Han Dynasty. She made great contributions to the relationship between Han and Xiongnu, and in the following more than 40 years, no wars broke out and people of both countries lived a peaceful life.

Paragraph 4

N那达慕大会
adam Fair

The Nadam Fair, a traditional Mongolian festival, falls in warm and sunny July and August in Inner Mongolia. Organized by the Qi (county) Government it usually lasts for seven days. "Nadam" in the Mongolian language means "recreation" or "games". It first began in the Han Dynasty (206B.C.-220 A.D.). The main activities at the fair include horse racing, archery and wrestling.

Paragraph 5

G草原旅游区
rassland Tourist Zones

In the Inner Mongolia Autonomous Region, the area of grassland is 880 000 square kilometers, or accounting for 21.7 per cent of the nation's total, the

North China

leading of China's five largest grasslands. From east to west, are scattered grassy marshland, typical grassland, wideness grassland, grassy wildernessd desert as well as hilly grassy marshlands, low wet and grassy marshland, and marshy grassland, distributed randomly anywhere. Major grassland tourist zones include the Hulunbuir, Xilin Gol, Xila Muren, Huiteng Xile and Gegen Tala. From May to September, the lands are covered with green grass and flowers, with big herds of cattle and sheep grazing in the meadows, ribbon-like rivers, pearl-like lakes and yurts resided by the mongolians. They all constituted beautiful and majestic pictures.

Paragraph 6

Wudangzhao 五当召

Wudangzhao, or the Bad Ger Lamasery, lying 70 kilometers southwest of Baotou, is one of the best-preserved Tibetanstyle lamaseries and largest Tibetan Buddhist monastery of the Yellow Sect in the entire autonomous region. Situating on a hill slope and built during the Kangxi's reign (1662-1722) of the Qing Dynasty, it is a vast complex consisting of six main halls, three Living Buddha mansions and a mausoleum, and has a total of 2 500, rooms.

Cultural Links 文化链接

神奇的百灵湖

百灵湖位于扎赉特旗图木吉苏木境内。这里幅员辽阔,资源丰富,土质肥沃,交通便利。百灵湖是由哈达山下的马蹄泡子扩建而成。关于它的由来还有一段神奇的传说。

成吉思汗当年率领大军来到这里,由于闯关夺隘,日夜兼程,将士们都非常疲惫。一日,翻越哈达山时,将士们个个汗流浃背,气喘吁吁,口干舌燥,真是人困马乏。大队人马都想在阴凉处歇歇脚,喝喝水,休息片刻再向前进发。可是荒山野岭上,一无人家,二无水源,到哪里去找水喝呢?个个睁大眼睛前后左右看,人人东张西望伸着脖子找,但就是不见星点水源。将士们口渴难耐到了极点。

就在这时,成吉思汗的坐骑突然一声嘶鸣,停步不前了。长长的嘶鸣声惊天动地,把哈达山都震颤了。将士们不知发生了什么事,都抬头去看成吉思汗的战马。只见那匹战马两眼圆睁,鬃毛竖起,前腿使劲刨地,后腿拼命蹬土。一时间,尘土飞扬,沙石四溅。不一会儿,一个泡子就出现在马蹄下。说来也怪,眼看那泡子中间泉水喷涌而出,顷刻间就注满了泡子。将士们欢天喜地地喝了个够。

从此,这里便有了一个泡子,而且水源旺盛。后来人们就叫它"马蹄泡子"。

1996年,扎赉特旗政府投资开发旅游业,在原马蹄泡子基础上建成了百灵湖民族度假村。百灵湖三面环山,一处注水,水面3万亩,蓄水量7 000万立方米,最深处17米,平均水深7米。湖中放养鲤鱼、鲢鱼、大银鱼、草根鱼、武昌鱼、乌仔头鱼等鱼种,年均捕捞鲜鱼17.5万公斤,产值超百万元。百灵湖东依哈达山,山脚建有望湖亭、水上餐厅、蒙古包、跑马场等,湖面有游泳区、游船区、钓鱼区等。登上哈达山举目远眺,东部草原辽阔,绿草如茵,百花斗妍,牛羊成群;西面万顷碧浪,波光粼粼,游船往来频繁,真不愧为"草原上的明珠"。

Vocabulary
妙词连珠

Yu Mian Noodles 御面	Five-pagoda Temple 五塔寺
camel hoof 驼蹄	Hulunber Meadow 呼伦贝尔草原
The Great Mosque 清真大寺	Singing Sands Gorge 伊蒙响沙湾
Museum of Inner Mongolia 内蒙古自治区博物馆	grassland 草原
	Mongolian 蒙古语

Key Sentences
流畅精句

1. Tianjin is China's fourth largest city.
   天津是中国第四大城市。
2. Tianjin is good shopping city as well as a museum of 19th European century architecture.
   天津是个很好的购物城市,也是一个19世纪欧洲建筑博物馆。
3. During the Ming dynasty, city walls were built and the city was called Tianjinwei.
   明代,天津修筑了城墙,天津被称作天津卫。
4. Tianjin is rather smoggy.
   天津多雾。
5. It is worthing seeing for the models of a wedding sedan and a real wedding bed in Yangliuqing.
   杨柳青值得一看的是仿造的结婚花轿和真正的婚床。
6. Tianjin is the biggest industrial and commercial harbour city of north China.
   天津市是中国北方最大的工商业港口城市。
7. Situated in Tanggu District and Haihe River's entrance. Tianjin New Harbour is the largest man-made harbour present in China, as well as an international trade seaport, which has maintained trade relations with harbours in 150-odd countries and regions.
   位于塘沽海河口的天津新港是目前中国最大的人工港,也是以外贸为主的国际港口,与世界150多个国家和地区的港口有着外贸关系。

8. As one of national famous historical and cultural city, Tianjin is abundant in scenic spots and historical sites, which connect with scenes and sight in Beijing and Hebei, and form a big tourist zone.

   天津市是中国历史文化名城之一,辖区内名胜古迹众多,又与北京、河北的风景区相毗邻。

9. Major attractions in Tianjin are Tianhou Temple, Ancient Cultural Street, Dule Temple, Panshan Scenic Resort, Dagu Fort, Great Wall at Huangya Pass, Yangliuqing, a home to New Year Pictures and Yangcun Amusement Park.

   主要名胜古迹有天后宫、古文化街、蓟县独乐寺、盘山风景区、大沽炮台、黄崖关长城、年画之乡杨柳青、杨村小世界等。

Wonderful Paragraph
精彩片段

Paragraph 1

天津卫
Tianjin City

Tianjin as a military stronghold of ancient Beijing gradually grew into a city through history from the Sui Dynasty on, when the Great Cannel was built, to the prime time of the Tang Dynasty when Tianjin became a hub of communications for rice and cloth. In the Tongzhi Reign of the Qing Dynasty, the governor of Beijing and Tianjin cities and minister of Northern China were both stationed in Tianjin. Tianjin became the center of modernization campaign of Northern China and the base for developing capitalist industries.

Paragraph 2

盘山风景名胜区
Panshan Scenic Resort

Panshan Mountain, in Jixian County (historically known as Yuyang City)

North China

of Tianjin, is a National Scenic Area ranking among China's top fifteen scenic spots. It is also popularly known as the Number One Mountain of East Beijing and, from the Three-Kingdom Period through the late years of the Qing Dynasty (3rd to 20th centuries), had remained a favourite site of excursions by kings, emperors and celebrities. The mountain acquired the name of "Eastern Wutai Mountain" since the Tang Dynasty because of the multitude of Buddhist temples flourishing there. The summit of the mountain is 864 meters above sea level, and the five peaks, eight rocks and three Pans (twined pine trees) are the mountain's most wonderful vistas. In a distance, one sees a full panorama of seas of clouds and clusters of waving pine trees, and close by, one marvels at crystal-clear waters and odd-shaped rocks. Every step leads to a picturesque scene, and every scene tells a legend. After a tour to Panshan Mountain, an enchanted Emperor Qian Long of the Qing Dynasty sighed: "If I had known there is a Panshan, I wouldn't have made tours to the South."

Paragraph 3

黄崖关长城
Great wall at Huangya Pass

Around 120 kilometers north of Tianjin, there is a 42-kilometer section of Great Wall rarely visited by overseas tourists. Construction of the Huangyaguan Great Wall started in 557 under the Northern Qi Dynasty. It was rebuilt during the Sui and Ming dynasties, with 14 beacon towers and 52 guard towers, connecting Malanguan Pass in the east and Pinggu Jiangjunguan Pass in the west.

Paragraph 4

独乐寺
Solitary Joy Temple

Located in Jixian County, 113 kilometres from Tianjin city, the Solitary Joy (Dule) Temple, also known as the Big Buddha Temple, was first constructed in the Tang Dynasty and rebuilt in 984 in the Liao Dynasty. Dule means exclusive happiness. Legend has it that when An Lushan（安禄山？-757, a general of the Tang Dynasty) rebelled against the emperor, he held a meeting here at the temple before going to war and he gave the temple its present name because he wanted happiness exclusively for himself instead of sharing it with the people. The temple consists of an entrance gate, the 23-metre-high Guanyin (Avalokitesvara or Goddess of Mercy) Pavilion and the chambers on the east and west sides. The gate, the roof of which has give ridges and four slopes, is China's extant oldest. The pavilion, built in 24 different systems of brackets inserted between the top of a column and a crossbeam, is the cream of China's extant high-rise pavilions of wooden structure. On top of all this, it stands formidable despite 28 major earthquakes. Inside the pavilion is a 16-metre-high clay statue of Avalokitesvara, or the Goddess of Mercy, beautiful in shape and enchanting in mien, a rare treasure among clay sculptures following the style of the Liao Dynasty (907-1125).

Paragraph 5

杨柳青年画
The Yangliuqing New Year Picture

The woodcut New Year pictures of Yangliuqing have a strong flavor of life. People in the Yangliuqing village and 32 villages nearby, 20 kilometers from the west of Tianjin City proper, are all engaged in making New Year pictures. The New Year pictures are a unique art form with even arrangement, forceful stokes, elegant colors and beautiful shapes.

Yangliuqing New Year pictures are different from other New Year pictures, for it is Xylograph in terms of craft. Xylograph of Yangliuqing originated in the Ming Dynasty (1368-1644), and matured in the Qing Dynasty (1644-1911) when it was chosen as an article of tributes to the imperial family. At the end of the Qing Dynasty, it was on the decline due to the prevalence of foreign paintings. In the 1960s, it finally recovered its splendor and improved the craft with the support from the new government.

The process of making a Yangliuqing New Year picture has a dozen steps like plotting, craving, to name a few. It perfectly relates color and emotion, folk painting and standard paining, realism and romanticism. It covers an extensive range of subjects like folk custom, legendary stories, historic events, and opera, usually via emblems and symbols to deliver the theme.

Yangliuqing New Year pictures are a gem of art and loved by people both at home and abroad. It is exported to Italy, France, Britain, Belgium, Japan, Canada, the US, Singapore and Mexico, etc.

Cultural Links
文化链接

狗不理的传说

"狗不理"始创于1858年。清道光年间,河北一农家,四十得子,为求平安,取名"狗子",期望像小狗一样好养活(按照北方习俗,此名包含着淳朴的挚爱亲情)。狗子十四岁来津学艺,在一家蒸食铺做小伙计,狗子心灵手巧又勤奋好学,练就一手好活,不甘寄人篱下,自己摆起包子摊,它以水馅拌发面,口感柔软,鲜香不腻,形似菊花,色香味形都独具特色,引得十里百里的人都来吃包子,生意十分兴隆,狗子忙得顾不上跟顾客说话,这样一来,吃包子的人都说"狗子卖包子不理人",天长日久,都叫他"狗不理"。当年,袁世凯在天津编练新军,将"狗不理"包子带入皇宫,敬献慈禧,太后膳毕大悦,曰:"山中走兽云中雁,腹地牛羊海底鲜,不及狗不理香矣,食之长寿也。"从此"狗不理"名声大振。近一个半世纪,历代传人继承先辈的传统技艺并不断创新,使"狗不理"这个具有悠久历史的民族品牌更加绚丽。目前,"狗不理"已在国内外设立四十余家连锁店,其速冻产品远销世界三十多个国家和地区。

用英语说中国——旅游亮点
Introduce China in English—Scenic Spots

Vocabulary 妙词连珠

ingeniously 巧妙地
fascinating 吸引人的
nightfall 黄昏
roar 吼叫;咆哮
cascade 小瀑布
meander 曲流,河曲;蜿蜒而流
slope 倾斜
mystery 神秘,神秘的事物
antiquity 痕迹,古迹
eminent 著名的
villa 别墅
refined 精炼的;细雅地;细致的
internal 内部的;内在的
sitting stature 坐像
TV Tower Town 天塔城

Solitary Joy Temple 独乐寺
The Panshan Mountain 盘山
Yangcun Mini World 杨村小世界
Bohai sea 渤海
Yansan 燕山
Harbour 港口
smoggy 有雾的
year picture 年画
Huangya Pass 黄崖关
Dule Temple 独乐寺
fort 炮台
major 主要的
a famous historical and cultural city
   历史文化名城
spectacular 壮观的

4 西北
Northwest China

Unit 1 Shaanxi Province 陕西省

Key Sentences 流畅精句

1. As the gateway to Northwest China, Shaanxi is located on the middle reaches of the Yellow river in the north Loess land in Central China.
   陕西省位于中国内陆腹地,地处西北门户,黄河中游。
2. Mausoleum of Qinshihuang, the first Chinese emperor, rests underground near Xiahe Village, 5 km east to Lishan Township in Lintong District, Xi'an City, where Emperor Yingzhen, the first emperor of China was buried.
   秦始皇陵位于西安市临潼区骊山镇东 5 千米的下河村附近,为秦始皇嬴政的陵墓。
3. The Museum of Qin Terra Cotta Soldiers and Horses stands on the east side of the Mausoleum of Qinshihuang. As the attached part to the burial chamber discovered in 1974.
   秦始皇兵马俑博物馆在秦始皇陵东侧,是始皇陵的陪葬坑,发现于 1974 年。
4. Xi'an called Chang'an in ancient times is one of the most famous ancient capitals in China.

西安古称长安,是中国著名的古都之一。

5. Xi'an was the starting point of the well-known "Silk Road".
西安是中外闻名的"丝绸之路"的起点。

6. The terracotta army is a puzzle because the first emperor left no record of its existence.
兵马俑军阵如今仍是个谜,因为始皇帝没有留下任何记载。

7. Terra Cotta Warriors have been made one of the 20th century's greatest archaeological discoveries.
兵马俑被誉为20世纪最伟大的考古发掘之一。

8. Emperor Qinshihuang is the first emperor of the Qin Dynasty, the builder of the Great Wall, and the first unifier of China.
秦始皇是秦朝的第一个皇帝,他修建了长城,第一个统一了中国。

9. Numerous cultural antiquities and natural surroundings give people a panoramic view of the ancient city, Xi'an.
众多的文化遗址和自然环境可以让人们全景式地认识西安这座古城。

Wonderful Paragraph
精彩片段

Paragraph 1

秦始皇陵及兵马俑
Mausoleum of Emperor Qin Shihuang and Terra-cotta Warriors

Emperor Qin's mausoleum is the largest of ancient China, situated at the northern foot of Mt Li, Lintong County, some 30m east of Xi'an city, facing Weishui River in the north, close to the tourist resort Huaqing Pool in the west.

The huge and amazing satellite pit of terra-cotta warriors is 1 500m east of the mausoleum, discovered in March of 1974, by a group of farmers drilling a well against the draught. Archaeologist the unearthed the treasure of Qin dynasty hidden for over 2 000 years.

The pit is truly an underground military museum largest worldwide. Its design is rational and unique with a weight wall every 3m, dividing the deep pit into lanes of warriors neatly arrayed.

The satellite pits are 1 500m to the east wall of the mausoleum, right at the north side of the main road to the east gate. The pottery warriors were imitations of military arrays, the imperial guards of the underground royal city. Judging from the pit designs and warrior equipment, Pit I is that of the main force of infantry and chariots, Pit II the compound of infantry, cavalry, and chariots, and Pit III the headquarters of them all.

The life-sized pottery army, thousands in number, was deployed in practical battlement formation, hidden 5 to 7 meters underground in the three pits of varied sized and shapes.

Its discovery is a major achievement of the world's archaeology. Praised as world's 8th Wonder, it well matches the pyramids in Egypt and the Greek sculptures as the precious wealth of human culture.

Due to its hugeness and the lack of written data, Chinese archaeologists and historians have worked on the mausoleum for decades. Full scale excavation is left to the future, except some scientific unearthing of a few satellite pits, and visitors to the tomb see only a hill like mound, under with lies the emperor in his meticulous underground palace free of disturbance for over 2 000 years.

In 1961, the State Council recognized it as a historical site under state protection, and in 1987 UNESCO inscribed the mausoleum and its warrior pit in "World Heritage List".

Paragraph 2

Mount Hua

Mount Hua is located in the eastern part of Shaanxi Province belonging to the eastern section of Mount Qinling. Seen from a distance, it looks like a flower, hence the name Mount Hua. Its peak is Mount Taihua, known in the ancient times as the Western Mountain in Shaanxi Province at an elevation of 2 160 metres. In China there are Five Sacred Mountains (i. e. the

Eastern Mountain in Shandong Province, the Southern Mountain in Hunan, the Western Mountain in Shaanxi Province, the Northern Mountain in Shanxi Province, and the Central Mountain in Henan Province). Mount Hua is one of the key national scenic spots in China. Flight of Fancy—A 3.1-hectare (7.75 acres) heliport has been built at the foot of Mount Huashan, a renowned tourist destination in Shaanxi Province. Mount Huashan is one of China's five most famous scenic mountains, known for its steep and dangerous peaks. The new helipad is a strategic move by the provincial government to accelerate the development of local tourism.

Paragraph 3

大雁塔 Big Wild Goose Pagoda

Situated inside Ci'an (Thanks-giving) Temple, four kilometres south of Xi'an City, is one of the famous Buddhist pagodas in China. Sponsored by Tang Emperor Gaozong (628-683, reigned 650-683), the temple was first built in 652 during the Tang Dynasty as a symbol of thanksgiving to his mother for her kindness who had suffered an early death. To protect the scriptures and statues he brought back from India, Xuan Zang (602-664), a famous Tang monk, made a proposal to the court for a pagoda to be built inside the temple. The proposal was accepted and a pagoda, named the Big Wild Goose Pagoda was first erected in 652 during the Tang Dynasty. The pagoda experienced many vicissitudes in the past centuries. The present structure boasts five storeys with 59.9 metres in height and the base of the pagoda is 4.2 metres totalling 64.1 metres in height. Legend relates that one day a group of big wild geese flew over, suddenly one of them dropped from the sky and died on the ground. Monks were at a loss and did not know what to do. They said that the dead wild goose was a Buddha. They buried the goose and a pagoda was erected, hence the name, the Big Wild Goose Pagoda. The Big Wild Goose Pagoda of Xi'an is a structure of imposing grandeur.

西北
Northwest China

Paragraph 4

小雁塔
The Small Wild Goose Pagoda

The Pagoda was constructed in the period 707 to 709, though it acquired its present name only after its large neighbour to the southeast became known as the Big Wild Goose Pagoda. Its function was also to house Buddhist sutras. Although with a height of 43 metres it is shorter than the Big Wild Goose Pagoda, it has more tiers. In 1555 a big earthquake damaged the original 15-storey pagoda in the Ming Dynasty: A crack ran from the top to the base and the upper two tiers toppled off. Though the crack was revamped, the two top storeys were not replaced during the renovation. The present 13-tier pagoda is a tribute to some Tang architects, showing their skill in building a pagoda, which has witnessed dozens of other earthquakes during the last 200 years and is still standing. It was completely restored in 1965 and at the same time lightning arrestor and lighting equipment were installed on the pagoda. The Small Wild Goose Pagoda is a square brick construction, with each side measuring 11.38 metres. Its style is fine and delicate with a rhythmic series of projecting eaves. Above the north and south arched doorways on the first storey are the Tang engravings of ivy designs and Buddhist figures. Ming inscriptions describe the earthquakes, which the pagoda survived.

Paragraph 5

华清池
Huaqing Palace

Huaqing Palace South of Lintong County and 30 kilometers to the east of Xi'an, the Huaqing Palace sits on the northwest slopes of Mount Lishan, where served as a popular site to build temporary palaces by emperors of different dynasties for its hot spring for convalescence. The Huaqing Palace was built in 747, or the sixth year of Tang Tiaobao's reign. Emperor Minghuang of the dynasty and the Lady Yang, his favorite concubine, used to stay here for sightseeing and bathing.

Paragraph 6

黄帝陵
Tomb of King Huangdi

Tomb of King Huangdi, whose first name was Ji and nickname was Xuanyuan, was born in Shouqiu (Qufu City in Shandong Province), and buried on the slopes of Mount Bridge in Huangling County, Yan'an City. He ws believed the ancestor of Chinese. The tomb is 3.6 meters high, 48 meters in periphery, with a tablet pavilion in front of it, in which stands the tablet with inscription of "The Dragon's Burial Palace on mount Bridge". At the foot of the mountain stands the Temple of King Huangdi, Xuanyuan by name, in which grows the cypress tree planted by Emperor Wu of the Han Dynasty.

Paragraph 7

西安鼓楼
The Drum Tower

Situated on the northern side of the western street of Xi'an, the Drum tower was first built in 1380 in the reign of Emperor Ming Hongwu. It was later rebuilt in 1699 by Emperor Qing Kangxi and again in 1740 by Emperor Qing Qianlong Era. The tower is 33 meters high and 52.6 meters wide, covering more than 1970 square meters. It has two storeys with double eaves and Xieshan roof. The Drum Tower is of abundant vitality and of grandiosity. Made of and covered by only one piece of high quality ox hide, the big drum is 1.80 meters high and 2.83 meters in diameter with the total weights of 1.5 tons.

西岳巨灵擘山传说

很久很久以前,西岳华山和今天山西境内的首阳山连在一起,为一条山脉。由于大自然的恩赐与厚爱,这儿田土肥沃,风景秀丽,山上有皑皑白云,郁郁青松;山下有夭夭桃花,萋萋芳草。我们华夏民族的祖先就在这块土地上繁衍生息,他们"日出而作,日入而息",日子过得富庶而又祥和。然而,一场意想不到的灾难发生了。

传说天庭王母娘娘的蟠桃宴会上,老寿星因孙大圣一句玩笑的话,笑得手一抖,倾倒了半盏玉浆,酿生了人间洪祸。霎时间,一条大河自西向东而来,河水一路奔腾怒吼,横冲直撞,摧毁了庄稼,淹没了房舍。由于华山与首阳山的阻拦,河水不能直泻东海,于是华山脚下顿时成了一片汪洋大海……

主宰西土十二万里天地的白帝少昊,看到了民们流离失所、叫苦不迭的悲惨景象心急如焚,肝胆俱裂,他立即请求玉帝,派人治水。玉帝认为,惟有力大无穷的巨灵神可担此重任。

巨灵神名叫秦洪海,生得头如笆斗,眼似铜铃,毛发直竖,腰阔十围,貌似笨拙,行如猿猱。自领了玉帝旨命,就踏上华山峰头,居高临下,察看地形,以求为洪水找一条合适的出路。

经过细心地观察,巨灵神发现在首阳山和华山之间有一条狭窄的峪道,于是他走进峪道,左手托着华山的石壁,右脚蹬着首阳山的山根,使尽全身力气,大吼一声,只见迅雷劈空,电光闪耀,一声巨响,两山开裂,百丈高的一股黄浪汹涌澎湃从两山之间奔腾东流。巨灵神站在波涛之中,抬头看华山,已被推进秦岭深处;回首望首阳,已经藏在波涛之北,看着被淹没的田地又重新露出水面,欣慰地笑了。

如今,在华山北峰、苍龙岭一带东望华山著名景观"仙人仰卧",即是开山导河功成后、仰卧入睡化为山峰的巨灵神。西峰南端有巨灵神观察地形时留下的巨灵足迹;首阳山根有巨灵神开山时的脚印;华山东峰崖壁上有五指分明的巨灵仙掌。此仙掌已被世人公认为关中八景头一景。唐著名诗人王维还写诗赞美华山的高峻、仙掌的灵异:

用英语说中国——旅游亮点
Introduce China in English—Scenic Spots

昔闻乾坤闭，
造化生巨灵。
右足踏方止，
左手推削成。
天地忽开坼，
大河注东溟。
遂为西峙岳，
雄雄镇秦京。

Vocabulary
妙词连珠

Banpo Museum 半坡博物馆	The Qianling Mausoleum 乾陵
Great Mosque 大清真寺	Zhaoling 昭陵
Big wild Goose Pagoda 大雁塔	Famen Temple 法门寺
Small Wild Goose Pagoda 小雁塔	Mount Huashan 华山
Yellow Emperor's Mausoleum 黄帝陵	Mausoleum of Emperor Qin Shihuang 秦始皇陵
Medicine King's Mausoleum 药王洞	
Qiangling Mausoleum 乾陵	ancient Xi'an city 西安古城
Lady Yang's Tomb 杨贵妃墓	bury 埋葬
Black Dragon Temple 青龙寺	vault 墓穴
Temple of Prosperous Teaching 兴教寺	terracotta 赤土陶器，陶俑
Old Han Terrace 古汉台	aesthetic 审美的
Mausoleum of Hua Mulan 花木兰墓	warrior 武士
Mountain Huashan 华山	chariot 双轮战车
Pancake in mutton soup 羊肉泡馍	archaeology 考古学
Yan'an Pagoda 延安宝塔	array 排列
Huangdi Mausoleum 黄帝陵	layout 布局

Unit 2 青海省 Qinghai Province

Key Sentences 流畅精句

1. Qinghai Province is located in the northeast of Tibetan-Qinghai Plateau.
   青海省位于青藏高原东北部。
2. Qinghai Lake is the largest salt lake in China at the highest location above sea level.
   青海湖是我国最大、海拔最高的内陆咸水湖。
3. Qinghai Government was set up with Xining the capital.
   省政府驻西宁市。
4. With five islands each unique in its own way, especially the island of birds.
   湖中有五个形态各异的岛屿,尤以鸟岛闻名遐迩。
5. Qinghai's ninety-six percent land is pasture.
   青海 96% 的土地是草原。
6. Qinghai is famous for Ta'er Lamasery and the Bird Island in Qinghai Lake.
   青海以塔尔寺和青海湖上的鸟岛而闻名。
7. Qinghai is the source of both the Yellow and Yangtze rivers.
   青海既是黄河的源头,又是长江的源头。
8. Xining has a nickname of "World of Salt".
   西宁俗称"盐的世界"。
9. Qinghai is the main land gateway to Tibet.
   青海是通往西藏的门户。

用英语说中国——旅游亮点
Introduce China in English—Scenic Spots

Wonderful Paragraph
精彩片段

Paragraph 1

Qinghai Lake and Bird Island

Lying 180 km from Xining and 3 200 metres above sea level, Qinghai Lake is the largest salt water lake in China; not only that it is also the largest of all lakes, both salt water and fresh, in the whole country. In Qinghai Lake Bird Island is the most charming and attractive place. Situated on the western shore of Qinghai Lake, the island has largely due to the receding of waters off its shores, been turned into a peninsula. Though it covers an area of slightly less than 1 000 square meters it attracts many migrating birds in spring and summer. To these hundreds of thousands of migrant birds, the island has become a very important bird sanctuary. Thousands of birds of different species such as geese, gulls, sandpipers and cormorants, nest on the island and the sound of its calls, twitters is carried far and away. For these birds as well as bird watching enthusiasts, the island represents nothing short of a piece of heaven. Another attraction on the lake is Haixinshan where according to legend great horses were bred.

Paragraph 2

Ta'er Lamasery

Ta'er Lamasery derives its name from the Golden-roofed Lamasery's silver tower built in memory of Zongkaba, the founder of Huangjiao (the Yellow Section). The silver tower is called "Gunbenxianbalin" in Tibetan, meaning "a Maitreya Lamasery where 100 000 lions roar at a Buddha Portrait." Ta'er Lamasery is located in the Lianhuashan (Lotus) Mountain Valley in the southwest of Lusha'er Township in Huangzhong County. It is the

most important sight-seeing sport of Qinghai and one of the cultural relics under the state protection.

Paragraph 3

东关清真大寺
Dongguan Great Mosque

Dongguan Mosque is in Xining's Dongguan region which is mostly inhabited by Moslems. It is considered together with Huajue Mosque in Xi'an of Shanxi, Qiaomen Mosque in Lanzhou of Gansu, and Aitiga Mosque in Kashi of Xijiang as 4 largest mosques in Northwest China. It was built in the Hongwu Period of the Ming Dynasty and has a history of over 600 years.

Paragraph 4

昆仑山
The Kunlun Mountain Pass

The Kunlun Mountain Pass is a very important one along the Qinghai-Tibet highway at the altitude of 4 757 meters. In this area, there are many snow peaks and mountains. In June, the Spring brings green to trees, grass and flowers blossom everywhere in Golumd but at the Kunlun Mountain Pass, it is snowing heavily so that it has become the unique natural scenery of Golumd. During July to August, The Kunlun Mountain Pass becomes a green and blossom place for tourists.

Paragraph 5

三江源头
Tourist Area of the Sources of Three Rivers

This area mainly refers to the South Qinghai Plateau. It includes Guoluo Prefecture, Yushu Prefecture, south part of Huangnan and Hainan Prefecture, and Tanggula Mountain County in Golmud. The area is more than half of the whole province with the elevation above 4 200 meters. There are East Kunlun Mountains, and its branch ranges Buerhanbuda, Kekexili, Bayankela, Anyemaqen and Tanggula Mountain with the elevation almost above 6 000 meters. There are wide grasslands between mountains. It has long been known as "the sources of rivers" because of the great density of the network of waterways. Lakes spread all over the area. There are few people in most of the area. Even there are no people in some area. So the natural features of primitiveness and purely are retained. It is the paradise of plateau wild animals. There are many valuable and rare wild animals and valuable ingredients of traditional Chinese medicines. Tibetans are the major residents in the area with the population more than 70 percent of total in the area. Living in the area for thousands years, Tibetans become strong, bold and unconstrained and frank, who create splendid Tibetan culture, and make great contribution to the Chinese nation even to the whole humanity.

Paragraph 6

Snow Peaks of the Geladandong Mountains

The highest peak of the Geladandong, meaning high and steep peak, Mountains is 6 621 meters above sea level. Within an area of 50 kilometers from south to north and 15 to 20 kilometers from east to west, there are over 30 iced peaks whose altitudes are more than 6 000 meters. The ice or snow covered area is 790 square kilometers. Over 130 modern glaciers originate here. On the top of Jianggendiru Peak, which is 5 800 meters above sea level, one can see the glaciers shining under the sun like two silver dragons.

The glaciers move down at the speed of several meters or tens of meters or even faster every year. Below the snow line, the bottom edge of the glaciers has started to melt. Owing to the movement, breaking, and the repetition of melting and freezing, wonderful ice images have been formed in the area.

Cultural Links 文化链接

塔尔寺"三绝"

塔尔寺内的酥油花、壁画和堆绣,被称为"塔尔寺三绝",有很高的艺术价值。

酥油花相传是公元641年文成公主与吐蕃赞普松赞干布联姻时,当地佛教徒为表示尊敬,在公主从长安出发时带去的一尊佛像前供奉一束酥油花,后在西藏成为习俗。其后传到塔尔寺,而塔尔寺的酥油花塑得非常精巧,形象逼真,逐渐成为一绝。每年春节前几个月,酥油花艺人便将纯净的白酥油,揉以各色石质矿物染料,塑造成各种佛像、人物、花卉、树木、飞禽、走兽,有的还组成宗教故事、人间天上生活及神话故事等。每到农历正月十五日灯节会上将做好的酥油花展出,一年一度,成为寺内盛会。

壁画,有的直接绘于墙上,有的绘于栋梁上,更多的是绘于布幔上,悬挂或钉在墙上。壁画染料采用矿物染料,色泽鲜艳,经久不褪。每年六月观经会上,将绘有大佛像的数十丈长的布幔在山坡上高高挂起,谓之晒佛,围观瞻仰者常达数万人。

堆绣是用各色绸缎剪成各种形状,塞以羊毛、棉花之类的充实物,在布幔上绣成具有明显立体感的佛像、佛教故事、山水、花卉等,是一种独特的工艺美术品。

Vocabulary 妙词连珠

source 根源,源头	Ta'er Lamasery 塔尔寺
unique 惟一的,独特的	Dongyuan Great Mosque 东关清真大寺
salt 盐	
highway 公路	Qinghai Lake 青海湖
silver 银色的	Kunlun Mountain Pass 昆仑山
gobi desert 戈壁滩	Bird Island 鸟岛
Mekong River 湄公河(澜沧江)	

Introduce China in English—Scenic Spots

Unit 3　Gansu Province 甘肃省

Key Sentences 流畅精句

1. Located in Northwest China and stretching from Tibetan-Qinghai Plateau, to Inner Mongolia and then to Loess land.
   地处西北,跨青藏、内蒙古、黄土三大高原。

2. Gansu Province is the main channel of communication from Southwest China to Northwest China, once the Silk Road in the Han and Tang dynasties.
   甘肃省是我国西南部通向西北的交通要道,汉唐丝绸之路所经之地。

3. There are a lot of historic sites and cultural relics, such as Mogao Grottoes, Mt. Baita, Jiayu Pass and Mt. Maiji Grottoes.
   历史文物和古迹众多,有敦煌莫高窟、白塔山、嘉峪关、麦积山石窟等。

4. Singing Dunes—Yueya Pond is Situated in the south of Dunhuang.
   鸣沙山——月牙泉位于敦煌市城南。

5. The Yueya Pond is surrounded with dunes and it is so named because it looks just like a new moon.
   月牙泉被鸣沙山环抱,因水面酷似一弯新月而得名。

6. Dunhuang City is at the westernmost end of Hexi Corridor, Gansu Province.
   敦煌是位于甘肃省河南走廊最西端的城市。

7. Silk Road made it possible the eastward expansion of central and west Asian cultures with Indian Buddhism.
   丝绸之路的开通,使得西亚、史亚文化随着印度佛教文化东传。

8. In Dunhuang these different cultures met and melted together.
   在敦煌,中西不同文化在这里汇聚、碰撞、交融。

110

西北
Northwest China

9. Bingling Si Grotoes are 129 km southwest of Lanzhou.
   炳灵寺石窟在兰州城西南 129 公里处。
10. Tianshui was a trade-distributing center on the Silk Road.
    天水曾经是丝绸之路上的贸易集散中心。
11. There are 194 caves with over 7 200 stone and clay Buddhist statues at Maiji Mountain.
    麦积山有 194 个洞窟,计有 7 200 个泥塑、石雕佛像。
12. Many caves in Mogao Grottoes have a series of pictures telling stories.
    莫高窟的许多洞窟内有一系列记事壁画。
13. White Horse Pagoda commemorates the horse of the Indian monk Jiumoluoshi.
    白马塔是纪念印度和尚鸠摩罗什的马而建的。
14. The Yangguan Pass is just a beacon tower now.
    阳关现在只是一个烽火台。

Wonderful Paragraph
精彩片段

Paragraph 1

敦煌莫高窟
Mogao Grottoes in Dunhuang City

Mogao Grottoes is situated 25km southeast of Dunhuang city, Gansu province, in Daquan river valley at the foot of Echoing-sand Mountain facing Sanwei Mountain. On the cliff face over 1 600m long from south to north 492 caves survived the time, various in size and clustered higher or lower all over the cliff. In the caves are vivid statues, elegant apsaras, amazing murals, and exquisitely arranged lotus bricks, creating a holy world of Buddhism.

The first Mogao grottoes were carved in 366, and the carving went on through the following dynasties of North Liang, North Wei, West Wei, North

Zhou, Sui, Tang, Five Dynasties, Song, West Xia, and Yuan. There remain by now over 45 000m^2 murals and more than 2 400 statues, the tallest statue exceeding 30m and the largest mural covering about 50m^2. These statues and murals constitute a mirror of China in the thousand years from the 4th to the 14th century, reflecting the society, production, life, transportation, architecture, art, music, dance, customs, and religion of the people.

The artistic content of the grottoes is exceedingly rich as an integrated art of architecture, sculpture and fresco, reflecting not only the acceptance of Buddhism in Dunhuang area, but also the history and society as well as economy of the area, and providing a vivid illustration of the localization of Buddhism in China and the capacity of Chinese people in their absorbing and remodeling of foreign cultures.

These artistic creations of religion, grand in scale and stunning in number, provide the valuable data for the study of the social life, ethnic relation, and cross-culture exchange in ancient China.

In 1961, Mogao Grottoes was recognized by State Council as a key historical site under state protection, and in 1987, UNESCO inscribed it on World Heritage List as a cultural heritage of the world.

Paragraph 2

鸣沙山、月牙泉和雷音寺
Echoing-sand Mountain, Crescent Lake, and Leiyin Temple

Echoing-sand Mountain is located 6km south of Dunhuang city proper, and this ranges of sand dunes winds on from Mogao Grottoes in the east, to Danghe Reservoir in the west, altogether about 40km long, 20km wide, rising up at a relative height of dozens of meters. The highest spot is its Southwest Peak of the rear mountain, about . above sea level, while the primary peak of its front mountain is 1,240m above sea level. It is o named because, under the human tread or wind blow, the sand produces a sound like a string instrument, a horn, a drum, or that of rumbling thunder.

Descent Lake looks exactly like a beautiful new moon lying at the north foot of Echoing-sand Mountain. It is about 118m long from east to west, 54m wide, 5m deep in four wonders: for thousands of years its shape remains exactly the same, a clean and green oasis on the deadly land, right inside the threatening sand dunes but never filled up by the sand, and a dish of the old fish from the lake will keep one always young.

Leiyin Temple is north of Echoing-sand Mountain, built in 1991 and covering an area of 3 000m^2. The original temple, it is said, was buried under the Echoing-sand Mountain in a sandstorm. The new temple has over a hundred rooms, halls, pavilions, and houses, as well as 37 statues, of which the marble Sakyamuni was donated by overseas Chinese in Burma. At the moment a dozen of monk live in the temple and regularly hold Buddhism services. Now the temple is a key center in western China services. Now the temple is a key center in western China open to the world for Buddhist activities.

Paragraph 3

麦积山石窟 Maiji Mountain Grottoes

Located near Tianshui, a major city in Eastern Gansu Province, Wheat-Pile Mountain (The Maiji), reputed as the "Oriental Sculpture Museum," is 142 metres high. The name comes from the fact that the mountain looks like a stack of wheat. There are altogether 194 grottoes (the grottoes are divided into east grottoes and west grottoes) in all, and there are 54 grottoes in the east, and 140 grottoes in the west. All of them are cut on cliffs, 80 metres above the ground on the southern side of the mountain. The grottoes contain more than 7 200 clay or stone sculptures and over 1 300 square metres of murals, both of which are works of the 4th to 19th centuries (Northern Wei, Western Wei, Northern Zhou, Sui, Tang, the Five Dynasties, Song, Yuan, Ming and Qing dynasties)—making them a perfect example of China's sculpture through the ages. In addition to clay sculptures, there are more than 2 000 pieces of pottery, bronze ware, ironware, and jade articles, ancient books, documents, paintings, calligraphy and other cultural relics in the 194 grottoes. The highest figure is about 16 metres, and the smallest being only 10 centimetres. It exquisite clay sculptures are well known not only in China but also abroad. One salient feature of the grottoes is that the only means of communication between the caves is a plank road built on the face of a precipice. The gigantic road project must have taken on-lookers' breath away.

The grottoes have applied to the United Nations' Educational, Scientific and Cultural Organization (UNESCO) for admission onto the World Heritage List.

Paragraph 4

炳灵寺石窟
Bingling Monastery

Fifty kilometers west of the Yongjing County, the Thousand Buddha Caves of Bingling Temple is on the Jishi Hill. Bingling is a transliteration of Tibetan, which means Ten Thousand Buddha, just the common name of Buddhist caves in China. They were initially made in 420, and expanded several times through the ages. Nowadays, there still exist 183 niches, 694 stone statues, 82 clay sculptures, and 900 square meters of murals. All the statues, sculptures and murals exhibit superb craftsmanship, and have great artistic appeal. These caves, which stretch for 200 meters, include the caves of Western Qin, North Wei, Sui, Tang, and Song, Yuan, Ming, Qing dynasties.

Paragraph 5

嘉峪关长城
Jiayuguan Pass

Jiayuguan Pass is the first pass at the west end of the Great Wall of China and was built during the Ming Dynasty. It is located 6 kilometers southwest of Jiayuguan City which is in Gansu Province. It is located at the foot of Jiayuguan Hill, between two hills of which the Pass lies, so earned the name "The First and Greatest Pass under the Heaven". This is different

西北
Northwest China

from "The First Pass under the Heaven", which is located at the east end of the Great Wall near Qinhuangdao City in Hebei Province.

The Pass is located at the narrowest point of the western section of the Hexi Corridor, and Jiayuguan often has the meaning of "Nice Valley". It was also a must point of the ancient Silk Road.

The pass is trapezoid-shaped with a perimeter of 733 meters and with an area of more than 33 500 square meters. The total length of the city wall is 733 meters and the height is 11 meters. There are two gates-with one located on each of the east and west sides of the pass. On each gate there is a building. On the building at the west gate, the Chinese inscription of "Jiayuguan Pass" is written on a tablet. The south and north sides of the pass are connected to the Great Wall. There is a turret on each corner of the pass. On the north side inside the two gates, there are wide roads leading to the top of the pass.

The structure was initially built in 1372 during the Ming Dynasty and has a history of more than 600 years. A legend says that when Jiayuguan Pass was to be built, the official in charge of this project asked the designer to count how many bricks and other materials would be used precisely. The designer gave him a specific number. But when the project was finished, one brick was left which was placed on the pass as a symbol of commemoration.

Jiayuguan itself consists of three defense lines—an inner city, an outer city and a moat.

Paragraph 6

大、小盘城
The major Square City and the minor Square City

The major Square City was called Hechang City in ancient times, established in West Han Dynasty on a natural terrace of the ancient Shule River. Its name means "riverside warehouse", and it is a city of military warehouse in northwestern China rarely found elsewhere in the nation.

用英语说中国——旅游亮点
Introduce China in English—Scenic Spots

Three scenes of the city are worth visiting. The first is the survived city base, with the remaining area of about 600m². Those of the walls on the four sides are fairly well preserved, with the city gates, sidewalks, and horse road easily recognizable. The second attraction is the beacon tower of the city, standing near in the west of the city base. The third is the heaps of burning materials of the beacon scattered around the beacon tower, 15 in number. The largest of the heaps is about 2m long, 1.5m wide, and 13m high, lying neat as the best preserved heap of burning materials in China for beacon towers.

Paragraph 7

汉长城
Great wall of Han Dynasty

Great Wall of Han Dynasty began in the east from Lintao County, Gansu Province, the terminus of the Great Wall of Qin Dynasty, and ended in the west at Lop Nur of Xinjiang. The section of this Great Wall north of the minor Square City is the most intact of the Great Wall of Han Dynasty preserved so far in China.

Paragraph 8

黄河铁桥
Yellow River Iron Bridge

Located at the foot of White Pagoda Mountain, the Suspending Bridge was first built in the early Ming Dynasty (1368-1644). In 1907, it was rebuilt with iron, therefore it was renamed Yellow River Iron Bridge. It is the first big iron bridge over the Yellow River in Chinese history. The length of the bridge totals 250 metres with four bridge piers. Since the new China was founded in 1949, the bridge has been reinforced by adding curve steel arch beams, which looks more magnificent.

Paragraph 9

Gansu Provincial Museum
甘肃省博物馆

The Gansu Provincial Museum was built in 1959, encompassing 21 000 square metres, with an exhibition space of 13 000 square metres. The museum is in the shape of Chinese character "山" meaning "mountain". The museum has 5 floors in the middle, three floors on both sides. In the museum exhibit historical relics, the Wei (220-265) and Jin (264-240) murals, the chart of the Silk Road, and other revolutionary cultural relics. The museum boosts nearly 100 000 relics and specimens. A bronze horse poised as if flying, and one of his hooves rests lightly on a swallow with wings outstretched, suggesting in a beautiful and imaginative way the almost divine power which the Chinese at this time believed the horse to possess from an Eastern Han Dynasty (AD 25-220) tomb discovered in Gansu in 1969 has been selected as a graph symbol of China's tourism.

Cultural Links
文化链接

壁画故事

释迦牟尼传记故事：敦煌彩塑中有大量佛教创始人释迦牟尼生平事迹的"佛传图"和"说法像"，其中"佛传图"绘于第 290 窟窟顶前部人字披东、西两披，各分三层连续描绘了"佛教"中的 87 个情节，组成长达 27.5 米的长卷连环画。这是世界上现存早期石窟画中最完好的一幅"佛传故事画"。

尸毗王割肉救鸽：这个本生故事画最早见于北凉第 275 窟的北壁中层，只画了割肉和过秤两个情节。最精彩的当属北魏第 254 窟北壁前部的"尸毗王本生"。此画增加了鹰追鸽、鸽向尸毗王求救、眷属痛哭等情节，增大了内容和时空跨度。正中的尸毗王形体高大，把画面一分为二。被割肉的小腿抬起，尸毗王目视血淋淋的伤口，使割肉主题一目了然。由此可见，这幅画的构思表现出高超的才能，把不同时空范围内发生的故事情节有机地结合到一个画面上,使画面中心突出,容量增大,有条不紊。

五百强盗成佛:绘在第285窟南壁,是莫高窟西魏时期最大的一幅故事画,也是最早的因缘故事画。其手法采用横卷式直线型构图,以八个并列的画面表现了故事的发生、发展到结束的全部内容。

九色鹿:此故事绘于第257窟的西壁,是莫高窟最完美的连环画式"本生故事画"。画面从两头开始,到中间结束。

Vocabulary 妙词连珠

luminous jade cup 夜光杯	the Mogao Grottoes 莫高窟
mural 壁画	Dunhuang Art Research Institute of Cultural Relics 敦煌艺术研究会
red date 红枣	
oasis 绿洲	Dunhuang Research Institute of Cultural Relics 敦煌文物研究会
The Giant Buddha Temple at Zhangye 张掖大佛寺	
	Echoing-Sand Mountain 鸣沙山
diamond sutra 金刚经	Pavilion of the crescent Lake 月泉阁
Jade Gate Pass 玉门关	Yang Pass on the Great wall 阳关
New Moon Spring 月牙泉	Wild camels 野骆驼群
ride camel 骑骆驼	Painting 绘画
the Silk Road 丝绸之路	grottoe 石窟
wedding and funeral ceremonies 婚丧仪式	sitting stature 坐像
	sculpture 雕塑
cultural relics 文物	religion 宗教
Caves of a Thousand Buddhas 千佛洞	

Unit 4 宁夏回族自治区
Ningxia Hui Autonomous Region

Key Sentences
流畅精句

1. Ningxia Hui Autonomous Region Situated in the west of Hetao Corridor along the Yellow River, tilting from south to north.
   宁夏回族自治区位于黄河河套走廊西部,境内地势南高北低。
2. Yinchuan is the capital of the Ningxia Hui Autonomous Region.
   银川是宁夏回族自治区首府。
3. You can be adventurous for Ningxia's mysteries.
   你可探访宁夏的神秘。
4. Ningxia Hui Autonomous Region was founded in 1958.
   宁夏回族自治区成立于1958年。
5. Ningxia produces coal, petroleum, mica, asbestos, lime and Chinese wolfberry.
   宁夏出产煤、石油、云母、石棉、石灰和枸杞子。
6. Ningxia was home to the Rong and Di tribes in the Western Zhou dynasty.
   宁夏是西周时戎族和狄族的故乡。
7. Yinchuan is close to mountains and sandy deserts.
   银川市紧邻群山沙漠。
8. Yinchuan was founded in Tang Dynasty.
   银川建于唐代。
9. The Yellow River Festival is celebrated in Yinchuan every September.
   黄河节每年9月在银川举行。
10. Qingtongxia is a gorge and in impressive dam.
    青铜峡是峡谷,也是个宏伟的大坝。

11. There are 2 000-year-old rock paintings on Helan Mountain.
    贺兰山有2 000年前的岩石画。
12. Gao Temple is a temple for Confucianism, Buddhism, and Taoism. And it also has statues of the Jade emperor, the Holy Mother, and Guan Yu, the God of War.
    高庙是一座儒、佛、道三教合一的寺院。里面还供奉着玉帝像、圣母像、关羽像。

Wonderful Paragraph 精彩片段

Paragraph 1

Mausoleums of the Western Xia Kingdom
西夏王陵

Yuanhao assumed the imperial title, it was known as the Xia Kingdom. In 1227, Western Xia was conquered by Yuan emperor Tai Zu (Genghis Khan). The Western Xia had ten ruling emperors over a 190 year period. The sites of the imperial mausoleums were chosen nearby at the east foot of the Helan Mountains, 25 kilometers west of Yinchuan City. On the southeast corner at the foot of the Helan Mountains are two large mausoleums, probably Jialing and Yuling mausoleums of Li Jiqian and Li Demin, who were posthumously designated Emperor Tai Zu and Emperor Tai Zong. The architectural arrangement of the mausoleum area makes these two mausoleums most prominent, followed by others built later. Like other imperial tombs, Western Xia mausoleums were composed of two architectural units, the mausoleum gardens above ground and underground palaces. All the mausoleum gardens faced south, and their architectural forms above ground have some unique characteristics, though they are quite similar to mausoleums of the Tang and Northern Song dynasties in Gongxian County.

Mount Xumi Grottoes
须弥山石窟

Mount Xumi Grottoes are located on the eastern slope of the mountain about 60 kilometres northwest of Guyuan County, Ningxia Hui Autonomous Region. The ideal geographical position of the mountain has a close bearing on the building of the grottoes. The area used to be a key passage on the ancient Silk Road between the East and the West and also a thoroughfare for exchanges between the Han and other ethnic groups of China. Therefore, it was the scene of many battles. In the Sui (581-618) and Tang (618-907) dynasties, people built temples on the mountain in token of their appeal for peace and stability and against war and murder as well as their faith in Buddhism.

The most celebrated place of interest in the mountain is the Giant Sitting-Buddha Maitreya in Grotto No 2. The Maitreya measures 26 metres in height, with its ears the length of two adults put together. The Maitreya has a benign look. It is considered a representative masterpiece of the grotto in the mountain. Grotto No 5 is the biggest of its kind in the mountain. Made of a mound hollowed out, it is called the "Haloes of Xumi". The grotto consists of seven well-preserved Buddhist statues, each six metres tall, and seven Bodhisattva statue. These sculptures look mysterious and fascinating under a few rays of light that enter the grotto through a hold in the mound. Subjected to devastation by earthquakes and windstorms in its 1,400-year history, half of the grotto was caved-in, but it has recently been restored.

The grotto began its construction around the time of the Northern Wei Dynasty (368-534) and was completed in the Sui (581-618) and Tang (618-907) dynasties. The Buddhist statues, which were made with an artistic approach of realism, reflect the true features of people in the Northern and Southern Dynasties (420-581), the Sui and Tang dynasties.

High Temple

High Temple at Zhongwei Located north to Zhongwei County. The High Temple was first built in the period of the reign of Emperor Yongle (1368-1398) of the Ming Dynasty. The High Temple was originally called "the New Temple". By the Qing Dynasty, it became a large-scaled architecture complex. During the period of the reign of Emperor Kangxi of Qing Dynasty, it was renovated and renamed "Pavilion of Jade Emperor". The present complex were mostly constructed during and after Qing Emperor Xianfeng's reign. The temple is famous for its height. On a high terrace of about 4 000 square meters, buildings and pavilions involving more than 260 rooms were constructed. The High Temple is an outstanding representative of Ningxia's ancient architectures. It was a place for religious activities of Confucianism, Buddhism and Taoism. 174 statues of different religions are protected well in the temple.

Top of the Sand Slope Tourist and Scenic Zone

Shapotou (Top of the Sand Slope) Tourist and Scenic Zone is located in Zhongwei County, bordered the Tengger Desert in north and the Yellow River in south. A number of oases lie right in the heart of the area. One of China's four humming sand dunes, "the Golden Sand and Humming Bell", is situated at the top of Shapotou. Nicknamed as "the Deserts Capital of the World", it is famous for not only its unique natural scenes, but also achievements of subduing the deserts.

鎏金铜牛——一脚踢出镇馆之宝

宁夏博物馆展馆门口一座鎏金铜牛格外吸引人。只见它有真牛般大小,横着身子卧着,头上两角弧度优美,两只圆睁着的眼睛警惕地看着1 000多年后的世人,全身折射出柔和的金色,说起它的出土还有一个趣事。新中国成立后,一直到20世纪70年代才组织了考古队系统发掘西夏王朝遗迹,因为之前遗迹被帝国主义列强大肆掠夺破坏过,考古队员边挖边痛心。在一座陪葬坑里,队员一进去就看到几个倒在地上的盗墓者尸骨,而坑内早已空空。一名考古队员不禁狠命地踢着泥地说:"又被他们糟蹋了!"不料脚被硬物碰得生痛,原来是踢到了地下铜牛的两角。中大历史系博士王芳就此指出,中学历史教科书里谈到古代鎏金技术时,就是以它作为配图和解说对象的,它也是宁夏博物馆的镇馆之宝。

gorge 峡谷	North Pagoda 北塔
region 区域	Shahu Scenic Spot 沙湖旅游区
Yellow River Festival 黄河节	Xumi Mountains Grottos 须弥山石窟
Tang Dynasty 唐代	Chinese wolfberry 枸杞子
Helan Mountain 贺兰山	The Nanguan Mosque 南关清真寺
mausoleum 壮丽的陵墓	Haibao (Sea Treasure) Pagoda 海宝塔
Gao Temple 高庙	
South Gate Mosque 南门清真寺	The Western Xia Mausoleum 西夏王陵
Zhongda Mosque 中大清真寺	
Drum and Bell Tower 钟鼓楼	Mount Xumi Grottoes 须弥山石窟
Qingtong Gorge Hydropower Station 青铜峡水电站	Shahu Lake Tourist Area 沙湖旅游区

Unit 5 新疆维吾尔族自治区
Xinjiang Uygur Autonomous Region

Key Sentences
流畅精句

1. Xinjiang takes 1/6 of China's total territory.
   新疆占中国版图的六分之一。
2. Named Xiyu in ancient time.
   古称西域。
3. Tianchi Lake on Mt. Tianshan lies on the slope of Mt. Bogeda in Fukang City.
   天山天池位于阜康市境的博格达峰山腰地带。
4. Located in the valley of Mt. Huoyan (Mt. Flaming) with meandering waters from snowy Tianshan mountains.
   (葡萄沟)位于火焰山西侧的峡谷中。这里水渠纵横,终日流淌着天山雪水。
5. Xinjiang produces oil, ketchup, sheep, pears, grapes and grain.
   新疆出产石油、番茄酱、绵羊、珍珠、葡萄和葡萄干。
6. The Flaming Mountain is so named because the incessant sun is supposed to make the rocks seems on fire from a distance.
   火焰山之所以得名是因为阳光连续照耀,使得岩石从远处看,就像在火上一般。
7. You can identify people's nationality from their facial features and their distinctive dress in Kashi.
   在喀什,你可以从人们的脸部表情和他们独特的衣着辨别他们的民族。

Wonderful Paragraph
精彩片段

Paragraph 1

T吐鲁番
urpan

Hot is summer in this major tourist city of Xinjiang, situated in Turpan Basin, the lowest point on the mainland of China. The local people have developed karez, an irrigation system composed of wells connected by underground channels, to counter the heat and drought of the place. At the foot of the Flaming Mountain east of Turpan lies Grape Gully (nickname: Green Pearl City), an oasis where the scorching sun is shut off by luxuriant tree foliages and grapevine trellises that cover 220 hectares and are crisscrossed by irrigation ditches. No place in China is hotter in summer than the Flaming Mountain in Turpan, a mountain made famous by the classical Chinese mythological novel, Journey to the West. Xinjiang's largest ancient pagoda, Dorbiljin (Emin) Pagoda, (also called Sugong Pagoda) stands 2 km east of downtown Turpan. To the east lies Gaochang, which until the early Ming was a thriving town on the Silk Road; today it has been reduced to a 2 million-square-metre stretch of broken walls and deserted fields. The inexorable pace of history is even more keenly felt at Jiaohe, another ancient city that was deserted during the early Ming, leaving a pile of ruins west of Turpan.

Paragraph 2

F火焰山
laming Mountain

Scientific explanation cites tectonic plate movement on the earth's surface during the formation of the Himalayas 50 000 000 years ago. The mountain is barren and extremely hot in summer. During the trek approaching the mountain, visitors will find the soles of their shoes soften in the intense heat. With the red sun overhead, the red mountain looks like a fiery dragon-truly an unforgettable spectacle!

The mountain lies 10 km (6.2 miles) east of Turpan city, covering about 100 km (62 miles) from east to west with a width of 9 km (5.6 miles). The average height is 500m (1 640feet), while the 831-meter (2 726-foot) -high peak rises above Shengjinkou, a vital pass of the ancient city of Gaochang.

Paragraph 3

坎儿井
The Karez System

the karez system, an irrigation system connected by underground channels, is considered as one of the three great ancient projects in china, the other two being the great wall and the grand canal. there are nearly one thousand karez totaling five thousand kilometers in length in turpan.

The structure of the karez basically consists of wells, underground channels, ground canal and small reserstoirs. in spring and summer, a great amount of melting snow and rainfall flow down from the bogda and karawuquntag mountains north and west of the turpan depression into the valleys and then seep into the gobi desert. taking advantage of the mountain slopes, the working people ingeniously created the karez to draw the underground water to irrigate the farmland. the water in the karez will not evaporate in large quantities even under the scorching heat and fierce wind, hence ensuring a stable water flow and gravity irrigation.

As far back as the han dynasty, the karez was recorded in shi ji (the historical records) and then called "well canal". most of the existing karez in the turpan area were built during the qing dynasty and in after years. nowadays large stretches of fertile oasis land are still irrigated by karezes. the karez in the wuxing township are open to visitors.

西北
Northwest China

Paragraph 4

T天山天池
ianchi Lake

In the middle of Bogda Peak, 110 km (68 miles) east of Urumqi, nestles Heavenly Lake. Covering 4.9 square kilometers (1.89 square miles), this crescent-shaped lake deserves its name, Pearl of Heavenly Mountain (Tianshan Mountain). With melted snow as its source, Heavenly Lake enjoys crystal water.

Paragraph 5

K喀纳斯湖
anas Lake

The Kanas in Altay Mountain, north Xinjiang, is a lake which looks mysterious and elegant with the peaks around it reflected bewitchingly in its pellucid water. Inhabiting the place are Mongol nomads who have adhered to their incomparable habits and customs.

Paragraph 6

K克孜尔石窟
izil Grottoes

Kizil, 70 km from Kuqa County, is the venue of one of China's four grottoes which was built earlier than Mogao Grottoes of Dunhuang. The 10 000 square metres of murals kept in the 236 caves that are still there, are of high value for artists and researchers alike.

Paragraph 7

B巴音布鲁克草原
ayanbulak Grassland

Some 400 km from Urumqi lies the vastest and most beautiful grassland of Xinjiang-Bayanbulak, which formerly belonged to Hejin County of Bayangol Mongol Autonomous Prefecture. The charms of Bayanbulak are accentuated by the Swan Lake in its heart, a mating and incubating place for large flocks swans.

Paragraph 8

The Ruins of Jiaohe
交河故城

The Ruins of Jiaohe Lying in Yarnaz Gully 13 kilometers were of Turpan, the ruins used to be the capital of Yarkhoto, one of 36 kingdoms of West Territory. The ancient city was first established during the Han Dynasty as a garrison town on a 30-meter-high loess plateau bounded by two rivers—thus the name Jiaohe, which means "confluence of two rivers". Present ruin of the city, built during the Tang Dynasty, is 1,650 meters long and 300 meters wide. Debris and dilapidated walls and bare foundations are what remain of the place, but the inexorable pace of history is nevertheless keenly felt from the city layout and vestiges of yamens, monasteries, pagodas and back alleys.

Cultural Links
文化链接

火焰山

大名鼎鼎火焰山 山不在高,有仙则名。火焰山就是这样一座山。火焰山位于吐鲁番盆地北缘。古书称赤石山,维吾尔语称克孜勒塔格,意即红山。火焰山脉呈东西走向。东起鄯善县兰干流沙河,西止吐鲁番桃儿沟,长100公里,最宽处达10公里。火焰山重山秃岭,寸草不生。每当盛夏,红日当空,地气蒸腾,焰云缭绕,形如飞腾的火龙,十分壮观。

神话小说《西游记》中的火焰山 明人吴承恩著名神话小说《西游记》,以唐僧师徒四人西天取经的故事而脍炙人口。第五十九和六十回,写唐三藏路阻火焰山,孙行者三调芭蕉扇的故事,更给火焰山罩上一层神秘的面纱。书中写道:"西方路上有个斯哈哩国,乃日落之处,俗呼天尽头",这里有座"火焰山,无春无秋,四季皆热。"火焰山"有八百里火焰,四周围寸草不生。若过得山，就是铜脑壳、铁身躯，也要化成汁哩！"这段描写显系夸张，但高热这一基本特征与火焰山是完全符合的。

关于火焰山的传说之一 当年美猴王齐天大圣孙悟空大闹天宫，仓促之间，一脚蹬倒了太上老君炼丹的八卦炉，有几块火炭，从天而降，恰好落在吐鲁番，就形成了火焰山。山本来是烈火熊熊，孙悟空用芭蕉扇，三下扇灭了大火，冷却后才成了今天这般模样。其实，火焰山是由侏罗纪、白垩纪及第三纪沙砾岩和红岩泥构成的，年龄距今有两万万岁了。

关于火焰山的传说之二 维吾尔族民间传说天山深处有一只恶龙，专吃童男童女。当地最高统治者沙托克布喀拉汗为除害安民，特派哈拉和卓去降伏恶龙。经过一番惊心动魄的激战，恶龙在吐鲁番东北的七角井被哈拉和卓所杀。恶龙带伤西走，鲜血染红了整座山。因此，维吾尔人把这座山叫做红山，也就是我们现在所说的火焰山。

拴马桩和踏脚石 在吐鲁番市胜金乡西南10公里处，从312国道西北望去，峰峰的火焰山顶上，有一石柱，巍然矗立，形同木桩，人称"拴马桩"。据说当年唐僧西天取经，路过此处，曾把白龙马拴在石柱上，拴马桩由此而得名。在拴马桩不远处，有一巨石，相传是唐僧上马时用的踏脚石。拴马桩维吾尔人称之为"阿特巴格拉霍加木"。另有传说穆罕默德时代，有个圣人名叫艾力，来到火焰山，曾把马拴在石柱上，以后人们就把这根石柱叫"阿特巴格拉霍加木"（意为拴马桩）以示纪念。

唐僧取经群塑 由木头沟进入火焰山腹地西洲天圣园，就能看见唐僧师徒四人西天取经的群塑。只见孙悟空腾云驾雾，肩扛芭蕉扇在前开路，唐僧气宇轩昂带着猪八戒和沙和尚，牵着白龙马，慢步徐行。群塑形态生动，表情逼真。群塑是1989年修造的。来此观瞻照相的中外游人接连不断，是火焰山新辟的旅游景点之一。遗憾的是群塑人为地被高高的铁栅栏团团围住，形同囚犯，令游人驻足长叹。

Vocabulary 妙词连珠

peppercorn 小辣尖椒
mutton kebab 羊肉串
jeweled knives 嵌玉刀
boot 靴子
Nang bread 馕
mare's milk 马奶
dried sour cheese 干酸奶酪
donkey cart 驴车
Old City between the Two Rivers 交河古城
Thousand-buddha Caves, Baizeklik 柏孜克里克千佛洞
karez wells 坎儿井
Khazakh Nomads 哈萨克乡
The Red Mountain 红山
Suliman's Minaret 苏公塔
Turpan Cemetery 吐鲁番古墓
Astana Graveyards 阿斯塔那古墓群
Id Kah Mosque 艾提尕尔清真寺
Tomb of Abakh Hoja 香妃墓
Exhibition Hall of Ethnic Customs 少数民族风俗陈列馆
Red Hill 红山
The Aay Grotto 阿艾石窟
Turpan 吐鲁番
The Lop Nur Mummies 罗布泊木乃伊

5 西南
Southwest China

Unit 1 四川省 Sichuan Province

Key Sentences 流畅精句

1. As part of the ancient Chinese culture, that Bashu culture had developed into an advance phase 4 000 year ago on a pretty large scale.
   早在4 000多年前,巴蜀文化就已逐步形成且具有相当的规模,是中华文化的重要组成部分。

2. Located on the middle reaches of the Minjiang River, Dujiang Watercourse is 60km away northwest from Chengdu.
   都江堰位于成都西北60公里的都江堰城西,居岷江中游。

3. Located in Aba Qiang Autonomous Prefecture, Jiuzhaigou Valley is a fairyland without any contamination.
   九寨沟位于阿坝藏族羌族自治区境内,是一个不见纤尘、自然纯净的"童话世界"。

4. Water is the soul of Jiuzhaigou with lakes, falls and shoals everywhere, such as Wucai Pond, Wuhuahai Lake, Zhenzhu Shoal, Baojing Rock and Changhai Lake.
   九寨沟的精灵是水、湖、泉、瀑、滩。主要景点有五彩池、五花海、珍珠滩、宝镜岩、长海等。

5. Sichuan is a homeland of pandas.
   四川是熊猫的故乡。
6. There's a panda museum in Wolong Nature Preserve.
   卧龙自然保护区有大熊猫博物馆。
7. Sichuan grows rice, wheat, chilies, and sweet potatoes.
   四川出产水稻、小麦、辣椒和红薯。
8. Emei Shan is one of China' four great Buddhist Mountains.
   峨眉山是中国四大佛教名山之一。
9. Xichang has China's satellite launching center.
   西昌是中国卫星发射中心。
10. Sichuan is endowed with rich resources of tourism. The province is known for its breathtaking natural beauty and many historical and cultural sites. There are 9 national scenic resorts and 7 national famous historical cities in Sichuan.
    四川省旅游资源得天独厚,自然风光旖旎,名胜古迹甚多,有国家级风景名胜区9处,国家历史文化名城7座。
11. Dujiangyan Irrigation Project, Mount Qingcheng, Giant Buddha of Leshan, Mount Emei, Jiuzhaigou Valley and Huanglong scenic areas have been inscribed on the World Heritage List by the UNESCO.
    其境内的青城山、都江堰、乐山大佛、峨眉山、九寨沟风景区、黄龙风景区均被联合国教科文组织列入《世界遗产名录》。
12. Other key tourist spots are Du Fu's Thatched Cottage, Marquis of Wu's Temple, Wenshuyuan Mona-tery, Tower of Looking over the River, Salt Museam, Daocheng Scenic Area, Jianmen Pass, Bamboo Sea in south Sichuan, and Conch Gully.
    四川省主要风景名胜有杜甫草堂、武侯祠、文殊院、望江楼、盐业博物馆、稻城风景区、蜀南竹海、海螺沟等。

Southwest China

Wonderful Paragraph
精彩片段

Paragraph 1

Jiuzhaigou (Nine Fence Gully)
九寨沟

In the northern Sichuan, close to the border of Northwest China's Gansu Province, Jiuzhaigou is a breathtaking alpine valley discovered by lumberjacks in the 1970s. It now welcomes an annual influx of nearly one million tourists from home and abroad.

Jiuzhaigou Scenic area refers to the "Y" shaped three gullies of Shuzhen, Rize, and Zechawa, altogether covering an area of 720km^2 and stretching out for a total length of over 50km. It is a habitat of Tibetans, and geologically a cold alpine Karst topography in nature. The nine villages and the mountain lakes, called "haizi" (sea, or son of sea), shining like crystal mirrors, dot in the depth of forests and snow mountains. At the upper most lies the Long Lake, while the Grass Lake is the end of Rize Gully. The two gullies run down northward and join together at Nuorilang to form the beginning of Shuzheng Gully. The height drop amounts to 1 000m or more from the joint of the two gullies to the outlet of Shuzheng Gully. Lining along the distance are 114 stepped lakes, between which are 17 waterfall groups, 11 torrents, and 5 calcareous tufa shoals, forming "a fairy land under the sky" that features in alpine lake groups, waterfall groups, and calcareous tufa shoals, as well as snow mountains, virgin forests, and Tibetan folklore.

Jiuzhaigou Gully is rich with flora. At present it has 30 000 hectares of natural forests, 2 576 species of higher plants as well as 400 species of lower plants. With the numerous lakes and various vegetation, Jiuzhaigou has a self complete ecological system, which provides the best habitats for wild animals. Investigation shows in the gully there are 170 kinds of vertebrates, and 141 species of birds, of which 3 are under Class I state protection, 4 under Class II, and 10 under Class III.

用英语说中国——旅游亮点
Introduce China in English—Scenic Spots

In December of 1992 it was inscribed on World Heritage List by UNESCO.

Paragraph 2

黄龙 Yellow Dragon Scenic Area

Yellow Dragon Scenic and Historic Interest Area is located at the south section of Mt Minshan range, Songpan County, Aba Tibetan and Qiang Peoples Autonomous Prefecture, northern Sichuan Province, which is a geological transition from the eastern edge of Qinghai-Tibet Plateau towards Sichuan Basin.

The scenic area covers about $700km^2$, of which the Yellow Dragon Gully takes up $600km^2$, while the subdivision Mouni Gully occupies the other $100km^2$. The area has well preserved tectonic zones, glacial remains, and river source topography. It is well known for the "four wonders" of colorful ponds, snow mountains, alpine gorges, and forests. The huge travertine formation is like a golden dragon winding among the virgin forests, cliffs, and icy peaks, constituting the amazing, precipitous, majestic, and wild environmental features of Yellow Dragon scenic area.

The altitude of the area is over 3 000m above sea level, with snow peaks like a forest, of which 7 are over 5 000m high, while the highest Snow Treasure Peak (Xuebaoding) is 5 588m above sea level, which is the summit of Mt Minshan and capped with snow all year round. In the area are also preserved a wealth of rare plants and animals, including 1 500 species of higher plants, most of which are only found in China and 11 of them are under Class I to Class III state protection. As for the rare animals, there are giant panda, golden snub-nosed monkey, takin, cloud leopard, white-lipped deer, brown-eared pheasant, and white-eared pheasant, all under state protection as Class I to Class III endangered animals.

Here are landscapes comparable to the snow-white mountains in Canada, Great Canyon of Wyoming, virgin forests in Colorado, and travertine colored ponds of the Yellowstone Park. This area gathers all the best land-

西南
Southwest China

scapes which make it a rare scenic beauty in the world.

In October of 1982, it was listed as a key scenic area of the nation, and in December of 1992 UNESCO inscribed it on its World Heritage List as a natural heritage of the human world.

Paragraph 3

青城山
Mount Qingcheng

Next to Chengdu lies Mount Qingcheng, one of the birthplaces of Taoism (Daoism), China's only indigenous religion. It is still a religious centre sprinkle with caves and shrines venerated by Taosit. Founded in AD 143 in Mount Qingcheng, Taoism has developed into an important religion in Southeast Asia, exerting tremendous influence there. For ordinary tourists, Mount Qingcheng is an ideal summer resort. The four-hour trek to its summit, 1 600 metres above sea level, is a pleasant trip. Sixteen kilometres from Dujiangyan city, Mount Qingcheng has been known since ancient times as "the most tranquil place under heaven (青城天下幽)". Reaching the mountain on an earlyu spring or summer morning, the tourist will find it shrouded in mist, which moistens stone steps rising up towards the summit. Forests of pine, Chinese fir, cypress and all kinds of fragrant undergrowth make up a deep green world. The only sounds the tourist hears are birds, waterfalls and the tourists' footsteps. Chinese hermits and men of letters have long cherished the perfect sense of peace there. There are four famous Taoist mountains such as Mount Qingcheng in Sichuan Province, Mount Wudang Hubei Province and Mount Laoshan in Shandong Province. UNESCO inscribed the Mount Qingcheng-Dujiangyan Irrigation Project on the World Heritage List in 2000.

Paragraph 4

都江堰
Dujiang Weir

Dujiang Weir, or Dujiangyan Irrigation System, is located west of Dujiangyan City, Sichuan Province. Originally it was called Du'an Weir after the name of the ancient Du'an County, where the weir was situated. Since Song and Yuan Dynasties its was given the present name Dujiang Weir, honored as the "Guarding Treasure of Sichuan Province" that is "ingenious of all times".

The irrigation system was constructed in 227 BC by Li Bing, governor of Shu Prefecture, over 2 200 years ago. It is not only the earliest water control project in China, but also the only and the oldest remain of such in the whole world. Characterized in its successful control of water without any blocking dam, Dujiang Weir is a milestone in the history of technology in China.

In December of 2000, Dujiang Weir was inscribed by UNESCO in World Heritage List as cultural heritages of the human world.

Paragraph 5

峨眉山 Mount Emei

Mount Emei (an elevation of 3 099 metres), located 165 kilometres from Chengdu, capital of Sichuan Province, draws the most attention for its 154-kilometre spread, attracting tourists since ancient times with phenomenal views all the year round.

Mt. Emei is known as one of the four primary shrine mountains of Buddhism in China and the famous national park, situated 7km southwest of Emeishan City, Sichuan Province. The mountain stretches out for 23km from south to north, occupying an area of about 115km^2. Viewed from afar, its catchy Da'e and Er'e hills stand side by side in quite a symmetry, long and thin like the delicate eyebrows of a beautiful maid, hence the name, which literally means "the charming eyebrow of a beautiful maid" in Chinese.

The long extending range of Mt Emei lies between Mt Liangshan and Mt Laishan, referred to as "Mr Emei block belt" in geology. In its very long development, the mountain has gone through various ice invasion, water erosion, and wind sweeping of the nature, and finally presents itself with a rich diversity of miraculous scenes. The altitude difference of thousands meters brings about a temperature drop as sharp as 15℃, and atop the mountain it is rainy and foggy, with an average of 263.5 raining days a year, hence the mountain is veiled behind misty cloudsalmost all year round, and it is a rare opportunity to have clear glimpse of the entire mountain.

Mt Emei is a world famous site of tourism, with a miraculous view for each of its hills and a surprise every few steps. There are the recognized top ten scenes of Sunny Clouds over Luofeng Peak, Evening Bells at Shenji Monastery, Clear Sound under Twin Bridges, Morning Rainat Hongchun Terrace, Autumn Breeze over Baishui Monastery, Nine Sages' Residence, Elephant Pond in Moonlight, Overhanging Greenery at Linyan Rock, Snow World at Daping Monastery, and Buddha's Halo at Golden Summit. There are the four natural wonders of Buddha's Halo, Cloud Sea, Sunrise, and Holy Lamps. And there are the series of interesting sites such as Nation Dedicating Temple, Tiger Taming Temple, Myriad Years Temple, Clear Sound Pavilion, Immortal Peak Temple, Elephant Bathing Pond, Hongchun Terrace, and Golden Summit.

Featured with the graceful natural beauty, the long Buddhist culture, the rich resources of wild life, and the singular topography, Mt Emei wins itself the honor of "Top Elegance under the Sun".

Paragraph 6

乐山大佛
Leshan Giant

Leshan Giant Buddha is a huge statue of Maitreya cut out of a hill in accordance with the terrain, an amazing project in the 8th century that lasted for 90 years. The statue measures 71m in total height, or 59.96m for its sitting proper, which entitles itself as the tallest stone carved statue of Maitreya in the world. The carving is smooth and proportional, and the Buddha looks solemn and majestic. On the cut-out walls at its south and north sides are over 90 stone figures carved in Tang Dynasty, of which the shrine of

"Sutra Illustration of Pure Land" and "Trinity Budda" are particularly cherished for their high artistic values.

The surrounding of Leshan Giant Buddha combines the charm of both the mountains and the rivers. Moreover, it integrates both the beauty of a natural heritage and the gems of human culture. Within $2.5 km^2$ there are 2 sites under Class I state protection and 4 sites under Class II state protection. The Giant Buddha enjoys a favor of its own, lacing the historic and cultural Leshan City on the other side of the river. As the center of the scenic area. the Giant Buddha is accompanied with a number of sites of interest nearby, such as the Detached Mound from the irrigation system of Dujiang Weir by Li Bing in Qin Dynasty, the cliff tomb clusters of Han Dynasty, Buddhist figure carvings, pagodas, and temples of Tang and Song Dynasties, as well as architectural groups of Ming and Qing Dynasties.

Paragraph 7

四姑娘山
Siguniang (Four Girls) Mountains

Siguniang Mountains are as beautiful as their name, but uncovering their veils and appreciating their many charms can be exhausting. Located in Xiaojin County of the Aba Tibetan and Qing Autonomous Prefecture in western Sichuan Province, the Siguniang Mountains are about 220 kilometres away from Chengdu. The mountains stand in the remote distance, like fou beautiful Tibetan girls dressed in white scarves. Legend has it that many years ago, there lived a mountain god named Balang who had four beautiful daughters, and the youngest was the tallest and had the most graceful figure. A devil admired the girl's beauty and wanted to marry them. So the devil suggested to the mountain god that they fight a duel. If he won, he would get the four girls. The mountain god was killed by the devil. And the four girls fled and eventually died from cold weather. Their bodies became the Siguniang Mountains and their father became the Balang Mountains. But another tale holds that the four girls were later saved by a hunter and became fairies. The Siguniang Mountains resemble four graceful fairies

Southwest China 西南

wearing white mantles and waving to guests from afar.

The Siguniang Mountains area consists of the Siguniang Mountains, Shuangqiao Gully, Changping Gully and Haizi Gully. The mountains are 6 250 metres high, reputed by some to be the "Oriental Alps." Snow covers the mountaintop all the year round. Under a blue sky and white clouds, the dark rocks and clean rivers are coated with green moss and various flowers, or golden grass and leaves, milky fog, white snow and crystal-like ice.

Paragraph 8

B 蜀南竹海
Bamboo Sea in South of Sichuan

Bamboo Sea in South of Sichuan The Bamboo Sea sprawls on the border of Changning and Jiang'an counties in Yibin. It is the only major scenic area in the country proclaimed by the State Council stressed on bamboo scenery. 28 peaks scatter over the 120-square-kilometer area. The entire area is, as its name suggests, a vast stretch of bamboo groves. There are above 30 kinds of bamboos such as Nan Bamboo, Flower Bamboo, Cotton Bamboo, Imperial-Concubine-Xiang Bamboo and so on. The air is fresh, while streams run with a rich susurrus, and waterfalls tumble and splash—all these qualify the Bamboo Sea as an ideal bio-tourist destination. In a boundless expanse of green waves there are a lot of scenic spots, such as Heavenly Emperor Temple, Arhat Cave, Heaven Palace, Pavilion of Viewing Cloud, and so on.

Cultural Links
文化链接

清明放水节

都江堰是天府源头,建堰的功臣李冰受到了世人的顶礼膜拜。

东汉李冰圆雕石像的出土说明在1 800多年前,灌区人民已经开始纪念李冰了。唐太宗时褒封李冰"神勇大将军"。宋太祖赵匡胤曾治修崇德庙，扩大了庙基，增塑了二郎像。伏龙观也成了纪念李冰的庙宇。

清雍正五年(1727年)，四川巡抚奏请颁定每年"春秋仲月"，照吉致祭二郎。祭祀时，先到伏龙观祭李冰，再到二王庙祭二郎。官祭一般是在清时岁修完毕时结合放水庆典一道举行的，祭完李冰父子后即到江边鸣炮放水。

官祭之外，还有民祭。传说农历六月二十四是二郎生日，后两日则为李冰生日。因此每年六月二十四前后，川西受益区人民不辞艰苦跋涉，扶老携幼，带着祭品，来庙祭祀，每日多达万人以上。至今民祭之日，二王庙里人山人海，香烟缭绕，虔诚之态，令人感动。

近年来，都江堰市恢复了都江堰清明模拟放水活动，活动丰富多彩，还恢复了仿古祭祀表演。

妙词连珠

Mount Emei 峨眉山	the Tiger-Taming Temple 伏虎寺
geographic location 地理位置	the Giant Buddha of Leshan/Leshan Dafo 乐山大佛
ecological environment 生态环境	Storehouse of Heaven 天府之国
vast expanses of clouds 云海	Precious Light Monastery 宝光寺
Buddha's light 佛光	Cultural Park 文化公园
the evening glow 晚霞	River View Pavilion 望江楼
the Elephant Bath Pond 洗象池	Sansu Shrine 三苏祠
Cave of Nine Old Men 九老洞	Manjusri Temple 文殊院
the Hongchunping Mountain Glen 洪椿坪	Grand Buddha Temple 大佛寺
the Ten-Thousand-Year Temple 万年寺	Two King's Temple 二王庙
	long chao dumplings 龙抄手
the Temple of Serving the Country 报国寺	dan dan noodles 担担面
	hot pepper 辣椒

Unit 2 贵州省 Guizhou Province

Key Sentences 流畅精句

1. Guizhou is multinational province with 37.8% of it population ae ethnic.
   贵州是多民族的省份,少数民族人口占全省总人口的37.8%。
2. Roaring down from the precipice to the Rhino Pond in the southwest of Zhenning Buyi & Miao Autonomous County, Huangguoshu Fall is the largest in China, 77 meters high and 101 meters wide.
   黄果树瀑布位于镇宁布依族苗族自治县城西南,是中国第一大瀑布。高77米,宽101米,河水从悬崖绝壁上直泻犀牛潭中。
3. Guizhou comprises a vast plateau of hills, there being almost no level ground in the entire region.
   贵州全境皆是高原山区,几乎没有平地。
4. Guizhou is rich in many watercourses, streams and rivers.
   贵州水利资源丰富,有众多大河小溪。
5. In Guizhou, the high rainfall and fertile land bring in abundant crops.
   雨水充足,土地肥沃,使贵州可种多种庄稼。
6. In Guizhou, rice and wheat are grown in the lowlands, while corn and rapeseed are produced in the uplands.
   在贵州,低凹地带种植水稻和小麦,高坡上则出产玉米和油菜。
7. Deposits of coal, silver, copper, manganese are being mined in Guizhou.
   在贵州,煤、银、铜和锰矿被开采出来。
8. Because the rock structure is largely limestone, there are many underground rivers and even vast underground lakes in Guizhou.

因为岩石大多是石灰岩,所以贵州有许多地下河,甚至巨大的地下湖。

9. Guiyang is on a tributary of the Wu River in the center of the Guizhou province.

贵阳位于乌江支流上,居贵州省的正中央。

10. Standing at an elevation of 3 000 feet, Guiyang is dominated by the mist-shrouded hills.

贵阳海拔3 000米,周围全是云雾笼罩的山峰。

11. Huangguoshu Falls is the largest waterfall in China.

黄果树瀑布是中国最大的瀑布。

Wonderful Paragraph 精彩片段

Paragraph 1

Huangguoshu Falls 黄果树瀑布

Huangguoshu Falls, the largest waterfall in China, is located on the Baishui River of Guizhou Province.

Here the rough and rapid water of the Baishui River rushes down directly from the cliffs to form waterfalls of 9 steps. The falls have a drop of 105.4 meters. From numerous whirling vortices the falls send out a thunderous roar which can be heard from long distances. When the sun shines over the falls, the mist appears changeably colorful through refraction of the sun.

Huangguoshu Falls is listed in the national register of key scenic spots. Three sites for viewing the falls have been provided: Guanpu Pavilion, Shuilian Cave and Tiansheng Bridge.

Guanpu Pavilion is built for observation of the falls. The rough water, 81 meters wide, falls, roaring down from a 68-meter-high cliff. The big water column plunges into the Xiniu Pool and produces 10-meter-high sprays

of waterfall. The river seems covered by a vast mist. With mountains, farms, forests and houses appearing vaguely as dream images. In summer a colorful rainbow arches in front of the falls. At this time the whole valley seems to be decorated with a piece of fine golden veil.

Shuiliang Cave is situated closely behind the fails. It is a cave constructed of several small natural ones, connected together. Openings in the caves allow observation of the failing water. Thin as small pearls and thick as giant poles, the water pours down continuously.

Tiansheng Bridge is in the lower reaches of the falls. Above it extends a stone forest. The strange stones and rank trees give a sense of remote antiquity. The stone forest is like a maze in complexity, creating a bewildering labyrinth of endless passageways.

Paragraph 2

黔灵公园
Qianling Park

It is one of the biggest inner-city parks in China. It is a natural forest park in Guiyang with high mountains and a crystal clear lake. In addition to such natural scenes as ancient trees, lakes, ponds and lotus, the park boasts many spots of historical interest. On the cliffs of the hills, there are inscriptions by ancient calligraphers. The largest inscription is the 6.2-meter-high and 2.7-metre-wide character hu (tiger) written by a calligrapher in 1860.

During the Anti-Japanese War, the famous patriotic generals like Chang Hsueh-liang (1901-2001) and Yang Hucheng (1892-1949) were jailed one after another in the Shuiyue Nunnery. The nunnery is now developed into a museum. The park is also home to some 400 monkeys. The 3 900-hectare Forest Park is located in the southeastern part of the city. It is China's earliest and largest forest park ever built in a city. In summer, as the temperature is two degrees lower than the other part of the city, the park is an ideal summer resort.

红枫湖
Hongfeng (Red Maple) Lake

Located about 32 kilometers (20 miles) west of Guiyang is the Hongfeng (Red Maple) Lake. It is considered to be the pearl of the Guizhou Plateau, and is the most fascinating among the three lakes in this part of Guizhou. The other two are Baihua (Hundred Flowers) Lake and Dongfeng (East Wind) Lake.

Hongfeng Lake is the largest artificial lake on the Guizhou Plateau. Its surface covers 57.2 square kilometers (22 square miles) and in area is twelve times the size of the Ming Tombs Reservoir in Beijing and six times as large as the famous West Lake in Hangzhou. The lake and the surrounding scenic area occupy a total of 240 square kilometers (93 square miles). There are many red maple trees on the surrounding mountain ranges whose leaves turn red every fall-hence the lake's name.

The Hongfeng Lake Scenic Area consists of four parts: the North Lake, the South Lake, the Rear Lake and the minority ethnic villages. The North Lake is the smallest and is famous for its various islands such as Bird Island, Snake Island and Tortoise Island. Along the shore there is a historic complex of ancient tombs left by the Western Han Dynasty.

Hongfeng Lake is beautiful and serene. It is an ideal tourist destination and can be conveniently included in an itinerary that includes the Dragon Palace and Huangguoshu Waterfall.

织金洞
Zhijin Caves

Located about 150 kilometres west of Guiyang, the capital of Guizhou Province, the Zhijin Caves are also known as the Daji Caves. With a total area of 700,000 square metres, the series of underground caverns stretch nearly 13 kilometres through the plateau rising about 1 300 metres above

Southwest China

sea level. At present, 47 caves and halls have been divided into 12 scenic areas opened to the public.

Paragraph 5

C草海 aohai Lake

Caohai Lake, located in the outskirts of Weining County with an elevation of 2 200 meters, is a natural freshwater Lake found on Guizhou Plateau. Covering a total area of more than 45.5 square kilometers, this lake is also the largest plateau lake in Guizhou.

According to local historical records, there used to be four lakes in each direction. At a later date, these lakes became land. During the reign of Emperor Xianfeng of the Qing Dynasty (1644-1911), mountain torrents occurred and the floods poured into the basin making the basin become a vast lake.

The lake is abundant in various kinds of seaweed, hence the name Caohai Lake (Grass Lake). Caohai Lake is also abounds in fish, waterfowls and many other aquatic animals and plants. It provides a winter habitat for over 100 species of birds, including the black-necked crane.

Besides the wildlife, Caohai Lake also offers an enchanting view all year round.

Paragraph 6

D龙宫 ragon Palace Cave Scenic Spot

In the western suburbs of Anshun in Guizhou Province, there exists a magnificent underground cave system with lakes, waterfalls and stalactites, covering an area almost 60 square kilometers (about 23 square miles). Because the main cave looks like the crystal palace where the dragon king lives, it is known as Dragon Palace Cave.

The scenic spot has four main areas, namely, the Rape Lake, the Whirlpool, the Leech Pass and the Dragon Palace itself. Among them, as the most famous and wonderful scenic spot, the Dragon Palace includes various Karst (Limestone) landscapes, solemn steep cliffs and jagged stone forest. The longest underground river in China, some 5 000 meters (over 5 468 yards) in length flows beneath more than 30 hills connecting over 90 limestone caves within this scenic spot.

The Dragon Palace can be divided into five groups of limestone caves connected by the underground river. The depth of the river can reach to 28 meters (about 15 fathoms) and the width can expand to over 30 meters (about 32 yards). Therefore, it is a fascinating adventure for visitors to float past the magnificent and ever changing views as you journey deeper into the cave by boat.

Besides the gate of the Dragon Palace, a waterfall pours straight down along the Dragon Palace from Tianchi Lake. The waterfall is 34 meters (over 37 yards) high and 25 meters (over 27 yards) wide and described as a white dragon leaving its cave by the locals, namely, the Dragon Gate Fall. This spectacular waterfall is considered one of the three natural wonders in the Dragon Palace by both geologists and tourists alike.

As a region inhabited by the Bouyei ethnic group in compact communities, the trip to the Dragon Palace is also a good chance for visitors to experience the charming and colorful life of this Chinese ethnic minority. At the same time, it is a comfortable place for people to relax because the radiation frequency in this region is the lowest in China.

"黄果树"的由来

传说吴三桂败退时,将一十八箱金银丢入犀牛潭中,从此,人们都想获得这些宝物。

过了若干年,这里首先搬来了一户人家,只是老两口。有一天,一个洋人来到犀牛潭边,用他的魔法看到潭中的财富,然而不知如何避开潭水捞取,因此在潭边徘徊三天。一天他突然发现瀑布上方侧面的悬崖上长的一棵黄树上结了一个仙果,此果是吸干潭水的神物,但时日不到,神功尚差,必须养足百天才行。于是,付钱请二老看守仙果,便回去准备取宝的工具了。

三个月过去了,仙果越长越大,形如升斗。然而未见洋人回来。到了九十九天仍不见洋人来,二老摘下仙果,抛入潭中试探。仙果入潭,只见光华四射,吸水有声,瀑水停落,潭水下跌。不到一个时辰,潭水全无,果见潭底金银财宝。正当他们惊喜无计之时,突然潭中响起天崩地裂似的巨声。吓得二老魂飞魄散。立刻瀑水下落,潭水涨满。一切恢复了原样。

第二天洋人到此,不见树上仙果,追问原因,才知情由。遂悔叹道:"仙果尚欠一日之功,可惜!可惜!"

后来这个地方的人多了,为了纪念这棵古老的黄果仙树,便把这个地方取名"黄果树"。

Vocabulary
妙词连珠

overall 全面的	White Dragon Cave 白龙洞
charm 魔力;魅力	Riverside Park 河滨公园
elegance 雅致;优美;高尚;优雅	Underground Park 地下公园
tranquility 平静;安静;安宁	Red Maple Lake 红枫湖
phase 状态,阶段	Hongfu Temple 弘福寺
bay 湾	Huaxi Park 花溪公园
balustrade 栏杆	Premier Scholar Pavilion 甲秀楼
verdancy 翠绿;未成熟;幼稚	Dragon Palace 龙宫
permeate 渗透;渗入	Qianling Park 黔灵公园
splendor 光辉;壮丽,显赫	Zhijin Cave 织金洞
thereby 因此;从而;在那方面	batik crafts 蜡染工艺
likewise 同样地;也;而且	

用英语说中国——旅游亮点
Introduce China in English—Scenic Spots

Unit 3 云南省 Yunnan Province

Key Sentences
流畅精句

1. Yunnan is a multi-national border province of China.
   云南是一个多民族的边疆省份。
2. Yunnan, called "Dian" or "Yun" for short, is situated in the southwest frontier region of China, and is an important passageway to the outside world.
   云南简称滇或云,是祖国西南边疆的重要门户。
3. Yunnan has not only a variety of magnificent highland scene, but also charming frontier landscapes.
   云南既有雄伟壮丽的高原景观,又有妩媚迷人的边塞风光。
4. The Stone Forest in Lunan, Yunnan, enjoys a high reputation in the world. Every year over one million people, both from abroad and at home, come here to visit it.
   云南的路南石林享誉世界,每年要接待国内外游客百万余人。
5. Xishuangbanna, located at the extreme southern trip of Yunnan province with Burma and Laos to the south, is 730 kilometers from Kunming.
   西双版纳位于云南省最南部,和老挝、缅甸接壤,距昆明730公里。
6. For centuries Xishuangbanna had been a hidden land and it was almost inaccessible.
   多少世纪以来,西双版纳一直都是一片鲜为人知的土地。要抵达西双版纳几乎难于上青天。
7. Down in the deep valley in the northwest of Shigu Township in Lijiang County, Hutiao (Tiger-Leaping) Gorge is the deepest comparatively in the world. Well known for its grandeur.

Southwest China

虎跳峡位于丽江县石鼓镇东北,是世界上落差最大的大峡谷,以奇险雄壮著称于世。

8. The ancient Lijiang is the best-preserved ancient town of the Ming and Qing dynasties in China.

丽江城是我国保留的明清年代城市风貌最完整的古城镇。

Wonderful Paragraph
精彩片段

Paragraph 1

三江并流自然景观
The Protected Areas of Three Parallel Rivers

This scenic area is in northwestern Yunnan Province, covering the three prefectures of Diqing, Nujiang, and Lijiang, including, specifically, Deqin County, Lisu Autonomous County of Weixi, Shangri La County, Derung-Nu Autonomous County of Gongshan, Fugong County. Lushui County, Bai-Pumi Autonomous County of Lanping, and the northwestern part of Naxi Autonomous County of Yulong. It borders with Burma in the west, whereas neighboring with Sichuan and Tibet in the north. With a total area of about 1.7 million hectares, it ranks as a vastest national scenic site in the world.

The three rivers refers to Nujiang, Lancang. and Jinsha, which flow to the south side by side along the deep gullies between the three lofty mountains of Gaoligong, Nushan, and Yunling, covering an area as wide as 150km or so from 98％ 101°30′ eastern longitude to 25°30′ -29° northern latitude. Gushing southward with awing power in parallel like the Roman numeral "Ⅲ", the three large rivers of Asia offer a singular geographical scene.

The charm lies in the unique spectacles of the alpine gullies. A bird's view of it would show that the majestic Himalayas on the Qinghai-Tibet Plateau rolling on from west to east is suddenly blocked by the north-south going mountains and gullies, where Lancang River, Nujiang River, and Jinsha

River from Tanggula Mountains in the northwest have to make an abrupt narrow-in and squeeze themselves into the sheer-cut gullies of Hengduan Mountains, with the shortest distance between them about a dozen kilometers only, a consequence from the mountain-making by the Himalayas that distorted this part of the land into various shapes beyond imagination.

In 1988, the area was listed among the key scenic sites of the nation, and in June of 2003 it was included in World Heritage List by UNESCO.

Paragraph 2

丽江古城
Lijiang Ancient Town

To add to its list of attractions, UNESCO recognized the Ancient Town of Lijiang as a World Heritage site in 1997. Nestled beneath snow-capped peaks, Lijiang is a living museum as it is home to the Naxi people who have steadfastly preserved their centuries-old heritage. They still live in traditional homes, play ancient music and celebrate ethnic festivals with vitality. It is such qualities which now make Lijiang a prized draw card for Yunnan's tourism promoters. Tourism in Lijiang a prize draw card for Yunnan's tourism promoters. Tourism in Lijiang experienced sharp growth in the past few years thanks to its rich tourist resources. Lijiang's charms are due entirely to jes remaining an ordinary town and home to one of the China's 55 ethnic group communities. Thanks to Lijiang's remoteness, the Naxi people have successfully resisted the type of development, which is rapidly changing the face of China.

For the most part, it is ancient town of Lijiang, which is the magnet that pulls in tourists. The Naxi people settled in the town, formerly called Dayan, about 800 years ago. More than 4,000 families still live in the town. All the houses, both look like they did centuries ago. They have been built with the same rooftops, stones, and tiles and are linked together by a web-like network of narrow, criss-crossing pathways. And just as they did several hundred years ago, the canals still run past the households. Apart from the architecture, the Naxi's cultural inheritance is very much evident in its music, which was brought into Lijiang during the Ming Dynasty. While the music died out in central China during the warring years. From the Qing Dynasty onwards, it has survived relatively intact in remote and peaceful Lijiang. Lijiang lies 590 kilometres from Kunming and 196 kilometres north of Dali.

Paragraph 3

玉龙雪山 Jade Dragon Snow Mountain

The mountain is 15km north of Lijiang city, a modern oceanic glacier nearest to the equator in Northern Hemisphere, and a state scenery site of tourism in China. The mountain has 13 peaks extending for 35km from north to south, along side the deepest gorge in the world: Tiger Leaping Gorge. It is snow clad year round, with grandeur and sublime. Fan Steep, its top peak, is 5 596m above sea level against the sky. The mountain is precipitous, picturesque, and peculiar, charming with the scenery sites of Yunshan Spruce Meadow, River of White Water, Ganhaizi Lake, Serac Forest, and so on, to make the mountain a tourists' resort for sight seeing, exploration, scientific survey, or just holiday enjoyment.

Paragraph 4

老君山 Mt Laojun

The mountain stands 70km upward the First Bend of Yangtze River. It is regarded as the "Grandfather of all mountains in Yunnan Province", after the folklore that the magic mirror of Supreme Laojun (Laozi, the Supreme Patriarch Of Taoism, regarded as a god) fell down out of his carelessness, and the 99 broken pieces turned into the 99 clean Dragon Ponds on top of the mountain, hence it is named as that.

The Ninety-nine Dragon Ponds, the god of Supreme Laojun, and the Danxia topography are regarded as the top three treasures of this tourist site, with a number of other interesting places like Mt Jinsichang, South Heaven Gate, Azalea Bush, Yellow Dragon Pool, Meile Peach Garden,

Mountain of Five Immortals, Buddha Rock in Morning Sunshine, Mountain of Bird King, Ninety-nine Dragon Ponds, Black Dragon Pool, Sishiluo, and Anqilin.

Paragraph 5

虎跳峡
Tiger Leaping Gorge

Jinsha River (upper course of Yangtze River) cuts spectacularly through Jade Dragon Snow Mountain and Haba Snow Mountain to form this deepest gorge of the world. It is 18km north of Lijiang city, between peaks of over 3 000m above the river, which is 80m or more at the widest, or only about 30m at the narrowest, a most dangerous section of Yangtze River about 17km long. At the entrance right in the middle of the river lies a huge rock, and the rushing water has to squeeze through a 13m passage at both sides. Folks say that tigers often leap to the other side of the river by this rock, thus the gorge earns this name. A more recent discovery is the ancient rock paintings on cliffs of the gorge, which add wonders to the grand gorge of the world.

Paragraph 6

石林
The Stone Forest

More than 120 kilometers from Kunming stands the Stone Forest, well known at home and abroad. It lies within Shilin Yi Autonomous Country. And it is a most enchanting sight of fantastic stone pillars, and is reputed as the Number One Grand Spectacle on Earth. The moment a tourist enters the forest, one miraculous view after another will catch his eyes. Countless stone peaks seem to have sprung from the ground, assuming a thousand different shapes, all fanciful and picturesque, as if lying with each other in their sublimity and grandeur. Among the sights in the stone forest proper and on its periphery the most splendid ones are "Sword Peak Pond", "Jade Lake in the Stone Forest" and "the Underground Stone Forest in Ziyun Cave".

Southwest China

Paragraph 7

T 大理三塔
hree Pagodas in Dali

These pagodas are situated north of Dali City. The three all and ramrod pagodas stand at the foot of Lan Peak of Cangshan Mountain, making the landscape more beautiful and adding grandeur to the ancient city. The major pagoda, Qinxun Pagoda, was built in the period 824 to 839 in the Tang Dynasty. It is rectangular in shape; 69. 13 metres high and divided into 16 tiers, while the two smaller ones, octagonal in shape have a height of 42. 19 metres each and 10 tiers. In 1978 discovered during restoration efforts, are more than 600 cultural relics of the Tang and Song dynasties, including Buddhist scriptures, Buddhist statues, Buddhist musical instruments and copper mirrors. The renovation was completed in December 1980.

Paragraph 8

E 洱海
rhai

Erhai Just as its name implies, the Erhai (Ear Lake, literally), a freshwater lake two kilometers northeast of Dali, is similar in form of that of an ear. Covering 250 square kilometers and an average altitude of 1 966 meters, the blue, rippling lake and the snow covered Mt. Cangshan, located on the western shore, add radiance and beauty to each other. The scene is, therefore, described as "Silver Mt. Cangshan and Jade Erhai".

Paragraph 9

N 怒江大峡谷
ujiang Grand Canyon

Nujiang source of the Qinghai-Tibet Plateau Tanggula mountain slopes, upstream called Heishuihe, Tibet was "pulling song cards." After Tibet, Yunnan, exit from Burma, known as the Salween river. It stands 3 200 km, with 1 540 km in China. As a result water rushing current, the roar was called "Nujiang." Nujiang strait, the east is Nushan (also known as Biluo snow), the West Side is trained, and many peak altitude of over 4 000 metres, equivalent snow snow white, and only about 800 meters altitude Nujiang river, valley and mountain Gaochai 3 000-4 000 metres, a famous Nujiang Grand Canyon. Nujiang Grand Canyon in southern Hengduan Shan valley area Sanjiang and flow Strip, Canyon-621 km, in Yunnan, more than 300 kilometres long, with an average depth of 2 000 metres, the deepest in Gongshanbingzhongluo area, 3 500 metres, "the East Grand Canyon" reputation.

Paragraph 10

西双版纳
Xishuangbanna

Xishuangbanna is the southernmost prefecture of Yunnan Province. The prefecture is nicknamed " Aerial Garden " for its luxuriant and multi-layered primitive woods and tropical rain forests, which are teeming with animals and plants. Renowned as a huge natural zoo, Xishuangbanna's rain forest and monsoon jungles provide a habitat for nearly 1 000 species of animals. Within thick and boundless forests wild elephants and wild oxen ramble about, with peacocks in their pride, gibbons at play, and hornbills whispering. Thirteen species of wild life enjoy state protection, including loris, the gibbons, the red-necked cranes, the brown-neck horn-bills, and the green peacocks, which to the Dai people are a symbol of peace, happiness and good fortune and whose graceful postures can put professional dancers to shame. The region has 5 000 kinds of plants or about one-sixth of the total in China. This has earned it the renown and sobriquet " The moonstone on the Crown of the Kingdom of Plants". Among these are such fascinating ones as the "color-changing flower" whose colors change three times daily and the "dancing herb" whose leaves rotate gently. Then there is " mysterious fruit" which reverse tastes, turning sour to sweet. Species of trees that go back a million years are still propagating themselves. The "King of Tea Trees," which authorities say is at least 800 years old, continues to sprout, adding extraordinary splendor to the homeland of the famous Pu'er tea. In Xishuangbanna, there is a saying: "Even a single tree can make a forest and an old stalk can blossom and beat fruit."

Cultural Links 文化链接

纳西民风

在纳西族传统中,有男人是天、女人是地的说法。古代纳西族的母系氏族社会制度延续了相当长的时间。到如今,大多数纳西妇女仍担当家庭里既主内又主外的角色,形成了古城里女人当家、男人赋闲的奇特风俗。

古城里的中老年妇女至今仍穿着传统的民族服装。前短后长的大褂上总爱配上一件红坎肩,白色的围腰上配系羊皮坎肩,前胸用深色的布带交叉出一个"X"形。相比起妇女,古城里的男人们则是最悠闲的了。纳西族男人大多体格精壮,脸膛黑红,颧骨高突,头发柔软而卷曲,性格热情、豪爽。因有女人内外持家,男人们的生活过得十分逍遥。他们常在河岸边或柳树下,提着鸟笼或托着猎鹰游来荡去,或三五成群谈天说地。他们之中很多人都痴迷于纳西文化,精通音乐、绘画,知识广博。

Vocabulary 妙词连珠

clint 石芽	virgin forest 原始森林
geomorphologic 地形学的	luxuriant 繁茂的
magnitude 巨大	Olive Plain 橄榄坎
manifestation 显示,表现	Calabash Island 葫芦岛
uncanny 离奇的	Wild Elephant Valley 野象谷
overpowering 无法抵抗的,压倒性的	Golden Temple 金殿
	the wonder on earth 人间奇迹
miraculous 奇迹的,不可思议的	fairyland 迷宫仙境
Stone forest 石林	Butterfly Spring 蝴蝶泉
Naigu Stone Forest 乃古石林	Sword Peak Pond 剑峰池
The City of Daybreak 黎明之城	

Unit 4　Tibet Autonomous Region
西藏自治区

Key Sentences
流畅精句

1. Situated in southwest China, Tibet Autonomous Region is also called "Zang" for short. The region covers 1.2 million square kilometers, and has a population of 2.62 million, which includes Tibetan, Han, Monba, Naxi, Lhoba and Hui. The capital is Lhasa.
   西藏自治区简称藏,位于中国的西南边疆,总面积120多万平方公里,人口262万,包括藏、汉、门巴、纳西、珞巴、回等民族。首府拉萨市。
2. Besides the spectacular sceneries, the long history and unique religious culture have bestowed Tibet colourful folklore and customs, and numerous culture relics.
   悠久的历史和独特的宗教文化造就了西藏色彩缤纷的风俗民情以及众多的人文景观。
3. Main tourist cities are Lhasa, Xigaze and Gyangze, and so on.
   主要旅游城市有拉萨、日喀则、江孜等。
4. Tibet is one of the most exotic places in the world to visit.
   西藏是世界上最神奇的旅游胜地之一。
5. Tibet is an important touring place because of its unique culture, its celebrated monasteries, and its stark, spectacular scenery.
   西藏独特的文化,有名的寺院以及庄严、壮观的景色使其成为了一个重要的旅游胜地。
6. Lhasa, the capital of Tibet, is the main point of entry to the roof of the world.
   拉萨,西藏的首府,是走进"世界屋脊"的主要通道。

7. The busiest tourist months of Tibet are April, May, and July through October.

   西藏的旅游旺季是4~5月和7~10月。

8. The Tibetan people are brave, strong and forthright, very kind and hospitable.

   藏族人民勇敢、刚毅、豪爽,又十分善良好客。

9. Buttered tea is a unique drink in Tibetan regions; it's also the main drink for the guests.

   酥油茶是藏区独具风味的饮料,同时也是藏家人待客的必备饮料。

10. The most important buildings to see in Lhasa are the Jokhang Temple, Potala Palace, Sera Monastery, and Drepung Monastery.

    拉萨市内要参观的最主要建筑有大昭寺、布达拉宫、色拉寺和哲蚌寺。

11. Besides the spectacular sceneries, the long history and unique religious culture have bestowed Tibet colourful folklore and customs, and numerous culture relics.

    悠久的历史和独特的宗教文化造就了西藏色彩缤纷的风俗民情以及众多的人文景观。

12. Tibet possesses more than 2 700 temples, among which the Potola Palace, Jokhong Monastery and the Norbulinka are UNESCO-endorsed world culture heritage sites. Main tourist cities are Lhasa, Xigaze and Gyangze, and so on.

    西藏共有寺庙2 700多座,其中布达拉宫、大昭寺、罗布林卡等均被联合国教科文组织列入《世界遗产名录》。主要旅游城市有拉萨、日喀则、江孜等。

Wonderful Paragraph

Paragraph 1

布达拉宫
Potala Palace

  The palace is 3 700m above the sea level, covering an area of over 360 000m² with an interior space of more than 130 000m², about 360m long from east to west, and the 13-story main tower is 117m high. It is comprehensive with halls, stupas, Buddhist chambers, chapels, monk dormitories, and courtyards, a palace complex largest and highest in the world reputed as "pearl on the world roof".

  Potala Palace is the winter palace of the Dalai Lamas of all times, and the governing center of the former rulers of Tibet, both political and religious. Since the 5th Dalai Lama, all important religious and political ceremonies were held here. Kept in the palace are the imperial edicts of entitlement by emperors of Ming and Qing Dynasties, seals, gold album and jade album, handicrafts, sutras, and all kinds of book, as well as the funerary stupa of the deceased Dalai Lamas.

  Potala Palace is the masterpiece of Tibetan buildings and the gem of ancient Chinese architecture. The palace integrates with the hill, standing aloft with grandeur and majesty. The walls alternating in red and white, the golden roofs shining with brilliance, it demonstrates in full the appealing charm of ancient Tibetan buildings. It is not only the symbol of the creativity of Tibetan people, but also the unique cultural heritage of human beings on this high and snowy plateau.

  In 1994, UNESCO inscribed it in World Heritage List as a cultural heritage.

J 大昭寺
Jokhang monastery

It lies at the center of the old Lhasa. Built in 647 by Songtsen Gampo and his two foreign wives, it has a history of more than 1 300. It was said that Nepal Princess Tritsun decided to build a temple to house the Jowo Sakyamuni aged 12 brought by Chinese Princess Wencheng. Princess Wencheng reckoned according to Chinese astrology that the temple should be built on the pool where the Jokhang now locates. She contended that the pool was a witch's heart, so the temple should be built on the pool to get rid of evils. the pool still exists under the temple. then goats were used as the main pack animals, as is the reason the city is called Lhasa. The construction took 12 months. However it was originally small and had been expanded to today's scale in later dynasties. When the Fifth Dalai Lama took reign, large-scale reconstruction and renovation had been done. The temple is a combination of Han, Tibetan and Nepalese architectural techniques. Visitors will see sphinx and other weird and sacred sculptures.

The temple keeps many invaluable cultural relics. the most famous and valuable one is the Jowo Sakyamuni aged 12, which is circumambulate by thousands of pilgrims day and night. On his sides, there are altars of Songtsen Gampo and his two wives who introduced Buddhism into Tibet. the murals in the main hall are also worth seeing, depicting the procession of Princess Wencheng arriving in Tibet and the building of the Jokhang Temple while other murals tell Jataka stories. Two thangkas imaging Yamantaka and Chakrasamvara from the Ming dynasty (1368-1644) still remain in perfect condition. the gold bumpa (a vase) upon which the reincarnation of Dalai Lama and Panchen Lama are decided, musical instruments brought into Tibet by Wencheng and other important stuffs are also kept here.

Every year, the Great Prayer Festival will be held in the Temple. the rites of Dalai Lamas and Panchen Lamas' initiation into lamahood are also held in the monastery.

Ramoche Monastery (Xiao Zhao Si)

Ramoche Monastery is situated in the northwest of Lhasa, covering a total area of 4 000 square meters (one acre). This temple is one of the key cultural relic protection sites of the Tibet Autonomous Region as well as a hot attraction in Lhasa.

The original building complex has a strong Tang architecture influence, for it was first built by Han Chinese architects in the middle of the 7th century (during the Tang Dynasty). Han Princess Wencheng took charge of this project and ordered the temple be erected facing east to show her homesickness.

Ramoche Monastery fell into ruins and went through many reconstructions, only the Buddha palace on the first floor is left in its original state. The present temple is the result of the large restoration of 1986. The main building in the temple has three stories. The first story includes an atrium, a scripture hall, and a Buddha palace with winding corridors. The third story was the bedroom once reserved for Dalai Lama. Upon entering the main building, one can see the ten pillars holding some of the remaining Tibetan relics such as the encased lotus flowers, coiling cloud, jewelry, and particular Tibetan Characters. The golden peak of the temple with the Han-style upturned eave can be seen from any direction in Lhasa city. Needless to say, the temple is a wonderful example of the combination of Han and Tibetan architectural styles.

One of the temple's prized artifacts is the life-sized statue of the 12-year-old Sakyamuni. The Wencheng Princess brought it from the capital Chang'an during the Tang Dynasty. As one of the precious cultural relics of Tibet, the statue is now placed in Jokhang Temple (Da Zhao Si), 500 meters (0.31 mile) south of Ramoche Monastery. Residing within the Ramoche Monastery is the life-sized statue of the 8-year-old Sakyamuni. Carried into Tibet by the Nepalese Chizun Princess, this figure is regarded as the

greatest saint in Ramoche Monastery.

Nowadays, the temple has become the very place for the Tibetan monks to study the Mi Zong (one of the sect of Buddhism).

Paragraph 4

S萨迦寺 akya Monastery

Built in 1073, the Sakya Monastery, located 450 kilometres west of Lhasa, has long enjoyed nearly the sam fame as the Dunhuang Grottoes for its large collection of Buddhist scripture esvaluable porcelain and vivid wall paintings dating back nearly one thousand years. The most valuable objects in the collection are ancient vases presented by emperors of different periods of the Yuan Dynasty to the leader of the Sakya sect. Other valuables include a jade bowl, a gold-plated Buddha, imperial shoes and a gold seal. Other exhibits, on display at the Tibet Museum to mark the 50th anniversary of Tibet's peaceful liberation, show that the Yuan Dynasty divided Tibet into three military areas with 15 districts. The museum contains letters of appointments of Tibetan officials by the Ming emperors and the certificates and seals of emperors of the Qing Dynasty used in appointing Dalai and Panchen lamas. It also has a picture showing the ceremony of the 14th Dalai Lama ascending the holy throne, presided over by Kuomintang government officials, as well as documents on the peaceful liberation of Tibet signed by the central government and the government of Tibet. An imposing array of valuable cultural relics on display at the Sakya Monastery in Lhasa prove that Tibet became part of China in the Yuan Dynasty (1279-1368) and has remained under the administration of the central government of China since that time.

Paragraph 5

N罗布林卡 orbulingka

Located in the western suburbs of Lhasa, Norbulingka (Norbu means treasure in Tibetan; lingka means garden in Tibetan) was built in 1740s during the reign of the seventh Dalai Lama. Later it was renovated and enlarged and became the Dalai Lama's Summer Palace. It was here that from April to September each year the Dalai Lama would handle political affairs and hold festive celebrations. Encompassing 360 000 square metres, the park consists of three parts: the palace district, district in front of the palace and the forest district. Forests take up about half of the park. Its main buildings are Golden Palace, Sutra Hall, and the New Palace constructed in 1954. UNESCO added Norbulingka Park to the List of World Heritage as an extension of the Potala Palace in December 2001.

Paragraph 6

雅鲁藏布大峡谷
Yarlung Zangbo River Grand Canyon

Yarlung Zangbo River Grand Canyon in the "roof" above the Qinghai-Tibet Plateau, with an average altitude of 3 000 meters, a 496.3 km, dangerous remote and quiet, the erosion of Ben 5 382 metres, Grand Canyon embrace Najiabawafeng difficult mountain areas, ice-covered snow freeze it cleave the Qinghai-Tibet Plateau and the Indian Ocean aqueous exchanges mountain barriers, like a long wet day to plateau internal transmission aqueous flow to the south-east of the Qinghai-Tibet Plateau thus become a green world. Yarlung Zangbo River Grand Canyon in the most dangerous and most core lot, a white horse black bear down from the pool of approximately 100 km, Canyon remote and quiet, torrents roar, and still no one can through the difficult and dangerous, which is called "human final tight."

Paragraph 7

珠穆朗玛峰
Mt. Qomolangma

Soaring into the sky at the borderline between China and Nepal, Qomolangma Peak is 8 843.13 meters high above sea level. As the highest, it is an ideal place for mountaineering and scientific exploration. Rongbu Temple is the only sitting at such a attitude, where one can get best view of Mt. Qomolangma.

Paragraph 8

Y 羊八井
angpachen

Yangpachen, 110 kilometers (68 miles) north of Lhasa, is famous for its hot springs. It is said that a long time ago, before the sky and the earth was separated, the whole world was in total darkness. People living at the foot of Mt. Nyainqentanglha were suffering. One day, a golden phoenix flew into the area, determined to create brightness by sacrificing its' self. It threw one of its bright eyes onto the ground. A fairy caught the eye, and then a bright lamp arose in the air. Snow capped peaks of Mt. Nyainqentanglha appeared; grassland like huge carpet emerged; happiness came to the Tibetan people. However, a greedy man near Yangpachen coveted the lamp. He took a witch man's idea to sharpen his hatred into an arrow to shoot the lamp. The lamp was broken then, the pieces of the lamp dropped onto the ground, turning into hot springs and burned the man to his death. People said that the hot springs were the fairy's tears.

The town lies on a high and cold plateau. However, people approaching will see some hot springs blowing out steam rising up to sky. While the surrounding area was barren and extremely cold, Yangpachen is green with grass and highland barley growing abundantly. Steam emitting from the springs covers the small town. Now it has a thermoelectricity plant, green houses and hot spring bathrooms, attracting more and more tourists.

Paragraph 9

B 帕廓街
arkhor Street

Barkhor, a circular street at the center of Old Lhasa, is the oldest street in a very traditional city in Tibet. It is a place where Tibetan culture, economy, religion and arts assemble and a place to which a visit must be paid.

It has been said that in the seventh century Songtsen Gampo, the first Tibetan King (617-650) who unified Tibet, married Chinese Princess Wencheng and Nepal princess Tritsun. Later Princess Tritsun built Jokhang Temple to accommodate the twelve-year-old Jowo Sakyamuni, brought to Tibet by Princess Wencheng.

Barkhor is the road which pilgrims tramped out around Jokhang Temple through centuries. Buddhist pilgrims walk or progress by body-lengths along the street clockwise every day into deep night. Most of Lhasa's floating population is comprised of these pilgrims. The pilgrims walk outside four columns on which colorful scripture streamers are hung, a custom which began in the Tubo period (633-877) as a way to show respect.

To the west of the north street of Barkhor, in front of a juniper hearth, the annual ceremony to hail Maitreya (Buddha of the Future) is held. Tibetans pray before the hearth to expect fortune in the next year. A yamun, which used to be the office of a Lhasa magistrate, squats nearby. A small lane leads northward to a nearby market, the oldest market in Lhasa. The pantheon of the three story temple built during the Tubo period retains its Tubo architecture after many renovations. It was said that characters used in Tibetan writing were invented in the temple. Barkhor, the sacred pilgrim path, is also a marketplace where shaggy nomads, traders, robed monks and chanting pilgrims join together. Clustered shops and stalls sell printed scriptures, cloth prayer flags and other religious vessels, jewelry, Tibetan knives, ancient coins and other Tibetan relics.

磕长头

"磕长头"是在藏传佛教盛行的地区,信徒与教徒们一种虔诚的拜佛仪式,有行进中磕长头、原地磕长头和围绕着寺庙磕长头三种形式。在各地

西南 Southwest China

通往拉萨的大道上，不时地见到信徒们从遥远的故乡开始，手戴护具，膝着护膝，前身挂一毛皮衣物，尘灰覆面，沿着道路，不惧千难万苦，三步一磕，直至拉萨朝佛。

Vocabulary 妙词连珠

gilded 镀金的	Dragon King Pool 龙王潭
deceased 已故的	Gandan Monastery 甘丹寺
sutra 佛经	Parknor street 八角街
stupa 佛塔	Baiju Monastery 白居寺
witness 目睹	Mt. Qomolangma 珠穆朗玛峰
Potala Palace 布达拉宫	Natang Monastery 纳唐寺
Tubo King Sontsan Gambo 吐蕃王松赞干布	Yangbajing 羊八井
	Tashilhumbu Monastery 扎什伦布寺
the Tibet Autonomous Region 西藏自治区	Yangzhuoyong Lake 洋卓雍湖
	Holy Mountain 神山
Princess Wen Cheng 文成公主	Sacred Lakes 圣湖
Dragon King's Pool 龙王潭	The Tombs of the Tuboking 藏王墓
the White Palace 白宫	Changzhu Monastery 昌朱寺
the Red Palace 红宫	MeiZhulin Monastery 梅株林寺
the Hall of the Buddha 佛教宫殿	Jokhang Temple 大昭寺
the Scripture Hall 圣经宫殿	Lhasa 拉萨
the Memorial hall 红念宫殿	Panchen 班禅

Unit 5　Chongqing Municipality
重庆市

Key Sentences
流畅精句

1. Chongqing Located in the south of the Sichuan Basin where the Jialing River joins the Yangtze.
   重庆位于四川盆地南部,嘉陵江入长江的入口处。
2. Chongqing is frequently misty in winter and in spring, hence the capital of Fog.
   因重庆冬春云轻雾重,又号称"雾都"。
3. Chongqing enjoys a time-honored history. It is ne of the famous Chinese cities endowed with historical and cultural significance.
   重庆市历史悠久,是中国历史文化名城之一。
4. During the Spring and Autumn and the Warring State periods, it belonged to the State of Ba; it was in the territory of Yuzhou in the Sui and Tang dynasties, and became the capital of the State of Daxia during the late Yuan Dynasty. In 1927, Chongqing is incorporated as a city. During the War of Resistance against Japan, it was the "provisional capital" of China under the Kuomintang's rule.
   春秋战国时期为巴国地域,隋唐时属渝州。元末明初为大夏国的国都。1927年设市。抗日战争时期为国民党政府陪都。
5. Major attractions include Dazu Rock Carvings, one of the UNESCO's world heritage sites, Yangtze River's Three Gorges, South and North Hot Spring Parks, Revolutionary Memorial Hall of the Red Crag Village, Bai's Mansion and Pipa (Loquat) Mountain.
   重庆著名景点有世界文化遗产大足石刻,长江三峡,南、北温泉公园,红岩村革命纪念馆,白公馆,枇杷山等。

西南
Southwest China

6. The Three Gorges of the Yangtze refers to the section between Baidi City in chongqing to Nanjinguan Pass in Hubei Province. Consisting of Qutangxia, Wuxia and Xilingxia gorges.
长江三峡是长江从重庆白帝城到湖北南津关之间的瞿塘峡、巫峡、西陵峡的总称,全长193千米,是著名的长江天险。

7. The Three Gorges are internationally known as a Mecca of tourism for its natural scenery with dozens of historic sites and lovely legendaries.
三峡以其奇异的自然风光,众多的历史古迹和优美的神话传说成为举世闻名的游览胜地。

Wonderful Paragraph
精彩片段

Paragraph 1

M 山城重庆
ountain City—Chongqing

  Chongqing, located in the southeast of Sichuan Basin, is an important industrial and economic center as well as a transportation point on the upper reach of the Yangtze River. In ancient times it was called Ba. It depends on mountains, so people call it Mountain city. And both in winter and spring, there has always been dense fog here, so it well known as a foggy city with a population of over 30 million, Chongqing is the biggest municipal city in China in terms of population.

  118AD, Emperor Zhanxian of the Song Dynasty was first made the prince here, and later crowned as the emperor. To celebrated this happy event, he gave the city it's present name Chongqing that means Double celebrations. As a famous mountain city, it has glorious night scenery with thousands of lights glistening in the river. In the suburbs, there are scenic spots, such as Shiyun Mountain, North Hot spring, Fishing Town and so on. A little far from the city, the remarkable scenic spots are Pipa Mountain, Futu pass, Jinyun Mountain, 4-sides Mountain, North and South Hot spring, Red rock Village etc.

Paragraph 2

Dazu Rock Carvings

Dazu is a county at the southeast corner of Sichuan Basin, 271km east of Chengdu, the provincial capital. In the county there are in over 20 sites several ten thousand of rock sculptures carved in Tang and Song Dynasties, those of Song Dynast are especially large in number, which are generally referred to as Dazu rock carvings.

The carving began in 650, the first year of Yonghui Period of Tang Dynasty, went on through the Five Dynasties Period and prospered in North and South Song Dynasties. The rock carvings are mainly clustered in Dazu County, at North Hill, Baoding Mountain, South Hill, Rock Gate Hill, and Shizhuan Mountain, which are the representation of the later and mature grotto art in China, renowned for their large scale, refined carving, and varied motifs. Altogether there are as many as 75 sites of grottoes with over 50 000 statues and inscriptions of more than 100 000 Chinese characters, reputed as "with everything found in all Buddhist classics" and with the prefect integration of humanization of deity and apotheosis of human beings in artistic creation.

Dazu rock carvings also differ from the earlier grottoes in bringing together the statuary gems of all the "three religions of China", namely Buddhism, Taoism, and Confucianism The statues on the cliff lace of South Hill, for example, are representative Taoist statues carved during the 11th to the 13th centuries, which are the most exquisite and complete of the time. The Confucian statues on the cliff face of Shizhuan Mountain, focused on Confucius, are seldom found in other grottoes. In addition, statues combining Buddhism, Taoism, and Confucianismcarved on Shizhuan Mountain, as well as those combining Buddhism and Taoism carved on the cliff face of Rock Gate Hill, are also very hard to find in grottoes elsewhere.

With a great wealth of visual images and written data, Dazu rock carvings reveal from all aspects the vital development of the art style of Chinese grottoes and the folks religious believes from the 9th century to the 13th century. They bear a historical, artistic, scientific, and aesthetic value that none of the earlier grottoes could possibly have.

"Pilgrimage to Mt Emei in Emei City if going up, or to Baoding Mountain in Dazu County if going down", this folk saying proves Dazu as a site of interest since ancient times, especially its North Hill and Baoding Mountain which are always crowded with tourists, pilgrims, and preaching monks. Every year on the 19th of the 2nd lunar month (believed to be the birthday of Avalokitesvara), tens of thousands of visitors would rush in to Banding Mountain, the "Holy Mountain on paradise land".

In December of 1999, UNESCO inscribed Dazu rock carvings on the World Heritage List as a cultural heritage.

Paragraph 3

长江三峡
The Three Gorges of the Yangtze River

The Three Gorges of the Yangtze River, a world-renowned tourist attraction, start at Baidicheng (White Emperor City) in Fengjie County (population 990 000) in the west and end at Nanjingguan (Southern Crossing) Pass in Yichang to the east, passing through Badong, Zigui counties and Yichang City in Hubei Province. The total length of the gorges extends 193 kilometres. Except the Daning River Valley and the Xiangxi (Fragrant Stream) Valley, the gorges themselves are 93 kilometres long. Te first gorge of the three from west to east, known as Qutang Gorge (瞿塘峡), is 7 kilometres, Wuxia Gorge (巫峡), the second one, runs west to east for 44 kilometres; Xiling Gorge (西陵峡), the last of the three, covers a distance of 42 kilometres.

The steep mountains, the dangerous rugged shoals and the turbulent waters are characteristic of the gorges. The perpendicular cliff and grotesque peaks with clouds wrapping them in a blanket of mist create one of nature's most majestic sights.

The gorges themselves are a long poem, a mysterious natural gallery. Qutang Gorge is famous for its magnificent precipices (以雄伟闻名), which form a colossal, nearly perfect gate over the river. Wuxia Gorge, with soaring fascinating mountain peaks rising from the riverbanks, is severe and secluded, and presents a panorama of lovely scenery (以秀丽见长). Xiling Gorge is noted for its numerous hidden rocks and perilous shoals (以险峻著称). The picturesque scenery along the river, which never fails to appeal to visitors, will surely make them admire the mysterious creative power of nature.

Paragraph 4

小三峡 Small Three Gorge

Small Three Gorge in Mt. Wushan Daning River Daning River, once called Wushui, originates from Mt. Daba, at the junction of Sichuan, Hubei and Shanxi Provinces. It flows into the Yangtze River through the western end of Wu Gorge. The meandering path of the Daning River and its soaring peaks form a unique landscape. The small Three Gorges are made up of Longmen Gorge, Bawu Gorge and Dicui Gorge. Although not the main three Gorges of the Yangtze, the beauty of the Small Three Gorges is thought by some to be even more spectacular.

Paragraph 5

张飞庙 Zhang Fei Temple

Opposite to the Yunyang town, the magnificent Zhang Fei Temple with glazed tile and red walls perches on the Flying Phoenix Hill on the southern bank of the river. The Temple was built to commemorate General Zhang Fei-one of the three sworn blood brothers of the state of Shu during the Three Kingdoms Period, (the other two were Liu Bei and Guan Yu). The Temple is a famous historical site along the Yangtze River.

Southwest China

Paragraph 6

Baidi City in Fengjie 白帝城

The city is located 4km east of Fengjie at the western entrance to the Qutang Gorge, by the junction of the Chaotang and Yangtze Rivers. In ancient times, revered poets such as Libai, Dufu, Liuyuxi and Fangchengdu visited and wrote famous poems during their sojourns here, making Baidi City the "Poem City." There are also many historic sites including Wuhou Ancestral Temple, Observing Star Pavilion and Mengliang Ladder. The legends of "Firing the 700 li long joint battalions" and "Liubei entrusting a son to Kongming," add fame to Baidi City.

Paragraph 7

Shibao (Treasured Stone) Stockade 石宝寨

The whole building, composed of a gate, gate tower, and an ancient Buddhist temple on the top, guards the only path up the mountain. The cultural relics and calligraphy and paintings by famous persons unearthed in Zhongxian County since the New Stone Age are displayed in the hall. It is called one of the "world's eight great majestic buildings."

Cultural Links 文化链接

千手观音

宝顶山大佛湾南岩有一尊共有1 007只手的摩崖石刻观音造像,为天下一绝。观音佛像身前有六只手,两手合十,两手结印,两手抚膝。头上还有一双手捧一坐佛。其余的手在身后像孔雀开屏一样巧妙分布在88平方米的崖石上。这些手千姿百态,无一雷同;手握法物各异,手心各有一只眼。千手表示法力无边,可以拯救众生于危难;千眼表示智慧无穷,可以普观世界,明察秋毫。

千手观音的出现,有一段动人的传说。传说千手观音原来是印度妙庄王的三公主妙善。妙善自幼出家修行,妙庄王坚决反对,一把火把妙善修行的庙给烧了,庙里的500和尚都被烧死在里面。妙庄王作了恶,身上长出了500个大脓疮。医生说要亲骨肉的一只眼一只手作药,才能医好。大公主不愿意,二公主舍不得。只有修行的三公主妙善听说后,自己就挖了一只眼,砍了一只手给父王作药。父王服药后,全身脓疮消失,身体康复。妙善的大孝行为感动了释迦牟尼,释迦牟尼就召见妙善公主:"你这大孝子,舍了一只眼、一只手,我就还你一千只眼、一千只手。"这样,妙善公主就成了千手千眼观世音菩萨的形象,为成千上万的善男信女所崇敬。宝顶山的千手千眼观音也就成了历代香火鼎盛,与峨眉山齐名的佛教圣地。

妙词连珠 Vocabulary

majestic 雄壮的;崇高的	underneath 在……下面
topographic 地形的,地志的	panoramic 全景的;连续转换的
remarkable 异常的;非凡的;卓越的	remains of Peidu 陪都遗址
transition 过渡(时期);转变;变迁	Loquat Hill 枇杷山
bestow 赠予;花费	the Gate to the Sky 朝天门
dense 浓密的	Red Crag Village 红岩村
cast 塑造	Immortals' Tower 会仙桥
combination 结合	Jialing River 嘉陵江
prefect 长官;提督	tourism through Three Gorges of Yangtze River 长江三峡游
renowned 有名望的;著名的	vicissitude 变化,变迁
peak 顶峰	topography 地质,地形(学)
nevertheless 不过;仍然,然而	eroison 侵蚀
offer 提供	unusual 稀有的,独特的
concave 凹的,凹面的	

6 华东
East China

Unit 1 山东省 Shandong Province

Key Sentences
流畅精句

1. Because of its location on the east side of Mt. Taihang, Shandong Province is so named.
   山东省因位于太行山之东而得名。
2. Ancient Shandong was the cradle of ancient Chinese Longshan culture and Qilu culture.
   古地山东,是中国古老的龙山文化、齐鲁文化的发祥地。
3. Mt. Tai stands in the middle west of Shandong Province with its Yuhuang Peak 1 545 meters high above sea level.
   泰山位于山东省中西部,主峰玉皇顶海拔 1 545 米,有"天下第一山"之美誉。
4. Mt. Tai is one of the cultural and natural heritages of the world approved by UNESCO.
   泰山已被联合国教科文组织列为文化和自然双重遗产。
5. Confucius Temple sits in Qufu City, where Confucius is worshiped in all times.
   孔庙坐落在曲阜城内,曾是历代祭祀孔子的地方。

6. Kong's Mansion, also named "Yansheng Mansion", is located east of Confucius, where Kong's family live.
   孔府位于孔庙以东,又称"衍圣公府",是孔子嫡系子孙居住的地方。
7. Konglin Mausoleum is in the northern suburb of Qufu City, where Kong's ancestors are buried.
   孔林位于曲阜城北,是孔子及其家族的专用墓地。
8. Jinan is at the junction of the Beijing-Shanghai and the Qingdao-Jinan realways.
   济南位于京沪铁路线和济青线的交汇处。
9. From September 6-8, there is the Mountain Climbing Festal in Tai'an.
   每年的9月6日至8日,泰安举行登山节。
10. Mountain Tai is 2.5 million years old.
    泰山已有250万年的历史了。
11. Qingdao is an important manufacturing center, ice-free port and pretty summer resort.
    青岛是重要的制造中心,不冻港和避暑胜地。
12. Weifang is noted for its international Kite Festival every year.
    潍坊每年举行的风筝节很有名。

Wonderful Paragraph
精彩片段

Paragraph 1

Mt. Tai 泰山

Also referred to as the Eastern Sacred Mountain, Mt Tai stands with grandeur in central Shandong Province, between Tai'an at its south foot and Jinan City at its north foot, covering an area of $250km^2$, with its summit Jade Emperor Peak 1 545m above sea level. Through history it has always been honored as "the first" and "most sublime" of the five sacred mountains in China.

East China

Mt Tai has a long history, ancient geological stratum, graceful scenery, and a wealth of cultural relics and sites. Apart from others, those that have been admired with a name amount to 112 peaks, 98 cliffs, 18 caverns, 58 weird crags, 102 streams, 56 ponds and falls, and 64 mountain springs, in addition to 22 ancient temples, 97 primeval sites, 819 stone steles, and 1 018 cliff inscriptions.

Mt Taishan has rich biological resources. All over the mountain are ancient trees and flourishing grass, and the vegetation covers 79.9% of the area. The zonal vegetation is warm-temperate deciduous broad-leaved forest, with a diverse flora comprising 989 species of seed plants in 144 families. Trees that are over 100 years old exceed 10 000 in number.

Mt Tai is a microcopy of the thousands years old civilization of China that contains a cultural wealth no other mountain in the world is comparable. Just like the Great Wall, Yellow River, and Yangtz River, Mt Tai is now the symbol of Chinese people.

In December of 1987, UNESCO inscribed Mt Taishan on the World Heritage List as both a natural and a cultural property of the whole world.

The origin of Mt Taishan as in legend is that it is the head of Pan Gu who opened up the sky and the earth of the human world and later turned his body parts into all the things of the world. Related with this is the saying that "At Mt Taishan the sky and the earth join", meaning the mountain is the highest spot where the sky and the earth meet together. Yet, with an altitude of 1 545m, Mt Taishan is actually second to Mt Huashan and Mt Hengshan in height as the third of the five sacred mountains. Nevertheless it is regarded as the top of all the five due to its peerless cultural bearings.

孔庙、孔林、孔府
Temple and Cemetery of Confucius and the Kong Family Mansion

The Temple of Confucius, the Confucius Family Mansion and the Confucian Woods are located in the city of Qufu, Shandong Province. They symbolize the Chinese people's remembrance of Confucius throughout the ages, and their respect to Confucianism. They are known for their cultural significance, agelong history, considerable scale, rich collection of relics and their scientific and artistic value.

According to historical records, in 478 BC, the year after Confucius' death, Lord Ai of the State of Lu had Confucius' house in the center of Qufu altered into a temple in commemoration of the sage.

After many rebuilds and expansions, it reached its present scale in the Ming Dynasty. Covering 140 000 square meters of land it has over a hundred halls, towers, pavilions and other buildings clustering around 9 courtyards. There are also the Apricot Altar where Confucius had his school, the famous cypress and over a thousand stone tablets.

To the east of the temple is Confucius' house. It was once Confucius' eldest grandson's yamen and named Lord Yansheng's Residence. During the Han Dynasty Emperor Gao Zu, named Liu Bang, made offerings at Confucius' tomb in the highest degree. The emperor also conferred on Confucius' ninth generation direct grandson and his sons after him an official post supervising sacrifices to Confucius on behalf of the country. In the course of history, many titles were conferred on Confucius and his descendants. The title of Yansheng was given to his descendant in the Song Dynasty. In the 10th year of the Ming Hong Wu reign an independent Residence of Lord Yansheng was set up, with the yamen in the front and the domestic household at the back. It has 480 rooms and houses many files and relics.

Located in the north of Qufu is the Confucian Woods where the tombs of Confucius and most of his descendants are to be found. After Confucius' death in April 479 BC, (the 16th year of Lord Ai of Lu), his descendants buried with him and the place gradually grew into a cemetery with over 100 000 tombs and 4 000 steles. Zi Gong, Confucius' desciple, started planting trees at Confucius' tomb and now there are over, 10 000 trees in the woods. Kong Shangren, well-known literatus and author of the "Peach Blossom Fan", was buried here too.

In 1994, World Heritage Committee of UNESCO inscribed the three in World Heritage List.

Paragraph 3

B 趵突泉 aotuquan (Jet Spring)

Baotuquan or Jet Spring, is acclaimed not only as the first of the 72 springs in Jinan but also as the "First Spring Under Heaven". Together with its environs, it has been converted into a park of the same name. Baotuquan is located in the southwestern corner of the old city district. It used to cover only 0.26 hectare (0.67 acre) of land and was expanded the grounds to 3.33 hectares (8.22 acres) in 1949. All the old buildings and relics here have been renovated, the springs and ponds have been thoroughly dredged, and the banks lined with stones. Lawns and rockeries have been built and numerous trees and flowers planted. In 1956, the place was formally opened to the public as a popular park. There are four famous springs in Jinan, such as Jet Spring, Black Tiger Spring, Pearl Spring and Five-Dragon Pool.

Paragraph 4

M 崂山 ount Lao

Located about 30 kilometres southeast of Qingdao, Mount Lao is one of the national parks in China. It encompasses 300 kilometres. Standing on the north shore of the Yellow Sea, the majestic and beautiful mountain and the sea join together. Its highest point is Giant Peak (巨峰), commonly known as Peak Lao (崂顶) at an elevation of 1 133 metres. It used to be a sacred place of Taoism in North China. The mountain is noted for producing mineral water. Built in 1903, Qingdao (Tsingtao) Beer is made of quality oat, rice, hops and spring water from Mount Lao. It is rich of carbon dioxide, soft and refreshing, with white and fine foams and unique taste. The beer enjoys a high reputation both at home and abroad. Emperors of the Qin and Han dynasties, 2 000 years ago used to come here to visit the mountain. Temples were constructed after the Song Dynasty (960-1279) and there were more than 1 000 Taoist temples at a time and these temples have been well preserved.

Paragraph 5

蓬莱阁
Penglai Pavilion

Penglai Pavilion Sitting on summit Danya Mountain and 1 kilometer north of the city of same name, the magnificent Penglai Pavilion was first built in 1061. Legend has it that Emperor Qin Shihuang and Emperor Wu of the Han Dynasty once sought for the elixir of life here. The famous legend of "Eight Immortals Crossing the Sea" finds its origin here. It is a vast group of ancient buildings on land of 32 800 square meters, composed of the six buildings and their attached constructions: Penglai Pavilion, Tianhou and Longwu palaces, Luzu and Sanqing halls and Mituo Temple. Attractively on display in these buildings are works of calligraphy of famous literary writers, couplet hung on the columns and stone inscriptions.

Cultural Links
文化链接

泰山石刻

泰山石刻以石刻众多而闻名天下，有的为帝王亲制，有的则出自名流之手，大都文辞优美，书体高雅，制作精巧，成为登山途中一道绚丽的风景

线。据统计,从岱庙至岱顶沿途中就分布了多达823处的碑碣和摩崖石刻。

就这些石刻的时代而言,有秦李斯刻石、汉张迁碑和衡方碑、晋孙夫人碑、北齐经石峪摩崖石刻和岱顶唐摩崖石刻。宋代以后,帝王将相、文人墨客更是纷纷题刻于泰山。这其中,秦泰山刻石可谓是摩崖刻石之祖。

泰山摩崖,有的眯石成景,如"斩云剑";有的点题意境,如"呼吸宇宙";有的因景寓意,如"高山流水";有的因石赋形,如"醉石"等。这不仅丰富了泰山的景观形象,而且寓景观以文化内涵。

泰山石刻,除了具有重要的史料价值之外,同时具有很高的艺术欣赏价值。其规模之大、作品之多、年代之长以及艺术之精湛、构景之巧妙,都是其他世界名山所无法比拟的。

Vocabulary 妙词连珠

Baotu Spring 趵突泉	the Temple of Confucius 孔庙
Liubu HIstorical Site 柳埠古迹	the Confucius Family Mansion 孔府
Thousand Buddha Mountain 千佛山	the Confucian Woods 孔林
Ancient Naval Base 古代海军基地	throughout the ages 历代
Penglai Water City 蓬莱水城	the Apricot Altar 杏坛
Liang Gong Woods 梁公林	Peach Blossom Fan 桃花扇
Temple of Duke Zhou 周公庙	spectacular 壮观的,惊人的
Old Dragon Bay 老龙湾	sacrificial 献祭的
Pavilion of Lord Fan 范公亭	summit 顶峰
Toushan grottoes 驼山石窟	precipitous 陡峭的
Lu Xun Museum 鲁迅博物馆	commemorative 纪念性的
Pu Songling's Former Residence 蒲松龄故居	calligraphy 书法,笔迹
Qingdao Marine Products Museum 青岛海产博物馆	South Gate to Heaven 南天门
	Azure Cloud Temple 碧霞祠
	Sun Watching Peak 日观峰
Confucianism 儒学	Black Dragon Pool 黑龙潭
descendant 后代,弟子	

Unit 2 江苏省 Jiangsu Province

Key Sentences 流畅精句

1. Jiangsu province Lies on the lower reaches of the Yangtze River and the Huaihe River.
   江苏省地处长江和淮河下游。
2. Suzhou Gardens are mainly private-owned, mirroring the sentiments of their owners.
   苏州古典园林多为私家园林,园林造景多抒发了主人的情感。
3. Zhongshan Scenic Spot lies in the east of Nanjing City, made up of Mausoleum of Sun Yat-sen, Zijinshan Observatory, Mingxiao Mausoleum and Linggu Valley.
   钟山风景区位于南京市区东部,由中山陵、紫金山天文台、明孝陵和灵谷寺等景点组成。
4. Mausoleum of Sun Yat-sen is built in memory of Dr Sun Yat-sen.
   中山陵是孙中山先生的陵墓。
5. Zijinshan Observatory was once the only one in China before 1949.
   紫金山天文台,是解放前我国惟一的天文台。
6. Mingxiao Mausoleum is for Zhu Yuanzhang, the first emperor of the Ming Dynasty.
   明孝陵是明代第一个皇帝朱元璋的陵墓。
7. The Humble Administrator's Garden is a masterpiece among Chinese gardens.
   拙政园是中国园林的经典之作。
8. Marco Polo visited Suzhou in the latter half of the 13th century and proclaimed it another Venice.

马可·波罗13世纪下半叶曾游历过苏州,并盛赞其为另一个威尼斯。

9. The most important spots in Nanjing are Sun Yat-sen Mausoleum and Soul Valley Temple.

南京最著名的景点是中山陵和灵谷寺。

10. The Nanjing City Wall is believed to be the longest city wall in the world.

南京城墙据说是世界上最长的城墙。

11. Yangzhou is a little charming city on the Grand Canal.

扬州是大运河边上一个妩媚华丽的小城。

12. Suzhou is famous for its fans.

苏州以生产扇子而闻名。

13. Suzhou embroidery is famous for its delicate workmanship, beautiful designs and elegant colors.

苏绣以其精致的工艺、漂亮的设计和雅致的色彩而举世闻名。

14. The Humble Administrator's Garden. is the largest of Suzhou's old gardens, covering four hectares. Water is its chief feature, with ponds occupying three-fifths the garden area.

拙政园是苏州最大的古代园林,占地4公顷。水是这个园子最主要的特征,水域面积占整个园林的五分之三。

15. Suzhou deserves the fame of a human Paradise on earth.

苏州真不愧为"人间天堂"啊!

Wonderful Paragraph
精彩片段

Paragraph 1

苏州园林
Suzhou Classical Gardens

The sayings beginning from Song Dynasty that "Suzhou on earth matches paradise in heaven" and "bumper harvests in Suzhou alone are enough for the whole nation" are convincing evidence that the region was reputed as the "paradise" and "grain barn" of the nation. The revenue from Suzhou took up about one tenth of the national total in Ming Dynasty. Suzhou, fertile and resourceful, was advanced in handicraft, processing, and commerce from early times. Owing to the convenient watercourse and land transportation, literary talents as well as merchants also flourished in Suzhou, who brought about the birth and prosperity of Wu culture. All of these thus provided garden construction with favorite conditions.

Suzhou city is on the plain of Taihu Lake, without difficult mountains as its defense forts, and in old times the guarding troops actually could do nothing but surrender at the initial attack. Therefore Suzhou suffered much less from wars or battles, which, luckily, spared the gardens of many dynasties in the city, well preserved for later generations.

The history of Suzhou classical gardens dates back to the royal garden of King of Wu in the 6th century BC, whereas the earliest record of private gardens was found to be Pijiang (Territory Developing) Garden in East Jin Dynasty. Famous gardens grew in number with the time and by Ming and Qing Dynasties they were everywhere in Suzhou and dozens of them have survived intact to the present.

The top of these gardens, such as Humble Administrator's Garden, Lingering Garden, Master-of-Nets Garden, and Mountain Villa with Embracing Beauty, are works in the prime of the private landscape architecture, characterized as the model in their profound mood, delicate composition, elegant art, and cultural connotation. In December of 1997 World Heritage Committee of UNESCO registered them in World Heritage List with the conclusion that "the four classical gardens of Suzhou are masterpieces of Chinese landscape garden design in which art, nature, and ideas are integrated perfectly to create ensembles of great beauty and peaceful harmony, and four gardens are integral to the entire historic urban plan." Then in 2001 the committee approved the extension to include Surging Waves Pavilion, Lion Forest Garden, Garden of Cultivation, Couple Garden Retreat, and Retreat and Reflection Garden.

Paragraph 2

周庄——东方威尼斯
Zhouzhuang-Oriental Venice

Ancient Water Town of Zhouzhuang is located to the southwest of Kunshan City, with an area of 36 square kilometers. It has a history of more than 900 years, and has preserved architectural style and layout of the Song Dynasty—"land and water routes running parallel, and streets and canals neighboring each other". It is reputed as "the Heaven of Peace of Water". Spanning on the rivers are 14 stone bridges dating back to the Yuan, Ming and Qing dynasties. There are nearly a hundred of ancient residences and compounds, and the most famous ones are the mansions of Shen's Family and Zhang's Family.

The 14 ancient bridges on the river were built during the Yuan, Ming, and Qing dynasties. Residents of the ancient town built houses and streets along the river. Over 60 per cent of the town's houses date back to the early Ming Dynasty. Over recent years, more and more tourists have been coming to this town.

Paragraph 3

古镇同里
The Ancient Town of Tongli

An Ancient Town of Tongli Located on the lakeside of Taihu and the shore of the Great Canal, 18 kilometers to Suzhou, Tongli, a picturesque and elegant town covering an area of 62 square kilometers, has become world known for its wonderful scenery and classic buildings. It is surrounded by water on four sides. The proper of this town is divided into seven blocks by 15 rivers, and 49 ancient bridges in different designs and sizes combine them into a complete whole. With their dwellings built the stream, the locals all enjoys the convenience to travel by boat. Tongli is rich in both culture relics and traditional architectures, there are many classic buildings constructed during the Ming and Qing dynasties. The Tuisi Garden (the Garden of Retreat and Reflection) is the most famous one.

Paragraph 4

Qinhuai River 秦淮河

Southwest of the city of Nanjing and extending more than 100 kilometers, Qinhuai river is a branch of the Yangtze River. The inner section of the river used to be the most flourishing place of Nanjing. Pained boats shuttled to and flo and music sounded all night. Many love affairs and romances spread from here. Having been archaized and revived, nowadays, the region becomes the most characterized area of commerce, tourism and folklore and culture.

Paragraph 5

Ming Xiaoling 明孝陵

Lying on the south slope of Mount Zijin (Purple Gold), Ming Xiaoling Mausoleum it is the tomb of Zhu Yuanzhang, founder of the Ming Dynasty, and his wife. It was built in 1383, main buildings in the mausoleum include the Square City, Hall of Xiaoling, Precious City, and so on. On both sides of the 1800-meter-long winding sacred way are stone animal, minister and general statues. In 2003, UNESCO added it on the World Heritage List.

Cultural Links 文化链接

苏州狮子林的传说

苏州城里有一座园林叫狮子林,这是元朝时建造的狮林寺的后花园。狮林寺又叫画禅寺,相传是元朝的天如禅师创建的。

传说造狮子林的时候,请了不少能工巧匠,画了不少精巧的图样,天如禅师都不中意。后来大画家倪云林做了指点,才建成了这座狮子林。倪云林画的《狮子林图卷》一直流传至今。

  为啥叫狮子林呢?按照佛门的说法,狮子又名狻猊,是佛国之兽。狮子林的假山最出名,这假山堆的名堂多着呢!有的是大狮,有的是小狮,有的是狮舞,有的是狮吼,有的是雄狮蹲坐,有的是母狮沉睡,有的是狮子滚绣球,有的是双狮在搏斗,真是千变万化。假山有许多好听的名字:有的叫"含晖",有的叫"吐月",有的叫"玄玉",有的叫"昂霄",最高的一座假山叫"狮子峰"。据说假山中隐伏着五百罗汉身,可惜一般人眼里看不出。谁能全部看出来,谁就是"罗汉身",谁看出的越多就越聪明。走进假山,峰回路转,如入深山,半天也绕不出来,好比诸葛亮摆的"八阵图",真是奥妙无穷。

  假山中还有许多山洞,每换一洞,向外张望,景色不同,有"桃园十八景"之称。其中有一个山洞叫"棋盘洞"。传说,八仙中的铁拐李和吕纯阳,有一次结伴游园,一头钻进假山,绕了半天走不出来。铁拐李一瘸一拐走得很吃力,坐在一个山洞里不肯动,嘴里直喊:"走勿动哉!走勿动哉!"他对吕纯阳说:"我俩歇歇力,下盘棋,啥人输,就把赢家背出去!"铁拐李知道吕纯阳棋艺不高,一定输,哪里知道吕纯阳偏偏赢了这盘棋,铁拐李没办法,只好向吕纯阳求饶。吕纯阳到了洞口双手一拂胡须,口中念念有词,天上飘落两朵祥云,两位仙人这才驾云而去。狮子林中的棋盘洞,至今还留下了吕纯阳用宝剑刻的棋盘呢!

Vocabulary 妙词连珠

legendary scenic spots 传奇色彩	workmanship 工艺
picturesque scenery 风景如画	tasteful 雅致
palace lantern 宫灯	exotic 奇异
classical furniture 古代家具	layout 布局
miniature tree 盆景树	leaning pagoda 斜塔
arch 拱门	private garden 私家园
fans 扇子	charming 幽雅

unique 奇特
magnificent 宏大
silk-producing 丝绸
Confucius Temple 夫子庙
Mochou Lake 莫愁湖
canal 运河
settle 定居
mansion 官邸
rockery 假石,岩石庭园
Venice of the East 东方威尼斯
Pavilion of Surging Waves 沧浪亭
Humble Administrator's Garden 拙政园
Fisherman Garden 渔翁园
Lotus Garden 莲花园

all year round 一年四季
symbolize 象征
species 种类
expansion 扩建
characteristics 特性
scenic 自然景色的
significanism 意义;积淀
encompass 围绕,包含
unfold 展开;打开
fascinating 迷人的;醉人的
scroll 纸卷
coverage 覆盖
noted 著名的
acme 顶点;极度

Unit 3 Zhejiang Province 浙江省

Key Sentences 流畅精句

1. In the Warring Period, Zhejiang was part of the Yue and Wu kingdoms, while in the Ming Dynasty Zhejiang Pacific Commission Office and finally in the Qing Dynasty Zhejiang Province.
   浙江在春秋时期为越、吴国地,明置浙江布政司,清为浙江省。
2. Zhejiang is rich in history heritage and cultural tradition, with lots of ancient relics all over.
   浙江历史悠久,文化灿烂,文物古迹遍布各地。
3. Hangzhou is one of the most famous scenic spots of China because of West Lake.
   杭州因西湖而成为中国最著名的名胜之一。
4. Hangzhou began to prosper as a trading center after the completion of the Grand Canal in 610 A.D.
   公元610年大运河开通后,杭州渐渐成为商业中心。
5. Hangzhou has been a famous resort for centuries, attracting painters, poets, and retired officials as well as tourists.
   数百年来,杭州声名鹊起,吸引着文人墨客、官宦富商,也吸引着众多游客。
6. Villages in Hangzhou grow the famous Longjing tea and silk worms.
   杭州的村镇培植闻名遐迩的龙井茶,并植桑养蚕。
7. Today Zhejiang province produces one-third of China's silk.
   如今中国三分之一的丝织产品产自浙江省。
8. West Lake is now 15km in circumference, with an average depth of 1.8 meters.

Introduce China in English—Scenic Spots

西湖目前周长15公里,均深1.8米。

9. West Lake is now linked again with the Qiantang River and is usually renewed with fresh water once a month.

西湖如今又与钱塘江相连,湖水通常每月更新一次。

10. Shaoxing is famous throughout China for its distinctive Yue opera.

绍兴独具特色的越剧名扬中国。

Wonderful Paragraph 精彩片段

Paragraph 1

West Lake 西湖

Hangzhou's fame is largely due to the picturesque West Lake. Lying in the west of the city, and surrounded by hills on three sides, the West Lake is 3.2 kilometres from north to south and 2.8 kilometres from east to west with a circumference of 15 kilometres. Its water surface encompasses 5.8 square kilometres, while the islands on the lake occupy 6.3 square kilometres. Its average depth of water is 1.55 metres, the shallowest is less than one metre deep, and the deepest being about 2.8 metres. Its storage capacity is between 8.5 million and 8.7 million cubic metres. The Su and Bai Causeways, both man-made, divide the lake into five separate lakes: the Outer Lake, the North Inner Lake, the West Inner Lake, the Yue Lake, and the Lesser South Lake. There are scenes everywhere in around the West Lake. Apart from the ten scenic spots of Qian-Tang, eighteen attractions of the West Lake, the top ten famed attractions designated during the Southern Song Dynasty (1127-1279) are as follows: Spring Dawn at Su Causeway (the Su Dyke Enveloped in Morning Mist 苏堤春晓), Autumn Moon Over the Calm Lake (平湖秋月), Lotus in the Breeze at the Crooked Courtyard (a lotus spectacle at Quyuan 曲院荷风), Three Pools Reflecting the

East China

Moon（三潭印月）, Watching Goldfish in a Flowery Pond（Viewing Fish at Huagang Pond 花港观鱼）, Orioles Singing in the Willows（柳浪闻莺）, Snow Scene on the Broken Bridge（断桥残雪 the Broken Bridge Cocooned under a Snow Mantle）, Double Peaks Kissing the Sky（双峰插云）, Evening Bell Ringing at Nanping（南屏晚钟）, and the Lei Feng Pagoda in the Glow of the Setting Sun（雷峰夕照）. Incidentally, China boasts as many as 36 west lakes, and the one in Hangzhou undoubtedly exceeds all its counterparts. Deep-forested hills embrace the lake on three sides resembling an amphitheatre except the east side where the downtown area is located. It is not hard to find peace and contentment around this beautiful lake, where nature goes through an amazing repertoire of changing moods that turn the picturesque waterways into shimmering avenues of enchantment. The climate is mild all the year round, so it is with joy that tourists come here to forget the hustle and bustle of the city. The splendid views along the lake, running from the east to west, are a never-ending delight for tourists. It is hardly surprising that tourists flock to the West Lake all the year round to enjoy the glorious scenery and warm sunny days. A 1 300-metre-long cross lake underwater tunnel was opened to the public on October 1, 2003.

Paragraph 2

雁荡山 Yandang Mountain

Located to the north of Wenzhou, Zhejiang Province and covering an area of 450 square kilometers, Yandang Mountain encompasses over 550 scenic sights. Known as the "famous mountain on the sea" and "the unique spot under Heaven" it is noted for its sheer peaks, grotesque rocks, ancient caves, cascading waterfalls, flowing springs and verdant trees. Its main peak is a place with reed marshes where flocks of south-bound swan geese stop in autumn. Hence the name Yandang（swan goose and marsh）.

In his Dream Stream Essays Shen Kuo（1031-1095）records: "Cliffs sheer and bizarre soaring straight up and towering rocks and unfathomable valleys make it quite a unique mountain." It truly lives up to its fame as "a wondrous mountain under Heaven".

Paragraph 3

楠溪江 Nanxijiang River

Nanxijiang River One of the national scenic resorts, it is located north in Yongjia County, Wenzhou City, and famous for beautiful water, grotesque rocks, many waterfalls and ancient villages. Major attractions include Hundred Zhang Waterfall, Cave of Revered Mr. Tao, Stone-Gate Terrace, Twelve Peaks, and so on. The Cave of Revered Mr. Tao derived its name from Tao Hongjing (456-536), a noted thinker of Taoism of the Southern Dynasty. The conchlike cave is spacious and straight, and is reputed as "the Number Twelve Auspicious Land of the Taoism Under Heaven".

Paragraph 4

灵隐寺 Temple of Inspired Seclusion

It is one of the most famous Buddhist temples in China. It was first built in 326 AD and restored several times through the centuries. At the front of the temple is Tianwang Hall where there is a statue of Maitreya. Behind it is the Great Hall, where the magnificent 19-meter-high statue of Sakyamunisits. Facing the temple is The Peak That Flew From Afar (Feilaifeng) which is covered with sculptures, inscriptions and trees.

Paragraph 5

普陀山 Putuo Mountain

Putuo Mountain Located on the Lotus Flowers Sea, about 100 sea miles east to the Hangzhou Bay, Putuo Mountain, regarded as the Buddhist Rites for Avalokitesvara Bodhisattva, is one of the four most famous Mountains of

Buddhism. The island, covering an area of 12.76 square kilometers and rising about 300 meters above sea level, is reputed as the "Buddhist Kingdom on the Sea". Major attractions include Puji Temple, Fayu Temple, Chaoyin Cave, Fanyin Cave, Thousand-Pace Sands and Purple Bamboo Forest.

Local people in the past suffered much and yearned for release from worldly cares, therefore, they created an idol, the Guanyin (also Guanshiyin or Goddess of Mercy; Sanskrit 梵文 Avalokitesvara, literally "looking on or hearing the voices of the suffering"). Guanyin is said to be "greatly merciful" and will help the needy and relieve the distressed. "In India, Guanyin was regarded as of the male sex while in China he turned into a Goddess of Mercy. This is in line with the wish of the people".

Paragraph 6

T 千岛湖
he One-Islet Lake

Well known for its pristine water and picturesque scenery, the Thousand-Islet Lake, composed of 1 078 islands, has long been a popular tourist attraction. Forest covers nearly 93 per cent of the lake area, which is home to more than 1 800 varieties of plants and 2 100 wild animals. With an average depth of 34 metres, its water transparency reaches 7 to 12 metres. In the past years, the local government has spared no efforts in protecting the lake and its surrounding area. More emphasis will be put on developing eco-agriculture and tourism in the coming years.

Paragraph 7

E 东湖
ast Lake

East Lake The lake is located in the east suburbs of Shaoxing, three kilometers from the city. Featuring an elegant landscape of lakes an mountains and fantastic stones, the East Lake is known as one of the Three Famous Lakes in Zhejiang Province, the other two being the West Lake in Hangzhou and the South Lake in Jiaxing. The East Lake used to be a hill about 60 meters in height. From the Han Dynasty, stone-men had been there to quarry stones. After thousand years of excavation, parts of the hill were hollowed, forming a unique scene of lake.

Cultural Links
文化链接

浙江"马灯"

"马灯"是浙江省流传甚广的一大舞种。从平原到山区、海岛,几乎各县市都有它活动的足迹,马灯形式有:"竹马"、"跑五马"、"高跷竹马"、"车马灯"、"马灯戏"、"手马灯"、"小马灯"、"马灯"等。马灯舞队有八匹、十二匹、二十四匹;也有五匹,扮赵云、关羽、刘备、张飞、穆桂英等戏曲人物;还有马灯和车子灯一起表演的叫车马灯;更有用竹扎成轿形的车子灯,演员站在车子内,下肢装上假脚,外有车夫推车。大都扮演"关公送皇嫂"、"赵匡胤千里送京娘"、"土地公公/土地婆婆"等故事。表演中夹唱民歌小调。有的马灯有马夫作翻、滚、洗马、驯马等舞蹈表演,如常山县洗马舞和昌化县昌北马灯都以马夫表演技艺而闻名。"手马灯"是手提一盏马灯,"高跷竹马"是演员身系马灯道具,脚踩高跷,均为走阵的舞蹈。有的马灯班带有歌舞和小戏,作为开场,如金华、湖州、衢州、杭州等市不少马灯班称"马灯戏"。歌舞节目有"报花名"、"拜寿"、"下南京"等几十种,小戏有"南山种麦"、"卖草屯"、"大补缸"等。马灯班的歌舞和小戏往往又与采茶班、花灯班表演的节目相通用。杭州淳安县跳竹马又称竹马小戏,在清末,发展成为"三角戏"(即生、旦、丑),即后来的睦剧。马灯的道具,是用竹扎成马的前、后身(也有头尾相连的)系在演员腰上。这类马灯道具又分两种。杭州市淳安、萧山、临安县和金华市各县流传的马灯,是长头颈马灯。它的马身较短,头颈长100厘米,前身高150厘米。用一支宽竹片做颈背,具有古朴、写意的特点,舞蹈时甩动马头颈,昂首奔驰。另一种是宁波地区的马灯,头颈四周均有骨架,头颈硬直,造型与比例如现实生活中的马。眼睛和身内装上电灯,马鞍、项铃装饰如古代战马。金华市有一队马灯,相传是明代传下来的,马灯造型是颈长、身短,马脸扁平,演员身穿戏曲书生巾袍,演唱昆腔曲牌,由丝弦箫笛伴奏,有些词意涩奥难解。温州瑞安的小头马灯,头小如拳,造型奇特。浙江马灯的盛行和习俗、民间传说关系密切。如杭州萧

山县的竹马班有比颈长之俗，长者为粮食丰收的标志，连年丰收的马头颈可逐年加高，粮食歉收的村庄是不能舞竹马的。在杭州、嘉兴、宁波、金华等地区盛传南宋皇帝赵构南逃的"泥马渡康王"的故事。在金华传说赵构号称宋高宗后，为纪念泥马渡江（钱塘江）扎纸马以庆祝。当地马灯中的白马，即为康王之坐骑。在嘉兴传说康王渡江下水处即在海盐县，至今民间还有以一匹白马为演出单位的马灯。在杭州淳安县传有关北宋宣和二年农民领袖方腊的坐骑疑阵救方腊的故事等。

Paradise 天堂	watch local opera 看社戏
Solitary Hill 孤山	Shaoxing wine 绍兴酒
Su Causeway 苏堤	ancient towpath 古纤道
attractive 有吸引力的	Orchid Pavilion 兰亭
extremely 特别的，极其	Great Benevolence Pagoda 大善塔
illusion 错觉，幻觉	Flourishing Culture Pavilion 文昌阁
the West Lake Tour 西湖游	Yellow Dragon Cave 黄龙洞
Jade Spring 玉泉	Mount Putuo 普陀山
Soul's Retreat Temple 灵隐寺	Xitang 西塘
Monastery of Pure Compassion 净慈寺	Red Boat on the South Lake in Jiaxing 嘉兴南湖红船
Purple Cloud Cave 紫云洞	Liang Zhu Culture 良渚文化
Precious Stone Hill 宝云山	Yandang Mountains 雁荡山
Six Harmonies Pagoda 六和塔	The Thousand-Islet Lake 千岛湖
Hundred-Plant Garden 百草园	

Unit 4 Anhui Province 安徽省

Key Sentences 流畅精句

1. With the Yangtze and the Huihe River meandering through, Anhui lies in the geographic transitional belt between Northern China and South China.
   长江、淮河横贯省,安徽省是国内南北地理交汇过渡地带。
2. Anhui is the combination of the first two syllabi of the names of two cities: Anqing and Huizhou.
   安徽建省时以安庆、徽州两府首字组名。
3. Wengxian was once the capital of Huizhou Prefecture.
   歙县是历史上的徽州府所在地。
4. As a double entry on the list of UNESCO's Heritage of Culture and Nature, Mt. Huangshan is one of the top ten national spots.
   黄山已被联合国教科文组织列为自然与文化双重遗产,是中国十大风景名胜中惟一的山岳风光。
5. Hefei, capital of Anhui province, stands at the confluence of the north and south Fei rivers, hence its name.
   合肥是安徽省省会,它因南淝河与北淝河汇合于此而得名。
6. Jiuhuashan, one of the Four Buddhist Mountains, has 78 Ming and Qing temples, 6 800 buddhas, and 99 peaks.
   九华山,是四大佛教名山之一,有 78 座明清寺庙、6 800 尊佛像和 99 座主峰。
7. Wuhu, an old and beautiful river city, is where the Qingyi River joins the Yangtze.
   芜湖是一座古老而又美丽的城市,位于青弋江和长江的汇合处。

华东 East China

8. Tunxi is the administrative part of Huangshan City and is 60km from the Huangshan Mountain Scenic Area.
   屯溪为黄山市府所在地,离黄山名胜风景区有60公里。
9. The charm of Anhui province is its old architecture and its countryside.
   安徽的古建筑和乡村生活很有特色。
10. Two km south of Xiaoyaojin, the Lecturing Rostrum is where Emperor Cao Cao trained Wei troops in using crossbows. These sites are marked with pavilions is traditional architecture.
    逍遥津以南两公里外是教弩台,曹操曾在此训练强弩手。这里有古典建筑、水榭亭阁。
11. Mt. Huangshan, according to legends, was the abode of immortals.
    黄山,传说是神仙居住的地方。
12. Clouds on this mountain swirl around peaks and valleys, forming a "sea of clouds".
    黄山云流动在千峰万壑之间,或成滔滔云海,浩瀚无际。
13. The mountain is the watershed of the two rivers of the Yangtse and Qiantang.
    黄山是长江和钱塘江两大水系的分水岭。

Wonderful Paragraph 精彩片段

Paragraph 1

黄山 Huangshan Mountain

Huangshan Mountain is located in the south of Anhui Province, Spanning She, Yi, Taiping and Xiuning counties. It was called Yishan Mountain in the Qin Dynasty and acquired its present name Huangshan Mountain in 747 (the 6th year of the Tang Tianbao reign). Its scenic area, covering 154 square kilometers of land, encompasses fascinating peaks, rocks, pines, clouds, springs and other rare scenes.

用英语说中国——旅游亮点
Introduce China in English—Scenic Spots

Huangshan Mountain is celebrated for having four wonderful mountain scenes: odd-shaped pines, bizarre rocks, cloud seas and hot springs. Rare geological formation and spectacular clusters of peaks are the natural characteristics of Huangshan Mountain. In the scenic area, unique granite peaks dotting the summits and cliffs; ancient pines stretching their branches in every posture, bizarre rocks with strong resemblances to whatever in your imagination; and the seas of cloud so full of unpredictable changes—they combine to unfold a large scroll of Huangshan Mountain showing movement in tranquility and vice versa. Huangshan Mountain houses rich resources of protophyte and wild animals. The scenic area has a forest coverage of 83.4% and 1 452 species of protophytes falling into 203 families. Huangshan Mountain has a wealth of cultural heritage too. On his second visit to Huangshan Xu Xiake, noted traveller and geographer of the Ming Dynasty, exclaimed: "Huangshan Mountain in Anhui has no equal. Once on top, one finds no other match. This is the acme!" Later man made the following statement: "One visits no mountains after the Five Sacred Mountains. And after Huangshan, one has no eye for the Five Sacred Mountains."

Paragraph 2

九华山
Mount Jiuhua

Mt. Jiuhua is situated in the southwest of Qingyan Town in the west of Anhui province. There're a lot of temples. It is the sacred place where many faithful men and women went on pilgrimage, and is also the summer resort where the scene is splendid and the climate is moderate. Of the four famous Buddhist Mountains, Mt Jiuhua wins the first place and gains the reputation of "the first pilgrimage" and " the first mountain" in the southeast. It's also known for a large number of tourist attractions, such as the strange rock, formations, the flying falls, the hambokou peaks, the great celestial pond and the queer trees. Of all ages, many literary and refined

scholars or high-rank officials had been here, drinking and talking about Buddhism and composing poems which left behind many much-told tales.

Paragraph 3

皖南古村落——西递、宏村
Ancient Villages in Southern Anhui Xidi and Hongcun

Precisely speaking, ancient villages in southern Anhui refer to the architectural complexes with a historical, artistic, and scientica value, specifically the folk houses, shrines, schools, archways, towers, pavilions, and water outlet, etc., mainly found in the six counties of ancient Hui prefecture, namely the present Xi, Yi, Xiuning, Qimen, Jixi, and Wuyuan counties. Villages here are well preserved as they were built in Ming and Qing Dynasties, together with the folks' customs and life styles. Among the counties, Yi County has the largest number of the ancient villages survived most intact.

According to a survey in 1982 by the local government, Yi County still has 715 natural villages, with over 30 ancient houses of Ming Dynasty, 3 590 or more of Qing Dynasty, as well as 3 clan shrines of Ming Dynasty and 118 of Qing Dynasty. The most representative of the villages are Xidi and Hongcun villages, which remain fairly untouched in their format and style of Ming and Qing Dynasties.

The human civilization of the two villages is amazingly harmonious with the landscape. The planning of the village as a whole is clever, the courtyard design is complete and rational, the decoration and furnishing are typical of southern Anhui, —all these make the two outstanding of the many ancient villages preserved in this part of the province.

Paragraph 4

古牌坊群
The Complex of Seven Arches

The Complex of Seven Arches Built by Bao Clan, it is located in Tangyue Village, 6 kilometers west of Shexian County. Three of the seven arches were built during the Ming Dynasty, and the other four were built during the Qing Dynasty. These memorial arches wind their ways into a simple and elegant group, and they are outstanding stone carving of Hui school.

Paragraph 5

包公祠
Baogong Memorial Hall

Baogong Memorial Hall, a special memorial hall to commemorate Bao Zhen (999-1062) in the Northern Song Dynasty (960-1127), is located in Fragrant Flower Mound of Baohe Park, Hefei. It was first built in the period 1488 to 1505 of the Ming Dynasty (1368-1644). These buildings were rebuilt in 1882 and 1946 respectively. Fragrant Flower Mound used to be the place where Bao Zhen studied. During the Ming Dynasty, Song Guangming, the governor of Hefei, saw this scenic spot and the ancient temple into Baogong Academy. In the memorial hall display the statue of Baogong, stone carved image, cultural relics and relevant materials. By the side of the memorial hall, there is a pavilion with a well in it. The well is named Honest and Clean Well (Incorruptible Well). Legend has it that those officials who have not been honest and clean dare not to drink the water from the well. Bao Zhen, popularly known as Bao Gong (Lord Bao), was prefect of Kaifeng, capital of the Northern Song Dynasty. He was famous in popular legend as an upright and capable official and fearless, impartial judge with a knack of passing true verdicts in all the cases he tried. The people called him "Just Judge Bao" in the Northern Song Dynasty.

Cultural Links
文化链接

黄山的景名和摩崖石刻

黄山的景名和摩崖石刻体现了壮观的文化特色。在主要景区,就有摩

崖石刻200处。遍布黄山的摩崖石刻,有两个显著的特点:一是它们分布在道路的近旁,与游览路线紧密结合,游人可以就近欣赏,增加游兴;二是均刻在石壁上,与山体结合在一起,浑然天成。

从黄山的景名和题刻内容来看,它们均抓住自然景物和环境气氛的特点,进行艺术概括,起到画龙点睛、烘托景物的作用,以帮助游人领悟自然美景的特征,启发人们联想,激发游人对景生情。如"立马空东海,登高望太平"刻在青鸾峰上,每字6米见方,是黄山规模最大的石刻。有的还能发人深省,启迪人生,追忆往事。如"大如河山"是因景寓意,"万山拜其下,孤云卧此中"富含诗情画意,"不垢不净"发人深省等。黄山的大量摩崖石刻以及它们所表现的深邃意境,反映了中国自然风景的民族特色。

geographic 地理	Water Pavilion in Xiaoyaojin 逍遥津水榭
location 环境	Cloud Valley Monastery 云谷寺
lie 位于	Fantastic view 奇景
Jade Screen Pavilion 玉屏楼	Li Taibai Pavilion 李太白楼
Watching Cataract Pavilion 观瀑亭	Baogong Memorial Hall 包公祠
Thousand Feet Spring 百丈泉	Mount Huangshan 黄山
Singing String Spring 鸣璇泉	Mount Jiuhua 九华山
Three Fold Spring 三叠泉	Wuhu Yangtze River Bridge 芜湖长江大桥
Cloud Dispersing Pavilion 排云亭	Shouxian County 寿县
Beginning the Believe Peak 如信峰	
Jadeite Pond 翡翠池	

Unit 5　Fujian Province
福建省

Key Sentences
流畅精句

1. It is so named Mountain Kingdom of Southeast China, for mountains and hills takes 90% of the of Fujian Province.
   丘陵、山地占福建全省总面积的90%以上,有"东南山国"之称。
2. In the Southern Song Dynasty, Fujian had the jurisdiction over eight prefectures, thus another name Bamin for Fujian, referring the eight prefectures as a whole Fujian Province.
   南宋福建置8个辖区,故有八闽之称。
3. Standing in Longyan Prefecture, Yongding Hakka Circular House is a unique folk dwelling.
   永定土楼是世上独特的山村民居建筑,位于龙岩地区。
4. Featured with green mountains and blue waters, Mt. Wuyi stands on the upper reaches of Chongyangxi Stream in the northwest of Fujian Province.
   武夷山位于福建省西北部,崇阳溪上游,以碧水丹山为其特色。
5. It is on the list of cultural and natural heritage with lots of natural spots, such as Shaibu Rock, Jiuqu Brook, 36 Peaks and Ancient Ziyang Academy.
   被列为世界文化和自然双重遗产,主要风景有:晒布岩、九曲溪、三十六峰和紫阳书院等。
6. Wuyi is a place for hiking and bamboo rafting down the jade-green Min River.
   武夷山是个远足的好去处,可乘竹排在翡翠般的闽江上漂流。

7. The Fujian dialect is distinct, neither Cantonese nor Mandarin.
   闽方言独具特色,既不是广东话,也不是普通话。
8. Xiamen is a port city and an important trading city.
   厦门是个海港城市,也是重要的商贸城市场。
9. The 1 000-year-old Nan Putuo temple is named after at home of the Goddess of Mercy.
   千年古寺南普陀是大慈大悲的观音菩萨的道场。
10. Zhangzhou enjoys a reputation of "A Land of Flowers and Fruits".
    漳州素有"花果之乡"的美誉。

Wonderful Paragraph 精彩片段

Paragraph 1

Mt. Wuyi 武夷山

Mt. Wuyi is located in Fujian Province at its boundary with Jiangxi Province, running along for about 500km at an average altitude of over 1 000m. The legend says that in the era of Tang Yao a senior man called Peng Zu took hermitage in the mountain with his sons Wu and Yi, who first developed this area, therefore the mountain was referred to as Mt Wuyi in their honor. Yet other folks say that this was once the settlement of the ancient Minyue people governed by their King Wuyi, hence the mountain's name.

Mt Wuyi scenic area is in the southern suburb of Wuyishan City, Fujiang Province, the southeastern section of northern Mt Wuyi ranges, a strap about 14km long and 5km wide, covering an area of 70km^2 about 350m above sea level in average. Geologically, the mountain is made up of low hills of red sand rocks, namely the Danxia landform. For the crustal movement of hundreds of millions of years, the topography had been changing all the time that finally created the present shooting peaks flanked by clear streams, which brings to the mountain the honor of "the most miraculous

用英语说中国——旅游亮点
Introduce China in English—Scenic Spots

and graceful in southeastern China".

The total area of this heritage is 999.75 km^2, the second vast in China that have been included in World Heritage List. In accordance with the features of the resources, the area is subdivided into four parts: Bio-diversity quarter in the west, Nine Bends Ecology quarter in the center, Natural and Cultural Scenery quarter in the east, and Chengcun Village of the ancient King Minyue.

On visiting the mountain, a high official of World Tourism Organization remarked, "Unpolluted Mt Wuyi is a good model for the world environmental protection," while an expert from World Heritage Committee of UNESCO said, "Mt Wuyi is the everlasting symbol of Chinese natural resources which can be applied continuously."

In December of 1999, UNESCO inscribed Mt Wuyi on its World Heritage List as a cultural and natural property of the world.

Paragraph 2

M鼓山ountain Drum

Mountain Drum Located 17 kilometers east from Fuzhou, the beautiful and secluded Drum Mountain with an elevation of 969 meters above sea level is centered by the Yongquan (Bubbling Spring) Temple. The temple built in 908, or the second year of the Later Liang's Kaiping reign during the Five Dynasties, is reputed as "the Number One of all Temples in Fujian". An ancient stone path with more than 2 500 steps stretches along the slopes of the mountain to the temple. On both side of the path are luxuriant cypresses and pine trees, secluded streams and flowing springs. There are 50-odd scenic spots, such as Huilong Pavilion, Fangsheng Pond and Incense Burner Peak.

Paragraph 3

G鼓浪屿 ulangyu Island

Gulangyu Island Covering an area of almost 1.8 square kilometers, Gulangyu Island is situated in the southwest of Xiamen proper. The blooming flowers, flourish trees and beautiful scenery win her a name of "Garden on the Sea". The Sunlight Rock, the highest point on the island, offers you a panoramic view of the sea and the city. Shuzhuang Garden is elaborately designed with artificial rocks, zigzagging bridges, beautiful pavilions and ancient caves, all setting off harmoniously.

China's first piano museum opened on Gulangyu, on December 22, 2001, an island of Xiamen in East China's Fujian Province. The museum displays 70 famous-brand pianos from the Unite States, Britain, France, Austria and Australia. They are all over 100 years old. Hu Youyi (胡友义), born in Gulangyu, collected the pianos, and now lives in Australia. According to an agreement between Hu Youyi and the Gulangyu district government, the pianos will be on display at the museum for 10 years and will then be donated to the local government. Gulangyu had been dubbed "Piano Island" because its 20 000 permanent residents own 620 pianos.

Paragraph 4

N南普陀寺 anputuo Temple

Nanputuo Temple On the southeastern outskirts of Xiamen City is the Buddhist Temple called Nanputuo. The famous ancient temple was first built during the Tang Dynasty. It covers 30 000 square meters with four main buildings—Hall of Heavenly Kings, Shrine of Greatness and Magnificence, Hall of Great Compassion, and Sutra-Keeping Pavilion—on the north-south axis.

用英语说中国——旅游亮点
Introduce China in English—Scenic Spots

Paragraph 5

Jimei 集美

Jimei is a famous university town—an epitome of the educational set-up of modern China. It is here that are located the former residence of Mr Chen Jiageng (1894-1961), a celebrated patriotic overseas Chinese, an exhibition hall displaying his life story, Guilai hall, the all-embracing South Fujian Stone Carving Museum—Aoyuan Garden, the unique south Fujian building groups, and also Dragon Boat Pond, the former Yanping fortress and the shopping street. Visitors will feel contented to buy some handicrafts articles and fashionable dresses s/he likes after the visit.

Paragraph 6

Hakkas and Their Earthen Buildings 客家土楼

Dotted around the mountain triangle where Fujian, Guangdong, and Jiangxi provinces meet, the so-called earthen buildings (tulou in Chinese) are attracting more attention in China and the other parts of the world. Architects consider them to the cream of traditional Chinese residential architecture. Scholar shave discovered that they embody a distinctive culture while local governments have realized that they can lure tourists like magnets. Bearing all this in mind, local architects, scholars and government officials are working together to try to put the buildings on the World Cultural Heritage List of the United Nations Educational, Scientific and Cultural Organization. The huge buildings, which resemble fortresses, are called earthen buildings because of their tall and strong earthen outer walls. The walls, often propped up by a frame of bamboo and wood chips, are made of earth, fine sand and limestone. The largest concentration of the buildings is in western Fujian Province, especially the areas inhabited by the Hakka people—a group belonging to the Han Chinese family, who can trace their ancestors back more than 1 500 years ago to Central and North China.

"茶中之王"——大红袍

　　大红袍茶树生长于九龙窠最后一窠之岩脚下。九龙窠是一个幽奇深邃的峡谷。九座嶙峋的岩峰,犹如九条将要腾空而起的游龙,蟠绕在它的两旁。峡谷里,巨石错落,细泉潺流,到处布满了丛丛簇簇的茶树。大红袍茶树之所以有获得"茶中之王"的美称,是因为它生长的环境得天独厚。茶树所处的峭壁上,有一狭长的岩罅,岸顶终年有水自罅滴落。

　　而随水流落又有苔藓之类的有机物,因而土壤润泽肥沃。而且两旁岩壁直立,日照不长,气温变化不大。再加之平常茶农精心管理,以上种种原因,自然就使大红袍的成茶具有独到的品质和卓著的药效。大红袍冲泡时散发出桂花香,经茶师评定,大红袍茶冲至九次,尚不脱原茶之真味。而其他名茶,最多冲至七次,味就极淡。因此,大红袍有"茶中之王"的桂冠。来武夷山的旅游者,无不以一睹大红袍树为快。

Horse's Tail Port 马尾港	bamboo raft 竹筏
Jimei School Village 集美学村	natural preservation area 自然保护区
island 岛	
tourist resources 旅游资源	Mount Drum 鼓山
history 历史	The Yu Hill 于山
karst 喀斯特地形、岩溶地形	scenic spot 景点
biosphere 生物圈	marsh 湿地;沼泽
Mount Wuyi Scenic Spot 武夷山风景区	erosion 腐蚀,侵蚀
	landscape 风景
Jiuquxi River 九曲溪	possess 拥有
above the seal level 海拔	originate 发源,发生

Unit 6　江西省 Jiangxi Province

Key Sentences
流畅精句

1. Lying on the southern bank of low-middle reaches of the Yangtze River, Jiangxi Province was once called Jiangnan Xidao in the Tang Dynasty.
   江西省地处长江下游南岸,唐代称江南西道,故而得名。
2. Poyang Lake is the largest fresh water lake in China.
   鄱阳湖是我国最大的淡水湖。
3. Jiangxi was part of Chu, Wu and Yue kingdoms is history, and in the Qin Dynasty, it belonged to Jiujiang Shire and Jiangxi Province in the Yuan Dynasty.
   春秋为楚、吴、越三国地,秦属九江郡,元置江西行省。
4. Jiangxi was the revolutionary center of the second civil war after Nanchang Uprising, and especially when Jinggangshan revolutionary base was established.
   八一南昌起义后,特别是井冈山革命根据地建立后,江西成为第二次国内革命战争时期的革命根据地中心。
5. King Teng's Pavilion was first built in Tang Dynasty.
   滕王阁最初建于唐代。
6. In Jingdezhen, the factory's craftsmen often spend weeks at a time hand painting the objects.
   在景德镇,工厂的艺人们经常花费几周的时间来手工制造瓷器。
7. Jiujiang has been an important trading center for Jingdezhen pottery, porcelain, and tea.
   九江一直是个很重要的贸易中心,经销景德镇的陶器、瓷器和茶。

8. Mount Lushan is located in the north of Jiangxi Province, with the Yangtze River flowing by just in the north and the Poyang Lake lying in the southeast.
庐山,位于江西省北部,北濒长江,东南临鄱阳湖,自然风光奇特秀丽。
9. White Deer Cave Academy, the most important of the four ancient academies of China, enjoys fame in the history of Chinese education.
白鹿洞书院列我国古代四大书院之首,在中国教育史上享有盛誉。
10. Guling is well known in Lushan Mountains because Chiang Kai Shek once had a summer villa there.
牯岭在庐山很有名是因为这里曾经有蒋介石的夏季别墅。

Wonderful Paragraph
精彩片段

Paragraph 1

Mt Lushan 庐山

Mt Lushan is south of Yangtze River and west of Poyang Lake, well known since ancient times for its magnificence, marvel, precipice, and grace.

The scenic area covers $302 km^2$, and the buffer zone extends out for $500 km^2$. Here there is the unusual glacial traces of the Quaternary Period, and a rich collection of landforms such as rivers, lakes, slopes, and peaks, regarded as a garden of geology. It has 171 peaks recognized with a name long ago, of which the summit Dahanyang Peak rises up for 1 474m above sea level Scattered among the peaks are 26 groups of grotesque rocks. Waters gush down the mountain and form 22 falls, 18 streams, and 14 ponds or lakes. Its Three-stepped Fall is reputed worldwide and has a height difference as big as 155m.

Mt Lushan has a wealth of biological resources in an integrated ecological system. About 76.6% of the area is covered with forests, providing a

paradise for over 3 000 species of plants, 2 000 insects, 171 birds, and 33 animals. At the foot there is also the Poyang Lake Migrant Birds Reserve, protecting the largest community of white crane in the world, and other rare birds such as white-naped crane and white head stork, amounting to over 4 000 individuals.

The climate of Mt Lushan is that of subtropical monsoon, typical of mountainous areas. The temperature drops as the mountain rises higher. In summer it is exceptionally cool, and has long been reputed as a world famous resort from the summer heat.

Out of the precipitous peaks, grotesque rocks, graceful waters, and dangerous ravines, grows up the colorful history and culture of Mt Lushan. It is the cradle of the pastoral poems of China, and the headstream of Chinese landscape poems and paintings. Numerous celebrated figures of all times paid their visits to Mt Lushan, from Li Bai in Tang Dynasty (618-907) to Guo Moruo of modern China, who left behind them an ample wealth of frequently cited lines and stanzas.

Mt Lushan is a holy site of religions as well, and in one mountain there hosts five major religions of the world.

Well preserved in Mt Lushan are over 20 sites of ancient times, as well as 600 or more sites of the mediaeval times. The scenic quarters boast for its 16 natural wonders 474 sites of interest, 900 cliff inscriptions, 300 stone steles, and 600 villas of modern times in various Chinese or foreign styles.

Mt Lushan is recognized as one of the first group of the key scenic sites in China. In 1991 it was award with the honor of one of the "Top Forty tourism sites of China". In December of 1996, Mt Lushan was inscribed in the World Heritage List as a world natural scenery. And in February, 2004, Mt Lushan National Geopark was approved by UNESCO as a site of the World Geological Parks on its list of World Network of Geoparks.

East China

Paragraph 2

石钟山
Stone Bell Hill

Stone Bell Hill Situated at the mouth of Poyang Lake by Hukou County, the Stone Bell Hill is no more that 70 meters in height. Water of the lake, lapping into the cracks and crannies around the base, produces a bell-like sound hence the name. Su Shi, a noted literati once wrote the famous article of "The Notes of Stone Bell Hill". It was also a military strategic spot in ancient time. Zhou Yu, a famous general of the Eastern Wu during the Three KIngdoms drilled the navy on the Lake here; and the Taiping Rebel once defeated Qing armies leaded by Zeng Guofan here.

Paragraph 3

龙虎山
Longhu Mountain

Longhu Mountain Located west to Guixi County, the Longhu (Dragon and Tiger) Mountain having a typical danxia landform belongs to the Wuyi Mountains range. It is noted for lush-vegetation-covered peaks, graceful rivers and abundant cultural relics. As the birthplace of the Zhengyi Sect of the Taoism, the mountain is dotted with Taoist buildings including Shangqing Palace, Tianshi Mansion mainly. More than a hundred coffins are seen suspended on the cliffs of Xianshui Rock, which could date back to 2 600 years ago during the Spring and Autumn and the Warring States periods. Situated on the eastern part of the mountain are the ruins of "Xiangshan Academy", which was established by Lu Jiuyuan, a celebrated scholar of Confucianism.

Paragraph 4

井冈山
Jinggang Mountains

Jinggang Mountains Located in southwest Jiangxi and the middle part of Luoxiao Mountains where Hunan and Jiangxi provinces meet, the Jinggang Mountains covers an area of more than 660 square kilometers. With an altitude of 1 841 meters, the mountains look majestic and graceful. So many revolutionary sites, monuments, and museums indicate that Jinggang Mountains was a cradle of Chinese revolution. Major revolutionary sites are Jinggang Mountain Revolutionary Museum, five villages of Great Well, Lesser Well, Upper Well, Middle Well and Lower Well, Huangyangjie Post, and so on.

Paragraph 5

滕王阁 The Prince Teng Pavilion

The Prince Teng Pavilion towers at the bank of Gan River. The original pavilion was first built in 653 in the Tang Dynasty (618-907). It was rebuilt during the reign of the Ming emperor Jingtai (1450-1456) outside the Zhangjiang Gate. After the Qing Dynasty it was destroyed and reconstructed again. In 1926 a fire set by the Northern Warlords (1912-1927) again burnt it down. Reconstruction of the pavilion began in 1983, and was completed in 1989. Occupying an area of 43 000 square metres, the main structure of the pavilion covers 13 000 square metres. With double eaves, the pavilion boasts nine storeys, with a height of 57.5 metres. It looks even more magnificent and imposing.

Cultural Links
文化链接

庐山由来的传说

有一种传说早在周初(大约公元前十七、十六世纪),也有说在周威烈王时候(即公元前四世纪),有一位匡俗先生(亦称匡裕),在庐山学道求仙。据说他的事迹为朝廷所获悉。于是周天子屡次请他出山相助,匡俗也屡次回避潜入深山之中。后来,匡俗其人无影无踪。有人说他成仙去了,这自

然是无稽之谈。后来人们美化这件事，把匡俗求仙的地方称为"神仙之庐"。并说庐山这一名称，就是这样出现的。因为"成仙"的人姓匡所以又称匡山或称为匡庐。到了宋朝，为了避宋太祖赵匡胤的讳而改称康山。

另一种传说在周武王时候有一位方辅先生。同老子李耳一道骑着白色驴子入山炼丹，二人也都"得道成仙"，山上只留下一座空庐。人们把这座"人去庐存"的山，称为庐山。"成仙"的先生名辅，所以又称为辅山。但是老子与武王并不同时，这同样是神话故事。

第三种传说仍然是匡俗先生的故事，但时间较晚，情节也有些不同。说是匡俗的父亲东野王，曾经同鄱阳令吴芮一道辅佐刘邦平定天下，东野王不幸中途牺牲。朝廷为了表彰他的功勋，封东野王的儿子匡俗于鄡阳（鄡阳为今鄱阳县一部分，号越庐君。越庐君匡俗有兄弟七人爱好道术）都到鄱阳湖边大山里学道求仙。这座越庐君兄弟们学道求仙的山，被人们称为庐山。

East Lake 东湖	Jiangxi Provincial Museum 江西省博物馆
Badashanren Academy of Painting & Calligraphy 八大山人书画院	roar 吼叫；咆哮
Donglin Temple 东林寺	cascade 小瀑布
Dragon Pool at Xiufeng 秀峰龙潭	meander 曲流，河曲，蜿蜒而流
Fairy Cave 仙人洞	slope 倾斜
Yellow Dragon Pool 黄龙潭	mystery 神秘，神秘的事物
Dragon Head Cliff 龙首崖	antiquity 痕迹，古迹
White Deer Cave 白鹿洞	villa 别墅
Wulao Peak 五老峰	Mount Lushan 庐山
Former Headquarters of the Nanchang Uprising 南昌起义总指挥部旧址	the Poyang Lake 鄱阳湖
	natural wonder 自然景观

用英语说中国——旅游亮点
Introduce China in English—Scenic Spots

Unit 7　上海市　Shanghai Municipality

Key Sentences
流畅精句

1. The word "Shanghai" in Chinese means literally "a port on the sea".
   "上海"这个词在汉语里的字面意思是"海上之埠"。
2. It is experiencing double-digit economic growth and its average per capita income is one of China's highest.
   上海经济正以两位数的增长速度发展,人均收入居中国之最。
3. Shanghai is called the dragon's head of the burgeoning Yangtze River basin.
   上海如今是蓬勃发展的长江流域的龙头。
4. In Shanghai, the hottest temperature is 35℃ in July and August, and the coldest is −5℃ in January and February.
   上海天气最热是在七八月间,气温最高可达35℃,最冷则在一二月间,气温降至摄氏零下−5℃。
5. Nanjing Road is visited by at least 200 000 people daily.
   南京路每天人流量至少有20万。
6. Lujiazui District is situated in Lujiazui Financial Trade Zone in the newly formed Pudong District. It is also one of the most attractive tourist areas in Shanghai.
   陆家嘴地区位于浦东新区的陆家嘴金融贸易区,与外滩隔江相望,是上海新兴的最有吸引力的旅游区域之一。
7. Shanghai is internationally known for its historic position, commerce and trade, urban views, shopping and gourmandism.
   上海的旅游特色体现在其历史地位、商贸经济、都市风光、购物美食等方面。

8. Golden fall from September to November is nice and cool, during which most tourist festivals are held, such as culture and art festival, festival of ethnic customs, food festival and lots more of shopping promotions.

9~11月是金秋季节,天高气爽,上海较为盛大的特色旅游节大多在这段时间举办,如文化艺术节、民族风情节、购物节、美食节等系列促销活动。

Paragraph 1

外滩
The Bund

The Bund, which extends from Jinling Road in the south to the Waibaidu Bridge over the Suzhou Creek (the whole project of the cleanup of the Suzhou creeks is estimated to cost 20 billion Yuan or US $ 2.42 billion and by 2010 hopefully the river will once again be clean enough to encourage marine life back to the area) in the north, is on the western bank of the 114-kilometre-long Huangpu River, a tributary of the Yangtze River. It is a 1.5-kilometre boulevard and used to be called the Huangpu Shoal. Walking along Zhongshan Road, visitors can enjoy he fade grandeur of old Shanghai, for this was the Bund, where the great trading houses and banks had their headquarters. On one side is line of imposing 1930s European buildings, while the other is the Huangpu River. The Bund underwent a face-lift several years ago, which included raising the level of the breakwater to prevent flooding. The raised pedestrian promenade gives a wonderful view of the Huangpu River with the futuristic-looking buildings of the New Pudong Area rising on the other side. Across the Waibaidu Bridge is the Shanghai Mansions. On the 22nd Floor of the Mansions, you will find yourself above the tree line, and unfurling below you, a marvellous view of the bustling city of

Shanghai with a sea of buildings in all their majesty. The architecture, along the Bund is unanimously honoured as a "World Architectural Fair."

Paragraph 2

东方明珠广播电视塔
Oriental Pearl TV Tower

The Oriental Pearl TV Tower, completed in 1994 and standing 468 meters, is the tallest TV tower in Asia and the third tallest in the world. It stands by the bank of Huangpu River.

It covers a total area of 8 400 square meters. The monastery has three halls namely the Heavenly King Hall, the Grand Hall and the Abbot's Chamber. This famous Buddhist Monastery houses two jade statues of Sakyamuni. One is in a sitting position, and the other is a reclining position. Both statues are of great artistic value and are regarded as treasures of Buddhism in our country.

Paragraph 3

金茂大厦
Jinmao Mansion towers

As No. one tower in Asia and ranking 3rd in the world, Jinmao Mansion towers at Shiji Dadao in Pudong District. As a luxury hotel, the tower likes like a round gigantic column decorated with silvery marble slabs. With 88 floors above the ground and 4 floors underground, it is 420.5 meters high and fully facilitated with modern conveniences. There is a rotating dining hall on the top with a window view of the city down under and a garden around.

Paragraph 4

上海大剧院
Shanghai Grand Theatre

Shanghai Grand Theatre The theatre has become a representative building in Shanghai for its unique style and beautiful outlook. With a total

construction area of more than 62 000 square meters and a total height of 40 meters, it has 10 storeys 2 for underground, 2 for lofts and 6 on the ground. When night falls, the crystal-like theater glitters in infinite brilliance, giving people an impression of metropolitan art.

Paragraph 5

Y 豫园
u Garden

Yu Garden, a classical garden in downtown Shanghai, boasts a history over 400 years. Each pavilion, hall, stone and stream in the garden is expressing the quintessence of South China landscape design from Ming and Qing Dynasty. Over forty spots, divided by dragon walls, wound corridors and beautiful flowers, form an unique picture featuring "one step, one beauty; every step, every beauty."

It's reputed to be the most beautiful garden south of the Yangtze River. Built beside the Temple of the City God and covering only fives acres, it follows the Suzhou garden design of a world in microcosm, with 30 pavilions linked by corridors, artificial hills, bridges over lotus pools, groves of bamboo and walls occupied by stone dragons. The surrounding bazaar is packed with traditional and modern shops, restaurants and temples.

Paragraph 6

J 静安寺
ing'an Temple

Jing'an Temple is a popular temple, located at the entrance of Huashan Lu on Nanjing Xilu in Jing'an District. It is said that the temple was originally built in the period of Three Kingdoms named "Hudu Zhongyuan Temple" and renamed in the Tang Dynasty as "Yongtai Buddhist Temple". In 1008 (during the Song Dynasty), it got its present name and later burned down. Jing'an Temeple was rebuilt in the 6th year in the Guangxu Reign of the Qing Dynasty (1880), and renovated many times in the following decades, made up mainly of the Gateway, the Daxiong Hall, Guanyin Hall, Daming Bronze Bell and Stone Buddhas of the Southern and Northern Dynasties.

用英语说中国——旅游亮点
Introduce China in English—Scenic Spots

Paragraph 7

J玉佛寺
ade Buddha Temple

Yufo Temple is located on An'yuan Lu in Jing'an District. The temple was set up for the two jade Buddhas brought here by Buddhist Master Huigeng from Burma in 1882. The sitting Jade Buddha is 1.9 maters tall, made of a whole piece of jade. There is a set of Buddhist Scripture, 7 000 volumes in total, and other Buddhist items. The temple kitchen is popular for its Buddhist dishes.

Paragraph 8

L龙华寺
onghua Temple

Situated in the southwest part of the city, Longhua Temple is a major attraction of Shanghai. Though its popularity spread only after 1949, for foreigners living here in early 1900s, this biggest and oldest temple in the lower reaches of the Yangtze River Delta is very familiar indeed. Legend has it that it was first built in 242 during the Three Kingdoms period when Sun Quan (182-252, ruled 229-252), king of Kingdom Wu, had it built to show filial love to his mother.

Cultural Links
文化链接

城隍庙的故事

很早以前,有一年大旱,上海金山一带的农田干得开裂,田里的禾苗都快要枯死了。

农民们急得心里像着了火似的,整天坐也不是,站也不是,却也拿不出办法来,只得唉声叹气:"唉!要是能把黄浦江的水引到这里,就可以用水车里的水浇田了。"

"说得倒轻巧,开这么大一条河,得干多少年呀!"

正在这时,"霍"地站出来一位虎背熊腰的黑脸大汉,他说:"把这件事交给我吧,我保管一夜工夫就开好。"

"一夜工夫?"大家都简直有点不相信自己的耳朵,有人甚至还忍不住笑了出来。但是也没有别的办法,就随他去吧。

第二天早晨,农民们奔到田里一看,啊呀!果然,一条清澈的河流从黄浦江分出来,灌溉了几千亩良田。这时候,大家才知道那黑脸大汉原来是汉朝大将军霍光显灵。他带领子子孙孙开河灌田,解救了这场灾难。于是,人们就修筑了城隍庙,铸造了霍光将军的神像供在大殿。而那条河则被称为新开河。

Vocabulary 妙词连珠

enclosed 围着的	A night scene of Nanjing Road 南京路夜景
borderline 边界线	Shikumen Residences 石库门
extension 扩建	Site of the First National Congress of the Chinese Communist Party 中国共产党第一次全国代表大会会址
current 现在的	
erect 建立	
municipality 市政当局	
rustproof 不会生锈的	
resonant 嘹亮的	Jade Buddha Statue in the Yufo Temple 玉佛寺玉佛
Shanghai Concert Hall 上海音乐厅	Longhua Temple 龙华庙会
Shanghai Museum 上海博物馆	Shanghai Tourism Festival 上海旅游节
Shanghai Grand Theatre 上海大剧院	Shanghai International Tea Culture Festive 上海国际茶文化节
Shanghai Ocean Aquarium 上海海洋馆	
Wusongkou Port 吴淞口	Shanghai Osmanthus Festival 上海桂花节
Pudong 浦东	
Lujiazui 陆家嘴	Shanghai Nanhui Peach Blossom Festival 上海南汇桃花节
The Bund at Night 外滩夜景	
Nanpu Bridge 南浦大桥	

7 华中
Central China

Unit 1 河南省 Henan Province

Key Sentences 流畅精句

1. Henan Province lies on the middle lower reaches of the Yellow River.
   河南省地处黄河中下游。
2. Henan was part of Yuzhou in ancient China, and thus popular as "Zhongyuan" (Central China) since ancient times.
   河南自古属豫州,向有"中原"之称。
3. Longmen Grottoes is hidden is the cliffs of Mt. Longmen on both sides of the Yihe River.
   龙门石窟位于洛阳市南郊13千米的伊河两岸,龙门山上。
4. Henan is one of the cradles of China's civilization.
   河南是中国文明的摇篮之一。
5. It was in nearby Anyang that the oracle bones with the first Chinese writings were found.
   就在安阳附近,发现了中国最早的文字记载物龟甲。
6. China's earliest astronomical observatory is located in Henan.
   中国最早的天文台位于河南。

Central China

7. Songshan Mountain is one of China's five Sacred Mountains.
   嵩山是中国五大圣山之一。
8. Luoyang was the biggest city in China during the Tang Dynasty.
   洛阳在唐朝是中国最大的城市。
9. Xiaolangdi Dam project on the Yellow River is 154 meters high.
   黄河小浪底工程大坝有 154 米高。
10. Kaifeng is one of the 24 cities of historical importance protected by the State Council.
    开封是国务院重点保护的 24 个历史名城之一。

Wonderful Paragraph
精彩片段

Paragraph 1

龙门石窟
Longmen Grottoes

Longmen Grottoes is located at the foot of Yique Mountain 12km south of Luoyang City proper, where Yi River traverses northward between two mountain peaks which are just like a pair of Chinese gate towers. Indeed, Yique, the name of the mountain, actually means "gate of Yi River" in Chinese, and Emperor Yang of Sui Dynasty, when enjoying the beauty here, exclaimed with admiration, "Isn't this the Dragon Gate!" and that is the origin of the name: longmen, the "dragon gate" in Chinese.

The rocks of the mountain are hard and tough, quite ideal for stone sculpture, and Longmen Grottoes are the third cluster of cave temples commissioned by the imperial court, after Dunhuang Grottoes in Gansu and Yungang Grottoes in Datong of Shanxi. The caring began in North Wei Dynasty, and went on through East and West Wei Dynasties, then the dynasties of North Qi, North Zhou, Sui, Tang, and the Five Dynasties Period, lasting for over 400 years. During this long period, the full scale and efficient carvings account to about 150 years, mainly in North Wei Dynasty (over 40 years) and Sui and Tang Dynasties (about 110 years), and finally ranked Longmen Grottoes with Dunhuang Grottoes and Yuangang Grottoes as the Three Major Grotto sits of Buddhism in China.

Preserved in the grottoes are over 2 100 cave shrines sheltering 97 300 statues or more (the largest is 1 714m high while the smallest is less than an inch), as well as over 3 600 epigraphs or steles and 40 Buddhist stupas or pagodas. The sponsors of the caves were of all social status, not only the imperial rulers and nobles, but also civil associations and common folks, even some Buddhists from foreign nations.

Longmen Grottoes is truly a large museum of stone sculpture. Both an artistic expression on Buddhist culture and a reflection of the politics, economy, and social culture of the times, the caves have preserved for today a huge wealth of physical data of religion, fine art, architecture, calligraphy, music, costume, and medicine.

The landscape, mountain, and river of Longmen are grandiose and pretty, delightfully scenic as the first of the eight beauties of Luoyang. Bai Ju-yi, the celebrated poet of Tang Dynasty, wrote that "the landscape around Luoyang is wonderful, and Longmen is the best", which is still true for the present. Its ancient art, its splendid environment, and its convenient transportation,—all attract groups and groups of scholars and visitors from home and abroad.

In 1961 Longmen Grottoes were brought under the state protection as a key cultural site, and in November of 2000 the World Heritage Committee of UNESCO inscribed the site in its World Heritage List.

Paragraph 2

少林寺 Shaolin Temple

The world-famous Shaolin Temple is located at the foot of the Wuru Peak of the Shaoshi Mountain of Dengfeng, a little more than 50 miles southwest of Henan's provincial capital, Zhengzhou. Built in 495 during the reign of Emperor Taihe of the Northern Wei Dynasty, the temple was originally designed to house Batuo, a celebrated Indian monk, who, after many years of spreading Buddhism, was later known as Fo Tuo, or Grand Monk. Then in 527 AD, Bodhidharma, an ancient Indian monk known to the Chinese as Da Mo, came here and started the Zen sect, which is regarded as the "ancestral (first) court" of the Chinese Buddhism. It is reported that he lived here for nine years until his death in 535. Some accounts relate that Da Mo, seeing the monks becoming fat and lazy due to the sitting meditation, came up with walking meditations that imitated the natural motions of animals and birds that eventually evolved into a form of unarmed combat or martial arts (Wu Shu or Kung Fu). That started the kung-fu tradition at the temple. At the beginning of the seventh century, a tiny army of 13 Shaolin monks were reputed to have saved future Tang Dynasty emperor Li Shimin, by defeating an entire division of the ruling Sui Dynasty's army and helping him break out of prison. When he took power, Li showered favors, land and wealth on the temple. Shaolin then thrived as a center of kung-fu masters from around the country. At its heyday, it housed more than 3 000 solider-monks.

Paragraph 3

塔林
The Pagoda Forest

With a history of more than 1 000 years from the Tang Dynasty (618-907) to the Qing Dynasty (1644-1911), the Pagoda Forest has more than 230 pagodas for Buddhist abbots "住持", and is the largest one in China that has survived till now. Despite the difficulty, the temple has been making active moves to safeguard its intellectual property rights. The forest is a treasure house for the study of the ancient Chinese brick structure and sculpture art.

Paragraph 4

W 白马寺 hite Horse Temple

It is the birthplace of Chinese Buddhism and was the first Buddhist monastery established in China. It is said that in 67 AD two envoys who were sent to India to get the Buddhist scriptures returned with two Indian monks and had the temple built. As the scriptures were carried back on a white horse, two white stone horses were erected in front of the temple and the temple was named White Horse Temple.

Paragraph 5

B 白园 ai's Garden

Also referred to as Bai's Tomb, it is on the Pipa Peak of northern East Hill (also called Fragrant Hill) at Longmen, Luoyang City. The stele in front his tomb is inscribed "Tomb of Instructor Bai of Tang Dynasty". His full name is Bai Juyi, while his style name is Bai Le-tian. His ancestors moved from Taiyuan, Shanxi Province to Weinan, Shaanxi Province, but he was born in Xinzheng County, Henan Province. Bai was a well reputed poet in Tang Dynasty, and the highest governmental position he achieved was the director of criminal ministry, and was once an instructor of the prince. He settled down at Fragrant Hill in his later years, and titled himself as "Resident of Fragrant Hill". In literature creation, he advocated for the new form of Yuefu poems, and composed a lot of poems exposing the political evils or depicting the miseries of common folks. Pipa Peak, so named by folks because it looks like the Chinese musical instrument Pipa, is a quiet and peaceful mountain resort covered with old cypresses, which is now a key tour site of Luoyang City. In 1961, Bai's Garden, together with Longmen Grottoes beside it, was recognized as a key historical site under the state protection.

Central China

Paragraph 6

开封铁塔
Iron Pagoda

Built in the northern corner of Kaifeng in 1049, with drab, glazed bricks of 28 different patterns on the outside, the Iron Pagoda looks as if it were cast in iron, hence the name the Iron Pagoda. The 13-storeyed octagonal pagoda is 54.66 metres high. Due to the overflow of the Yellow River, the base of the pagoda has been buried underearth. More than 50 galled brick carvings including female performers, flying Aparas as in the frescoes of the Dunhuang Caves, kylin (Chinese unicorn, representing fortune and power in Chinese folk tales) Bodhisattvas, lions, ae vividly portrayed with exquisite craftsmanship, masterpieces of glazed brick sculptures of the Song Dynasty (960-1279). The view from the pagoda at the top sweeps over the whole city and down the Yellow River. The pagoda has become a popular tourist destination in its own right and draws thousands upon thousands of visitors each year. South of the pagoda stands an eight-sided pavilion. Inside the pavilion there is a bronze Buddha cast during the Song and Jin (1115-1234) period. There fore, it has been reputed as the "If you have not been up pagoda, you have not visited the city of Kaifeng (来开封不登铁塔, 等于没来过开封)."

Paragraph 7

宋陵
Song Tombs

The Song Tombs are scattered over an area southwest to Gongyi. Seven of the nine emperors of the Northern Song Dynasty (960-1127) were buried here; the other two were captured and taken away by the Jin armies who overthrew the Northern Song in the 12th century. There were over 20 tombs for empresses and imperial concubines in the area. And royal members and ministers of the dynasty, such as Kou Zhun and Bao Zheng (both were famous ministers), were also buried in the area.

Paragraph 8

Guan Lin 关林

Literally means Guan's Wood, it is said it's the tomb of the head and a carved wooden body of Guan Yu, a highly reputed general of Shu Kingdom in the Three Kingdoms Period, who, soon after his death, is regarded as the protector and the God of Loyalty in Chinese legend. Located in Guanlin Township about 7km south of the old city of Luoyang, it has the front court as the shrine, and the tomb lies in the rear quarter. The temple was constructed in Ming Dynasty, and pine trees were planted since its building. In Emperor Qianlong's reign, Qing Dynasty, it was expanded to the present size of nearly 7 hectares. With its wood of dark pines, majestic halls, huge tomb mound and big tomb steles, this reverend site is now an admired resort in Luoyang City to the fans of ancient architecture or tourists just for leisure.

Cultural Links 文化链接

龙门二十品

龙门二十品指龙门石窟中的20方北魏时期的造像题记,其中19品在古阳洞,一品在慈香窑。二十品的称呼最早见于清代康有为所著的《广艺舟双楫》和方若所著的《校碑随笔》。题记内容一般是表达造像者祈福消灾的美好愿望。就艺术形式而言,它是以汉隶为基础的书法艺术,结体用笔在隶、楷之间,既有隶书古朴刚健的风格,又有楷书端庄大方的神韵,是隶书向楷书过渡中一种比较成熟的独特字体。它代表了北魏时期书法艺术的最高成就,是"魏碑"体中的精品。在我国书法艺术发展史上占有重要的一页。

Vocabulary 妙词连珠

grotto 石窟	King Yu's Temple 禹王庙
treasury 宝藏	Tomb of Guan Yu 关羽墓
scripture 经文	Luoyang Folk Customs Museum
restore 恢复	洛阳民俗博物馆
preserve 保护	The First Founder's Hall in Honor of
Fawang Temple 法王寺	Dharma 初祖庵
Central Mountain Temple 中岳庙	

Unit 2 Hubei Province 湖北省

Key Sentences 流畅精句

1. During the Warring Period, It was the political and cultural center of the Chu State.
   战国时期,这里是当时楚国的政治文化中心。
2. Shennongjia Prime Forest in Hubei province attracts eco-travelers.
   湖北省的神农架原始森林吸引着生态旅游者。
3. Yellow Crane Tower of Wuhan City, Hubei Province, is one of the three famous towers in China.
   黄鹤楼位于湖北省武汉市,为中国三大名楼之一。
4. Gezhouba dam is one of the largest sluice gates on a inside river in the world.
   葛洲坝是世界上最大的内河船闸之一。
5. Yellow Crane Tower is a symbol of Wuhan.
   黄鹤楼是武汉的象征。
6. East Lake in Wuhan is bigger than West Lake in Hangzhou.
   武汉的东湖比杭州的西湖要大。
7. Also called Taihe Mountain and Xianshi Mountain, the Wudang Mountain is located in Danjiangkou City, Hubei Province.
   武当山旧称太和山、仙石山。位于湖北省丹江口市。
8. The Taoist music in the mountain is also a living fossil of the music of China.
   武当山的道教音乐也是中华音乐的活化石。

Central China

> 9. A lot of temples and mansions were constructed during the Tang, Song, Yuan and Ming dynasties, with Jindian Temple the most grand atop the Wudang Mountain.
> 唐、宋、元、明各代,均在武当山大兴土木,修建道观,主峰天柱峰顶的金殿尤为著名。

Wonderful Paragraph
精彩片段

Paragraph 1

W武当山
udang Mountain

Wudang Mountain, also called Taihe Mountain (Mountain of Supreme Harmony), is a well-known holy site of Taoism in China. It stands aloft in Danjiangkou, Shiyan City, Hubei Province, overlooking the vast water of Danjiangkou Reservoir in the front, and joining Shennongjia Forest Reserve at the back, covering an area of about 312km.² The highest peak is Peak of Heaven Pillar, about 1 612m above the sea level. Around it there are altogether 72 peaks, 24 streams, 11 caverns, 3 ponds, 9 springs, 10 pools, 9 wells, and 9 terraces, to form this beautiful and grand view of Wudang Mountain.

The large scale of its architectural complex was planned by the emperor himself, and the construction was supervised by imperial officials specially assigned for the project. The sites of the buildings were decided by gemancy experts, and the master craftsmen of the nation were summoned for the construction under the supervision of the minister of construction. Therefore the complex is grand and imperial, brilliant and glorious, with features that none is to match.

用英语说中国——旅游亮点
Introduce China in English—Scenic Spots

Paragraph 2

S神农架
Shennongjia

Located in Central China's Hubei Province, Shennongjia (Shennong's Ladder for the area to commemorate a legendary emperor, Shennong, believed to be the forefather of traditional Chinese herbal medicine and agriculture) covers an area of 3,250 square kilometres. Approximately 1.7 million years ago, because of a glacier of the Quaternary Period, at least one-third of the earth's land mass was covered with snow and ice about 1 000 metres thick, resulting in a heavy loss of life. It fortunately escaped the destruction of the glacier and became a haven to plants and animals, which have long perished elsewhere.

Home to 2 400 species of plants and 500 kinds of animals, Shennongjia is a natural botanical garden and zoo. In Shennongjia, 29 plants generally referred to as "living fossils" are found, including the dove tree, ginkgo and fir. Endangered animal species, such as the snub-nosed monkey, leopard and South China tiger, live there.

Shennongjia is also known for its many inscrutable caves. In one grotto, which can accommodate at least 10 000 people, the temperature varies so much that visitors can experience the four different seasons. Glaciers fill another grotto even in summer. Some of the caves are connected with subterranean rivers and fish teem in the sulterranean rivers. Each year, soon after the first spring thunderstorm, shoals of fish rush out of them. For visitors, a trip to Shennongjia's specimen hall can be a kind of compensation. Covering an area of 120 square metres, the hall displays specimens of 400-lus animals, birds, fish, butterflies and insects, which exist in Shennongjia. They include the snub-nosed monkey, white bear, South China tiger, wild boar, black bear, jackal, white stork and golden pheasant. Also on display in the hall is a mosquito 40 millimetres long and 98 millimetres wide when its wings are spread. It is said to be the largest mosquito in the world.

For researchers and visitors alike, the primitive forests of a Shennongjia

Central China

spell too many mysteries closely linked with its geological changes.

Shennongjia has been listed by UNESCO as one of nature reserves for wildlife protection in a global programme, the "Human Beings and Biosphere".

Paragraph 3

Y 黄鹤楼
ellow Crane Tower

Huanghelou (Yellow Crane Tower) of Wuhan City, Hubei Province, is one of the three famous towers in China. Built in 223 the tower has been a spot most frequented by men of letters, and, over the years, become the subject of more than a thousand poems and a hundred articles, the best known lines are "Long ago the immortal departed on the Yellow Crane, This Tower is all that's left." by Cui Hao of the Tang Dynasty. Merging perfectly with the natural scenery is the architectural complex of the tower—towers, pavilions, verandas, gateways and corridors etc. —built in proper distribution against the contours of the terrain.

Paragraph 4

G 葛洲坝
ezhouba Project

Gezhouba Project is located at Yichang, one of the largest hydropower projects in the world. With a storage capacity of 39.3 billion cubic metres of water the reservoir submerged 632 square kilometres of land, originally belonging to Chongqing Municipality and Hubei Province respectively, causing noticeable changes to the hydrology, chemical properties and sediment of the river in the reservoir area. The reservoir will also make local air moister and will bring more rain to the area. The reservoir's water surface and warm climate would form a "paradise" for birds. And it would also store abundant food for fish washed down from the local streams and rivers. It can generate 16 billion kilowatts of electricity every year.

用英语说中国——旅游亮点
Introduce China in English—Scenic Spots

Paragraph 5

T三峡大坝
he Tree Gorges Dam

The Three Gorges Dam, the largest water conservancy project ever undertaken in the world, is now being built at Sandouping in the middle of Xiling Gorge, the longest of the famous Three Gorges.

The three Gorges Dam will be 2 335 metres long, 185 metres high, and 18 metres wide on top and 130 metres wide at the bottom. The dam will raise the river to a level of 175 metres above seal level, creating a 600-kilometer long reservoir with a storage capacity of 39.9 billion cubic metres. Extending from the dam-site all the way to Chongqing 570.000 acres of farmland and towns and villages in 19 counties and cities will be flooded causing 1.3 million people to be relocated.

The construction of the project will cost 230 billion Chinese Yuan, an equivalent of 28 billion US dollars. The purposes for building this huge dam are flood control, electricity, Navigating and irrigation.

The construction of the dam formally began in 1994. According to the plan, the body or the dam will be completed in 2003 and the fist generator will begin to produce power. The whole construction will be completed in 2009.

Paragraph 6

A荆州古城
ncient City of Jingzhou

Ancient City of Jingzhou Situated on the northern bank of the middle reaches of the Yangtze River, Jingzhou is a city of great historical and cultural interest on the Jianghan Plain. It had been chose as the nations's capital by five Emperors from the Eastern Jin Dynasty (317-420) to the Five Dynasties (907-960). It was originally an earth city and rebuilt with bricks in the Qing Dynasty. The city holding access to the Yangtze River, had been a

Central China

place contested by all strategists since ancient times. The famous historical event, "General Guan Yu lost Jingzhou negligently", happened right here.

Paragraph 7

古赤壁
Ancient Chibi

Ancient Chibi is situated by Mt. Chibi on the southern bank of the Yangtze, 36 km from Puqing County in Hubei Province. Here are the remains of an ancient battlefield where the allied forces of Wu and Chu defeated the Cao army in the Three Kingdoms era. The story of the Chibi War is well known even by children today. Places of interest include the Yi River Pavilion, the River View Pavilion, the Wind-praying Terrace and Mountain Golden Imperial. The new-built Chibi war museum has an unique style, where there are sculptures of Zhouyu. There is a popular saying from a folk song in Chibi The book reviewers never go to Chibi because even 3-yean-old kids know the Three kingdom. So the story of the Chibi War in Three-kingdom's Era has been popular in the local area.

Paragraph 8

归元禅寺
Guiyuan Buddhist Temple

Guiyuan Temple, situated on Guiwei Street, is one of the four biggest temples for Buddhist meditation in Hubei as well as an important Buddhist temple in China. First built in the early Qing dynasty (1644-1911) by two monks named Baiguang and Zhufeng on the base of Sunflower Garden owned by a poet, the temple got its name form Buddhist chants: "With purity kept in mind, one has the thoroughfare everywhere." Guiyuan Temple has survived through more than 300 hundred years of repeated cycles of prosperity and decline, above all else, it is always leading the other temple in Wuhan with prosperous public worship, flourishing Buddhist ceremony and many pilgrims. The temple was destroyed and rebuilt for several times in its history and the present temple dates from the early Republic of China

(1912-1949). Covering an area of 46 900 square meters with a floor space of 20 000 square meters, the temple mainly consists of Daxiongbaodian Hall, Arhat Hall, Sutra Collection Pavilion, etc. Guiyuan Temple was in fashion for a time although its history was shorter than White Horse Temple, the best Buddhist Temple in China. It is famous not only for spreading Buddhism throughout the whole country, but also for perfect architecture, excellent sculpture and rich collection of Buddhist doctrine among Buddhist temples. In 1956 Guiyuan Temple was listed as preserved antiques unit of Hubei province and in 1983, it was appointed as one of the key Buddhist temple of Han nationality district in China by the State Council.

龟蛇二山的传说

　　武汉长江大桥横卧龟山和蛇山之间,极其雄伟、壮观。作为大桥南北基址的龟山、蛇山还有一段神奇的传说。

　　很久以前,东海龙王手下的龟、蛇二将不和,他们互相瞧不起,都自己夸自己的本事大,经常吵架。有一天,他们俩又吵得不可开交,龟将拿着宝剑,蛇将挺起长矛,打杀起来,搅得龙宫里波浪翻腾,连老龙王的宝座都晃荡起来,还误伤了一些鱼虾水族。老龙王大怒,降下旨来,派了二太子将他俩捆绑起来,到凡间的长江边上,一个镇在汉阳岸边,一个镇在武昌岸边,让他俩在这里思过。从此,它们就化作龟蛇二山,隔江对峙着。

　　他俩虽受到处罚,彼此还是不服,隔着江还互相赌气,看谁化的山长得快。于是龟、蛇二山便日长夜大起来,两座山的山头尽力往江中延伸,都想快点伸过江去把对方咬一口。这一来可坏了事,长江的水道越来越窄,不到半年功夫,已经窄得和汉水差不多了。上游宣泄不畅,许多良田村庄被江水浸没,人们怨声载道。

　　吕洞宾在吕祖阁里一觉醒来,知道了这件事。心想,他俩这样蛮干,那还了得,要让他们头碰住了头,岂不把大江拦腰隔断,上游的万顷田亩岂不尽成泽国!他化成一个采药老人,身背药袋,肩扛银锄,走出吕祖阁,来到蛇山中部,手举银锄,照定蛇腰挖了一锄。蛇将全身一展,腰部的蛇骨被挖

华中
Central China

断了,疼痛难忍,只好赶快缩头,一直缩到武昌岸上,再也不能动弹了。所以蛇山中间,至今还低很多,像断了的样子。

吕洞宾又过江到了汉阳,他请能工巧匠,一夜之间,在龟山头上造了一座"禹王庙",把大禹请来住在庙内,镇住龟将。龟将被压得浑身麻木,慢慢往汉阳岸边缩,刚刚缩到岸边时,再也没有力气缩了,所以至今龟山在江水中留下一个矶头,那就是龟头。

龟、蛇二将让开了水道,长江滚滚,东流千里,再也不受阻碍了。

refined 精炼的;细雅的;细致的	Chinese Sturgeon Hall 中华鲟鱼馆
internal 内部的;内在的	Dongpo Chibi 东坡赤壁
exotic sceneries 胜境	pharmacist 药学家
sitting stature 坐像	fossil 化石
Ancient Music Pavilion 古代音乐亭	Wudang Mountain 武当山
Endless Sky Pavilion 长天楼	Tianzhu Peak 天柱峰
Nine Heroines Monument 九女墩	medicinal herbs 中草药
Sparkling Lake Pavilion 湖光阁	frequent 常去
Guiyuan Buddhist Temple 归元寺	depart 离开,分开
Tortoise Hill 龟山	contour 轮廓
Ancient Copper Mine 古代铜矿	

Unit 3 湖南省 Hunan Province

Key Sentences 流畅精句

1. Hunan's embroidery is one of the four famous in China.
   湖南的湘绣是中国四大名绣之一。
2. Hunan is partly famous for Chairman Mao's birthplace.
   湖南之所以出名还因它是毛主席的故乡。
3. Changsha is also known for its important 2 100-year old Han Excavation.
   长沙还因其出土了2 100年前重要的汉墓而出名。
4. Chairman Mao studied and taught in First Hunan Normal School in 1913-1918 and 1920-1921.
   毛主席1913—1918年在湖南第一师范学院求学，1920—1921年在这里教书。
5. Yueyang is on the south shore of Dongting Lake.
   岳阳在洞庭湖的南岸。
6. Dongting Lake is the largest lake in China.
   洞庭湖是中国最大的湖泊。
7. Zhangjiajie National Forest Park is the first national forest park in China.
   张家界国家森林公园是中国第一个国家森林公园。
8. A Forest Protecting Festival takes place at the end of October annually in Zhangjiajie.
   张家界每年10月末举行森林保护节。
9. Hunan Huagu opera originated from local folk songs and ditties.
   湖南花鼓戏起源于当地民歌和小调。

10. There appeared lots of talents in history in Hunan, such as Mao Zedong, Liu Shaoqi, Cai E, Tan Sitong and Zeng Guofan.

古往今来,三湘四水涌现了不少人才,如毛泽东、刘少奇、蔡锷、谭嗣同、曾国藩等人物。

11. Located on the eastern side of Mt. Yuelu, Yuelu Academy is one of the famous four in China.

岳麓书院位于岳麓山东麓,是我国古代著名的"四大书院"之一。

Wonderful Paragraph
精彩片段

Paragraph 1

Wulingyuan Scenic Area
武陵源风景区

Wulingyuan is located in the northwest corner of Hunan Province, next to Cili County in the east, Yongding District of Zhangjiajie City in the south, and Sangzhi County in the northwest, covering an area of $369 km^2$ with more than 300 scenic spots.

The scenic area is distinguished for the quartzite sandstone peaks rare in the world, and well known for its five wonders of spectacular peaks, grotesque rocks, secluded ravines, graceful waters, and Karst caves. In addition, there are also dense forests, diversified streams and brooks, capricious mists, and plain pastoral landscape, to form the enchanting multi-dimensional scenery.

Wulingyuan is also a treasure house of plants and animals. The vertical distribution of the plants is distinctive with intact flora and balanced ecological system preserving a great number of rare plants and the botanic resources only found in Chian. The vegetation coverage is 88%, with over 3 000 species of higher plants, including woody plants in 107 families, 250 genus, and more then 700 species, and 35 species are inscribed in the Protective List of Rare and Endangered Plant Species in China as the first group un-

der key protection. As for the fauna in the area, there are 116 species of land vertebrates in 50 families, of which 3 species are under Class I state protection, 10 under Class II state protection, and 17 under Class III state protection.

Wulingyuan scenic area is reputed by the visitors as "Fairy World and Terrestrial Heaven", "No. 1 miraculous mountain under the sky", and "an enlarged bonsai and minified fairyland". The area consists of Zhangjiajie National Forest Park, Suoxi Valley Reserve, Emperor Mountain Reserve, and Yangjiajie Scenic Area. Since its accidental discovery in the 1970s, this hidden miracle of nature is now developed into a magnificent, comprehensive, and supreme tour resort peerless nation wide.

Paragraph 2

南岳衡山
The Southern Mountain Mount Hengshan

Also known as Nanyue, Hengshan Mountain, the most famous for its beauty in South China, is one of China's five most distinguished mountains across the country. It range beginning south from Huiyan Peak (Wild Goose Returning 回雁峰) in Hengyang city winds its way north to Yuele Mountain in Changshan City, stretching out 400 kilometres with 72 peaks rising from the horizon, of which five are the most well known such as Zhurong (God of fire 祝融), Tianzhu (天柱), Furong (Hibiscus 芙蓉), Zigai (紫盖) and Shilin (石廪) and with Zhurong (祝融) as its highest peak, 1 290 metres above sea level. It is 45 kilometres away from Hengyang City. In Hengyang Mountain there are many places of historic interest and scenic spots and is also an illustrious sacred place of religion in China. There both the temples of Buddhism and Taoism have long been scattering in the deep forests in the mountain and the two religions co-existed and flourished peacefully ever since, constituting a "miracle" in China's renowned mountains. The steles, stone inscriptions, sculptures are dotted everywhere in the mountain and it has got its reputation for being as mystery area of civilization since Tang (618-907) and Song (960-1279) dynasties. The mountain has been ac-

Central China

credited as one of the five celebrated mountains for its unique characteristic of incorporating into itself the antiquity, grace, serenity of seclusion, risk and wonder to form a marvellous spectacle for sightseeing The Visitor can enjoy himself/herself with different scenery in different seasons as s/he can have a beautiful sight of hundreds of flowers blossoming in spring, a good look of immense clouds floating and winding around the mountain valleys in summer, joyous watch of sunrise in autumn and pleasurably wandering in snow world in winter. It is indeed a very magnificent scenic spot for the tourist for sightseeing, for vocation and for summer resort.

Paragraph 3

岳麓山
Yuelu Mountain

Yuelu Mountain Situated in the west bank of Xiangjiang River, the Yuelu Mountain with an altitude of more than 300 meters, has been famous for secluded environment and beautiful scenery since ancient time. Tourist spots on the mountain are Pavilion of Loving to Evening, Gorge of Refreshing Breeze, Python Cave and Yuelu Academy. The Yuelu Academy, located on the east slopes of the mountain, was first built in 976, or the ninth year of Song Emperor Kaibao's reign, being one of the Four Most Famous Academies of the Song Dynasty. It was transferred to Institute of Higher Learning in 1903, and became the Hunan University in 1926.

Paragraph 4

洞庭湖
Dongting Lake

Dongting Lake, China's second-largest freshwater lake, is located in northeastern Hunan Province. It is a large, shallow body of water surrounded by mountain chains. It is also known as eight-hundred Li Dong Ting Lake (The Li is a Chinese length unit equal to 500 meters or about 1 640 feet). An impressive characteristic of the lake is it is inter-nested. Depending on the season, concentric ridges of land appear in the lake in many areas. This is because the lake acts as a flood basin for the Yangtze River. The appearance of Dongting Lake changes throughout the different seasons, sometimes even during the same day. Many ancient Chinese poems and stories were written about the beauty of Dongting Lake.

The climate of Dongting Lake is between middle and northern subtropical, so it is warm and humid, but there is also a draught window from which cold air from the north sometimes enters. So in spring and summer, the temperature is variable, while in late summer and autumn, it's sunny and hot with a little rain. Occasionally in autumn, it's a little bit cold and windy. The area around the lake has tremendous agricultural production ability with a long history of development. Since the plain is graced with fertile soil, proper temperature and plentiful rain, Dongting Lake is also called a land flowing with milk and honey.

Four streams including the Xiangjiang River, the Zishui River, the Yuanjiang River, and the Lishui River, all flow into Dongting Lake, and the lake is sometimes known as the holder of the four streams. Because Dongting Lake acts as a tremendous natural reservoir or flood-basin, it plays an important role in adjusting the flow of the Yangtze River. The Lake is sometimes known as "the taker and sender of the Yangtze River".

Paragraph 5

岳阳楼
Yueyang Tower

Standing in the western part of Yueyang City, the majestic Yueyang Tower overlooks Dongting Lake and faces Junshan Islet in the distance. Yueyang Tower is one of the three famous towers south of the Changjiang (Yangtze) River, the other two being Huanghe Tower in Wuchang and Tengang Pavilion in Nanchang. The predecessor of Yueyang Tower was a platform on which Lu Su, a general of Wu State (222-280) during the Three Kingdoms period, reviewed the navy in training. The tower was first built in 716. Both Li Bai and Du Fu, master poets of the Tand Dynasty descended it and composed poems there. In 1045 during the Nothern Song Dynasty,

Central China

Yueyang Tower was reconstructed, and Fan Zhongyan, a man of letters, was invited to write Notes on Yue yang Tower. "Being the first to show concern for the people and the last to enjoy comforts", a line from Fan's masterpiece essay, has made Yueyang Tower known through the ages. The tower has undergone many renovations but it maintains its architectural style and appearance. The tower we see today is a three-story wooden structure with four columns, upturned eaves, and a helmet-style top. It is a major historical relic under state protection.

Paragraph 6

F凤凰古城
enghuang Ancient Town

Fenghuang (Phoenix) Ancient Town The town is situated on the western boundary of Hunan Province and in the south of Xiangxi Tujia and Miao Nationalities Autonomous Prefecture. In an area of outstanding natural beauty where mountains, water and blue skies prevail, this ancient town with a history spanning 1 300 years has a number of remarkable old buildings, whose architectural designs date from the Ming and Qing Dynasties.

Paragraph 7

M毛泽东故居
ao Zedong Memorial Hall

The house where Mao Zedong was born and grew up boasts 13 rooms, including three bedrooms, a spare guest room, a rice granary, kitchen, adjoining bathroom, stable area, and sheds for cows, tools, and wood. Just in front of the house is a small pond with lotus flowers where Mao Zedong used to swim as a little boy.

张家界的"四怪"

1. 月亮垭——奇怪的月亮

太阳是红色的,月亮是白色的,这普通常识连三岁小孩都懂。可在武陵源的月亮垭,却能看到红色的月亮,真叫人惊奇不已。月亮垭的红月亮,一般是在春夏季的中旬,发生在久雨初晴的晚上八九点钟的时候。圆圆的月亮,像早晨初升的太阳,血红血红发出黄昏时的光环,把贺龙公园、石家檐、神堂湾一带照得通明如晨曦初照,给那直插云霄而静谧的大峰林染上一层金色。这种现象大约可持续1个多小时。

2. 神堂湾——奇怪的响声

座落在天子山上的神堂湾,自古以来蒙上一层神秘的色彩,其深不可测,神不可言传。它是一个天然的半圆形天坑,面积10余公顷,三面悬崖峭壁,湾内深不见底,神秘莫测;有时霞光万道,瑞气千条;有时又阴风惨惨,雾雨绵绵。更令人惊叹的是,只要你靠近潭边,耳边便隐隐约约响起一片鸣锣击鼓、人喊马嘶的声音,似有千军万马在鏖战……

3. 西海——奇怪的光环

茫茫西海,是一个奇特的石林海洋,石峰数以千计,千姿百态,有的如擎天柱有的如长鞭,有的如神剑,有的如棒槌……,十几个层次的景致,展现出一幅多姿多彩的画幅。在神堂湾与贺龙公园之间的风景地段,一根高约200米的石柱,峰顶叠翠,两个小石峰,中间钳着一块小石头。就这块神奇的石头,就这个奇妙的石峰,每年要发生一次奇迹——发一次光,光亮就像烧电焊那样,火光四射,四射的光芒照亮了神堂湾一带,把整个西海照得有如白昼,其光由小到大,由此及彼,最大的亮度大约持续三四分钟,最后由强变弱,再慢慢地消失。

4. 金鞭溪——奇怪的影子

武陵源金鞭溪那一人成三影的幻景,却是当地人幸福吉祥的佳话。金鞭溪,优雅清澈,像一条洁白的哈达飘动在武陵源,把景区装点得更加富有罗曼谛克的情调。秋天,当游客从水绕四门至张家界森林公园,沿途观赏五步一个景,十步一层天的景致时,溪水哗哗,鸟鸣蝉叫,山花新香,野果串串,如诗如画,好不惬意。当行至5公里许,若遇上秋高气爽晴空万里的好天气,你会惊讶地发现,你的影子由一变二,由二变三,人动影随,影随人至。

Vocabulary
妙词连珠

stone columns 石柱子	Academy 书院
ascend to heaven 升入天堂	calligraphy 书法
shelter 遮蔽	outstanding 杰出的,优秀的
steep 陡峭的;险峻的	adapt 使适合,使适应
slope 倾斜	yuelu Mountain 岳麓山
tinge 染	chairman 主席
Teat Peak Rock 乳峰石	talent 人才
cable car 缆车	birthplace 出生地,故乡
Henghshan Mountain 衡山	mystic 神秘的
Grand Temple of Nanyue 南岳大庙	Huagu opera 花鼓戏
Mawangdui Tomb of Han Dynasty 马王堆汉墓	laud 赞美
	originate 起源于
Mountain Tianzi 天子山	immortal 不朽的,永久的
Suoxi Valley 索溪峪	lush 茂盛的
porcelain factory 瓷厂	Forest Protecting Festival 森林保护节
Xiangjing River 湘江	
Dongting Lake 洞庭湖	

8 华南
South China

Unit 1 Guangdong Province

Key Sentences 流畅精句

1. Lying on the southern side of Lingnan Range and facing the South China Sea, Guangdong is regarded as the southern gateway to Mainland China with Hong Kong and Macao down below.
   广东省位于南岭以南,南海之滨,海岸漫长,毗邻港澳,是祖国的南大门。
2. The Pearl River is a rich lan crisscrossed with hundreds of water channels.
   珠江三角洲,河网纵横,是富饶的农业区。
3. With the longest coastline, there are over 700 islands scattered along the coast, ranking the 3rd in China.
   大陆海岸线漫长,居全国第一,沿海岛屿有700多个,居全国第3位。
4. It was called Baiyue in the Spring and Warring Period, thus Yue for short.
   春秋战国时为百越(粤)地,故简称粤。
5. Guangzhou is divided by the Pearl River.
   珠江横穿广州市。

South China

6. Guangzhou is known as the Goat City.
   广州被称作"羊城"。
7. Shenzhen is the fastest economy-growing city in China.
   深圳是中国经济增长最快的城市。
8. Zhuhai is one of the most pleasant cities in China.
   珠海是中国最令人愉悦的城市之一。
9. Chaozhou is one of the traditional Four Famous Ancient Towns is China.
   潮州是中国传统的四大古镇之一。
10. Foshan is important because of its Ancestral Temple and its handicrafts.
    佛山有名是因为这里的佛山祖庙和手工艺品。
11. Zhongshan Memorial Hall is located at Dongfeng Road, Guangzhou City and at the foot of the southern slope of Guanyin Mountain.
    中山纪念堂位于广州东风路,观音山南麓。

Wonderful Paragraph 精彩片段

Paragraph 1

星湖风景名胜区
Xinghu Scenic Area

Located in Zhaoqing City, Guangdong Province and with a whole thousand years' history in tourism, Xinghu Scenic Area is among the first batch of national key scenic areas. It consists of two parts. One being the Seven-Star Crags Scenic Area which is an integration of the charm of the West Lake in Hangzhou and the beauty of the mountains in Yangshuo, Guilin. The other is the Dinghu Mountain Scenic Area known as an emerald on the Tropic of Cancer. The attraction of Xinghu Scenic Area is its magnificent mountains, lovely waters, outstanding rocks and secluded caves. Although located in the desert zone of the Tropic of Cancer and in the near suburb of a city, Dinghu Mountain Scenic Area houses 1 700 species of higher plants and very precious primeval forests, making it China's first state-level nature reserve. In 1978 it was approved by UNESCO as a world nature reserve and a fixed location for scientific researches of "man and biosphere".

Paragraph 2

M 丹霞山
t. Danxia

54 km northeast away from Shaoguan City and as a sampler of red stone landscape of the world, Mt. Danxia is a national geo-park as well as a world geopark, with its Baofeng Peak 1 408 meters high above sea level. The landscape consists of the layer of red stone and pebbles formed in the Tertiary Period, as red as the rosy clouds.

Paragraph 3

W 白云山
hite Cloud Mountain

The name of the mountain is derived from the white clouds that fly over it and gather around its base. The magnificent scenery and abundance of historical relics have made this a famous scenic spot in Guangzhou since ancient times.

White Cloud Mountain is a park with natural hills and waters, ideal for sightseeing and as a summer resort, with a history of development of over 1 000 years. Locations such as Wind Soughing in the Pines on White Cloud Mountain, Pujian Spring, and Looking Afar in the Evening from White Cloud Mountain, the Returned Monk at Jingtai, the Splendid Mountain of Cloud, etc. are all famous scenic spots in this mountain. Renowned poets and scholars of past dynasties, such as Sushi, Yang Wanli, Wang Shizhen and others once came here and recorded their experiences in poetry and prose for posterity.

Paragraph 4

世界之窗
Window of the World

Window of the World is located in the west of Shenzhen Bay Holiday Resort and adjacent to Splendid Land of China and Village of Chinese Folk Customs. An imitation Golden Gate Bridge of San Francisco, USA at the entrance leads to the Asian District where one sees Angkor War of Cambodia—one of the four wonders of the East, Borobudur of Indonesia, Taj Mahal of India and Katsura Rikyu of Japan. Passing among rivers and lakes of Southeast Asia, one comes to the Sydney Opera House and the abodes of the Maori people of Oceania. On the axis of the Resort are the Eiffel Tower, the Arch of Truimph, fountains of the four continents and St. Michel's Convent. European architecture and sceneries line both sides of a garden carpeted with lawns and flowers. The African District is represented by a stretch of desert, ancient culture and primeval tribe life. The American District starts with the Grand Canyon and the Waterfall and followed by modern civilization represented by Mount Rushmore and Manhanttan in New York and finally returns to the mystery of Easter Island, and Nazca Lines. The ingeniously constructed scenic spots in Window of the World are fascinating. Even more so are the performances showing the customs of peoples in the world. At nightfall, the 200-meter-long Wall of Relief Sculptures lit up by fireworks highlights the jubilation of the jolly parade on the square, displaying to the full the main theme of the Resort

"the world rejoices with you".

"Give me a day, and I'll give you a world of wonders."

Paragraph 5

民俗文化村
China Folk Culture Villages

Situated by the picturesque Shenzhen Bay and adjacent to "Splendid China", the village is a museum of China's 55 ethnic groups with their distinctive architecture, customs and exotic flavor. Twenty-four life-size ethnic villages present various ethnic flavors from Beijing's courtyards and wooden archway to spectacular buildings of the Miao, Dong, Yao, Jingpo ethnic groups. From the wooded Banyans in Xishuangbanna to slender Suzhou bridges and mystery Lijiang houses, you can get a general idea about China's ethnic groups in just half a day.

Spectacular rocks and gushing waterfalls enhance the scenery. Visitors can participate in ethnic festive carnivals, observe the grandiose parade and taste ethnic delicacies as well.

Paragraph 6

Y越秀公园
uexiu Park

Yuexiu Park is the largest park in downtown Guangzhou. Covering an area of 860 000 square meters (212.5 acres), the park is made up of three artificial lakes and seven hills of Yuexiu Mountain; hence the name Yuexiu Park.

Yuexiu Park is a perfect combination of cultural relics and ecological tourism, reputed for its pretty water and hills as well as cultural relics. The main places of interest include the stone sculpture of the Five Rams, Zhenhai Tower, the site of the Ming Dynasty City Wall, and Square Cannon Site.

Paragraph 7

S孙中山纪念堂
un Yat-sen Memorial Hall

The Sun Yat-sen Memorial Hall, situated in the original site of Sun Yat-sen's Presidential Office on the southern slope of Yuexiu Hill, is a memorial building built in 1931 with the funds raised by the Guangzhou people and overseas Chinese in memory of Sun Yat-sen, the pioneer of China's bourgeois democratic revolution.

Sun Yat-sen, born on November 12, 1866 at Cuiheng Village of Guangdong province, was a leading figure in China's revolution against the

Qing government and the first President of the Republic. In August 1905, he formulated the Three Principles of the People—nationalism, democracy, and social well-being—which he believed were the guidelines for building a modern China, and as he had proposed, he truly contributed his whole life into the great task.

Completed in October 1983, the memorial hall, occupying an area of 12 000 square meters with a height of 46 meters, has magnificent exterior and elegant interior decorations. The whole building, octagonal in shape, is of a typical Chinese architectural style. The designer skillfully applied the structural theory of architectural mechanics taking full advantage of the benefits of reinforced concrete. He thus created a pillar less space with the span of up to 71 meters, its grandeur resembling a huge umbrella when seen from afar.

Above the entrance of the door, there is a plaque that bears in gold the words "Sun Yat-sen Memorial Hall" inscribed by Liao Chengzhi, the vice chairman of the standing Committee of the National People's Congress. At the central up-layer wall of the small hall hangs another plaque with the words "The Whole World as a Community" which was inscribed by Sun Yat-sen himself.

In 1956, a 5-meter-high bronze statue of Dr Sun was erected in front of the hall.

Sun Yat-sen Memorial Hall is the most symbolic building of Guangzhou, and a key venue for the city's large-scale meetings and performances.

Paragraph 8

W西汉南越王墓博物馆
estern Han Nanyue King's Tomb Museum

Located on Jiefang Bei Road, Guangzhou, the Western Han Dynasty Nanyue King Mausoleum Museum is the oldest and largest Han tomb with the most funerary objects in Lingnan (South of the Nanling Mountain) Area. As one of the 80 famous museums in the world, the museum covers

14 000 square meters (150 699.6 square feet) with 10 exhibition halls.

The owner of the tomb is the second king, Zhao Mei of Nanyue State of the Western Han Dynasty (206 B.C.-24 A.D.). Hidden 20 meters (65.6 feet) underground, the tomb is made up of 750 huge stones with colorful murals. The over 1 000 pieces of cultural relics, bronze ware and terra cotta ware in particular, feature the Yue Culture of south China (Nanyue Culture). Represented also are traces of central Chinese culture, the Chu culture of south China, the Bashu culture of southwest China, the Hun culture from the northern grassland, and even foreign cultures.

Highlighting the mausoleum is a silk-jade garment made up of 2 291 pieces of jade. Though jade garments with pieces connected by gold, silver, or copper are not uncommon, this garment with jade pieces connected by silk is the only one of its kind in the world. Nor are historical records available to verify other jade garments connected by silk thread. In addition, the style of buttons down the front is unique among unearthed jade garments. This silk-sewn-jade garment shows the early development of jade garments as well as development of the Nanyue culture.

In addition, three sets of bronze serial bells, thirty-six bronze vessels, thirty-six bronze mirrors, and three gold seals give visitors a glimpse of the ancient Nanyue Culture. The oldest and largest folding screen used in China is also here, as are two of the world's oldest bronze patterns for textile stamping.

Foreign articles excavated in the mausoleum indicate that Guangzhou was an ancient Marine Silk Road starting point. For example, there are five African elephant trunks, a silver box featuring Western Asian silver wares, and bronze incense burners and frankincense from Southeast Asia.

华南
South China

粤菜的起源

粤菜的起源，可远溯至距今二千多年的汉初。古代，中原的移民到来之前，岭南越族先民就已有独特的饮食风格，如嗜好虫蛇鱼蛤与生食。西汉时刘安曾有"越人得蟒蛇以为上肴"的记述。宋代周去非的《岭外代答》也记载广州人"不问鸟兽虫蛇无不食之"。这与广州所处的地理环境分不开。广州属于亚热带水网地带，虫蛇鱼蛤特别丰富，唾手可得，烹而食之，由此养成的喜好鲜活、生猛的饮食习惯。

自秦汉开始，中原汉人不断南迁进入广州。他们不但带来了先进的生产技术和文化知识，同时也带来了"烩不厌细，食不厌精"的中原饮食风格。到了唐宋时期，中原各地大量商人进入广州，广州的烹调技艺迅速得到提高，到了明清，广州的饮食文化进入了高峰。据清道光二年（1822年）的有关文献记载："广州西关肉林酒海，无寒暑，无昼夜。"

进入20世纪二三十年代，广州食俗，南北兼容，中西并蓄，极富特色的美食、小吃，大批大批地涌现出来。漫长的岁月，使广州既继承了中原饮食文化的传统，又博采外来及各方面的烹饪精华，再根据本地的口味、嗜好、习惯，不断吸收、积累、改良、创新，从而形成了菜式繁多、烹调艺巧、质优味美的饮食特色。近百年来已成为国内最具代表性和最有世界影响的饮食文化之一。这无论是按三大菜系，即黄河流域的"鲁菜"，长江流域的"川菜"、"苏菜"和"沪菜"，以及珠江流域的"粤菜"，还是按四大菜系（即鲁、川、苏、粤四大菜系），或者是八大菜系（即鲁、川、苏、粤、闽、浙、湘、徽八大菜系），粤菜都占有极其重要的地位。

Tianhe Sports Center 天河体育中心	Peasants' Movement Institute 农讲所
Mausoleum of Uprising 烈士陵园	The front of People's Park 公园前

用英语说中国——旅游亮点
Introduce China in English—Scenic Spots

West Gate 西门口
Chen Clan Academy 陈家祠
Railway Station 火车站
Yuexiu Park 越秀公园
Memorial Hall 纪念堂
Haizhu Square 海珠广场
Sun Yet-Sen University 中山大学
New Pearl River City 珠江新城
seep 渗透
crevice 缝隙
erosion 侵蚀
batch 一批
charm 魔力,魅力
stalagmite 石笋
Xinghu Scenic Area 星湖风景名胜区
the Dinghu Mountain Scenic Area 鼎湖山景区
under-ground worlds 洞中世界
heavenly residences 神仙府第
the earth crust 地壳

Unit 2　广西壮族自治区
Guangxi Zhuang Autonomous Region

 Key Sentences 流畅精句

1. As the Southwest China's main artery to the sea, Guangxi lies on the Beibu Bay in South China, bordering Viet Nam.
   广西壮族自治区地处我国南疆北部湾畔,西南面与越南接壤,是大西南的出海通道。
2. Lijiang Scenic Spot is the largest and most beautiful of all the karst scenic spots in the world.
   漓江风景区是世界上规模最大、风景最美的岩溶山水游览区。
3. Guangxi has a humid subtropical monsoon climate.
   广西属亚热带湿润季气候。
4. The Tropic of Cancer runs across Guangxi's central part.
   北回归线横贯广西中部。
5. In 1958, Guangxi Zhuang Autonomous Region was set up.
   1958 年,广西壮族自治区成立。
6. People in Guangxi enjoy a rich variety of cultural activities.
   广西人民的文化生活丰富多彩。
7. Guilin is also famous for its meandering Lijiang River and Peach Blossom River.
   桂林还以蜿蜒的漓江和桃花江闻名遐迩。
8. Guilin's scenes are the finest under Heaven, but Yangshuo's are still better.
   桂林山水甲天下,阳朔山水甲桂林。
9. Guilin has the finest mountains and rivers under heaven.
   桂林山水甲天下。

10. The Li River is limpid with crystal water.
漓江明洁如镜，清澈见底。

Wonderful Paragraph
精彩片段

Paragraph 1

Scenery of Guilin
桂林山水

Guilin situated in the northeastern part of Guangxi, Guilin proper covers an area of over 500 square kilometers. The world-renowned scenic city is one of the national famous historical and cultural city and excellent tourist city in China. A distinctive karst landmass is the reason behind Guilin's fabulous landscape that is characterized by green mountains, sparkling waters, strange caves and statuesque monoliths. Famous scenic areas in Guilin are Lijiang River, Elephant-Trunk Hill, Folded Brocade Hill, Whirlpool Hill, Reed Flute Cave and Seven-Star Cave.

Paragraph 2

Seven Star Park
七星公园

East of the Li River, Seven Star Park derives from the Seven Star Cave, is one kilometer away from the downtown. It occupies more than 40 hectares, which is the largest, most beautiful multiple park in Guilin. The park boasts of the green hills, crystal water, fantastic caves and beautiful rocks. The ancient Floral Bridge straddles at the southern entrance. Hidden-dragon Cave near the southern gate houses the Forest of Stone Inscriptions. To the east of Seven-Star Hill stands the Camel Hill, at the foot of which the US president Bill Clinton once made a public speech on environmental protection in 1998. Besides, the Seven-Star Cave, the zoo and potted landscape Garden are worthy of being seen.

Paragraph 3

H 琥珀山
upo Shan

Standing magnificently on the side of the river, this hill is so called because it serves to stem the torrents coming down the surrounding higher ground in summer, thus forming whirlpools. At its foot is Huan Zhu Dong (Returned Pearl Cave).

Paragraph 4

L 芦笛岩
udi Yan

Described as "Art Palace of Nature", the stalagmite and stone flowers of grotesque shapes in the caves create breathtaking spectacles which are really a feast for the eyes. Half way up the Brightness Hill, Reed Flute Cave is seven kilometers northwest of the center of Guilin. There used to be a special kind of reed growing outside of the cave which was an ideal material for making flute. Inside the U-shaped Karst cave are a large number of stalactites, stalagmites, stone pillars, stone curtains, and stone flowers, all glistening in colorful lights. In a distance of 500 meter between the entrance and the exit, there are more than 30 interesting sights, including " Pine in the Snow", "Mushroom Hill", "Virgin Forest"... The Reed Flute Cave is justifiably called the "Art Palace of Nature".

Paragraph 5

E 象鼻山
lephant Trunk Hill(Xiangbishan)

Elephant Trunk Hill is located on the western bank of Li River Scenery. The shape of the hill is just like a huge elephant drinking water from the river with its trunk, so it is called Elephant Trunk Hill.

Shui Yue Cave (Water Moon Cave) is between the trunk and the legs, which is a semi-round cave penetrated by water. The inverted reflection of the cave in water plus the part above forms a full moon. This phenomenon is unique and many laudatory inscriptions were found on the wall inside the cave. Visitors can boat through the cave to the river.

Another cave regarded as the eyes of the elephant lies in the hillside. It provides tourists an ideal position to enjoy the panoramic view of Guilin. On the top of the hill is a two-storey pagoda built in the Ming Dynasty (1368-1644) surrounded by green trees. The north seat of the second floor is inlaid with an image of Bodhisattva Puxian. The pagoda looks like a precious vase on the back of an elephant seen from distance and many beautiful legends about the pagoda with good wishes are said among people.

As the symbol of Guilin, Elephant Trunk Hill is the main scenic spot of the Elephant Trunk Hill Park, which also includes Yunfeng Monastery (a building with ancient style), Aiqing Dao (Love Island) and so on.

Paragraph 6

Y 阳朔风光
angshuo Scenery

Yangshuo, 65 kilometres southeast Guilin, is a county (population 300 000) directly under its jurisdiction. It is located in the upper reaches of Gui River and Li River runs through it. The county sits on a typical karst topography where there are green mountains and jade-like streams everywhere. The scenery along the Li River is superb, and a traveller of the Ming Dynasty Xu Xiake (1586-1641) described it as "the land of green lotus and jade-colour bamboo shoots (碧莲玉笋世界)." Yangshuo boosts four major scenic areas with over 20 scenic spots, each with its own peculiarity. Furthermore, the landscape changes colour and looks as the season and the day change, and gives different tastes in different weather. Of interest to visitors are Green Lotus Peak, Yangshuo Park, Mount Painting, and Mount Moon. There is a very popular saying: "Guilin's scenes are the finest under Heaven, but Yangshuo's are still better." It is a very popular travellers' destination in its own right and certainly a good place to live and work, with a diversity of opportunity. The town draws millions of visitors from both home and abroad. Undeniably, to live in Yangshuo is to be a lover of mountains. Which is not to say that all the people of Yangshuo spend their leisure hours gallivanting among the forests of the high country.

Paragraph 7

北海银滩
Beihai Silver Beach

Silver Beach on the southern coast of the city extends for 24 kilometers. It is a nature land bathing location and it's famous for its "long and smooth beach, white and fine sand, lukewarm and clean water, mild and gentle waves". It's known as National Holiday Resort and selected as The Key Scenic Spot of China in 1992. Facilities of traffic, communications, water and electricity, hotels, restaurants, entertainment are all provided conveniently in the holiday resort. Every year, millions of tourists are attracted here and it has became a newly risen idle place for holiday in the south of China.

Paragraph 8

德天瀑布
Detian Great Waterfall

Detian Great Waterfall Located in Daxin county of Nanning City in Guangxi, Detian Waterfall along the Sino-Vietnamese border is the second largest transnational waterfall in the world. The grand three-tier waterfall is about 200 meters wide during the flood season, making a deafening sound, which could be heard several kilometers away.

Paragraph 9

灵渠
The Ling Canal

The 34-kilometre-long Ling Canal was built in the period 219-214 BC. It is today's most complete ancient water conservancy project in the world still in existence. It was scientifically designed and exquisitely built, linking the two water systems of Yangtze and Pearl rivers, and has become the communication hub between the Central Plain and Linnan since the Qin Dynasty (221-206 BC). In recent years, Xing'an County (兴安县) of Guangxi Zhuang Autonomous Region invested 30 million yuan (US $ 2.6 million) for the environmental protection and tourism development. It has become a new tourist attraction for Guilin scenic area.

The four ancient water conservancy projects in China are the Ling Canal in Guilin, Guangxi Zhuang Autonomous Region (广西桂林灵渠), Dujiaugyan Irrigation Project in Chengdu, Sichuan Province (四川成都都江堰), the Grand Canal from Beijing to Hangzhou (京杭大运河) and the karez (坎儿井), an irrigation system of wells connected by underground channels used in Xinjiang Uygur Autonomous Region.

Cultural Links
文化链接

漓江九十九道弯

从桂林乘船到阳朔,百里漓江流水回环,弯多滩险。这和龙王的三公主还有关系呢!当初,三公主想帮助修筑万里长城的民夫,她从南海搬来石头,不料,经过桂林时被一位老公公道破,变成飞禽走兽的石头又变回石山,把一条好端端的漓江堵死了。

俗话讲,高山有清泉,江边有良田。相传桂林到阳朔原是一片平坦的田地。中间有一条六六三十六丈宽的大河。自从三公主赶来石头变成大石山把江河填满后,在这一带种田耕地就像在石板上面种花一样难了。有一年大旱了七七四十九天,山塘的水干了,田里裂开的缝放得下瓦钵,地里种的包谷、高粱干得伸手可以捏成粉末。人们唉声叹气,可又毫无办法。

有一天,大家坐在一棵大榕树下闲谈,有个白发老爷爷说:"诚心感天动地,我们明天破香柏树来作香,诚心诚意求天降雨吧。"但是,到哪里才能找到香柏树呢?白发老爷爷拿起斧头,一连走了七十二座大山,爬了八十一个悬崖,在一个峭壁上砍回了一棵杯口粗的香柏树。回来一烧,百里之内都香喷喷的。

这时,一股香气袅袅上升,飘到三十六天玉皇大帝的宫殿,他马上叫太白金星到南天门外察看。太白金星到南天门外转了一圈,马上回来告诉玉皇大帝,把前因后果说了一遍。玉皇大帝听说河流被石头堵死,就传来金龟将军,给它一支令箭说道:"你快去凡间扒开石山堵塞的江河,要扒得宽一些。"金龟将军急急忙忙跑到石山堵塞的漓江,舞动他的四只大脚,左一脚,右一掌,使劲扒起来。谁知这金龟将军平时倚老卖老,办事不认真,又有点老眼昏花,玉皇大帝原来叫它把河道扒宽一些,他误听成是叫它扒"弯"一些。所以,他把漓江扒得七弯八扭,从桂林到阳朔这一百六十多公里水路,就扒出九十九道弯,六十四条滩。

河道一扒开,水一流通,旱情就解除了。金龟将军高高兴兴地回到天廷交旨。玉皇大帝知道金龟将军违背了圣旨,就下令将它斩首。太白金星连忙启奏道:"金龟将军虽然把河道扒弯了,但总算扒开了河道,解除了百姓的痛苦,可以将功补过。"玉皇大帝这才免了金龟将军的死罪。罚他下界变成石龟爬山。

现在,我们乘船游漓江,船行到鸡笼淀一头,在左岸可以看到好像有一个石龟在爬山,那就是听错了玉皇大帝圣旨的金龟将军。

Vocabulary 妙词连珠

flow through 流经	Pearl-Returning Cave 还珠洞
divide into 分为,分开	the Wall of Thousand Buddhas 千佛岩
belong to 属于	
Elephant Trunk Hill 象鼻山	Pierced Hill 穿山
the Peach Blossom River 桃花江	Sky Light Hole 空月洞
Folded Brocade Hill 叠彩山	Moon Crag 月岩
Wind-Tunnel Hill 风洞山	South Stream Hill 南溪山
Osmanthus Hill 桂山	Dragon and Elephant Tower 龙象塔
Wind Tunnel 风洞	Yiling Stalactite Cavern 伊岭岩
Bright Moon Peak 明月峰	Very Bright Mountain 大明山
Seven-Star Hill 七星岩	Cliff of Thousand Buddhas 千佛岩
Wave-Subduing Hill 伏波山	Whirlpool Hill 伏波山

用英语说中国——旅游亮点
Introduce China in English—Scenic Spots

Pearl Returning Cave 还珠洞
West Hill of Guiping 桂平西山
Drum Festival 拉鼓节
Sowing Festival 芒歌节
Seedling Festival 新禾节
Horse-fighting Festival 斗马节
Reed-pipe Wind Instrument Festival 芦笙节
Zhuang brocade 壮锦

Unit 3 海南省 Hainan Province

Key Sentences
流畅精句

1. Hainan Province consists of the second largest island in China, Xisha Islands, Nansha Islands with reefs and sea territory around.
   海南省行政区域包括我国第二大岛——海南岛和西沙群岛、中沙群岛、南沙群岛的岛礁及其海域。
2. Zengmu Shoals is the furthest land of China.
   曾母暗沙是我国最南端的领土。
3. Hainan is the smallest province in China.
   海南是中国最小的省。
4. Hainan is 30km off China's southern coast.
   海南距离中国南海岸 30 公里。
5. The government has targeted Sanya and Yalong Bay as major resorts areas.
   政府的目标是把三亚和亚龙湾发展成重要的度假区。
6. Hainan Island produces tea, coffee, rubber, fish, sugar, coconut and rie.
   海南岛出产茶、咖啡、橡胶、鱼、糖、可可和水稻。
7. Sanya has 16 seaports 10 islands and 180km of coastline.
   三亚有 16 个港口,10 个海岛和 180 公里的海岸线。
8. Haikou is the capital of Hainan, wonderful in winter.
   海口是海南的省会,是个过冬的好去处。
9. Sanya is at the southern tip of Hainan Island. it's a famous coast resort.
   三亚在海南岛的最南端。那是一个著名的海滨度假地。

用英语说中国——旅游亮点
Introduce China in English—Scenic Spots

Wonderful Paragraph
精彩片段

Paragraph 1

A亚龙湾
sian Dragon Bay (Yalong wan)

Asian Dragon Bay (Yalong wan) is arguably Hainan's best beach and definitely the most pristine. Seven km of white sand stretch along beautifully clean blue water here, backed by palm trees and lush green hills. The beach sits roughly on the same latitude as Hawaii and enjoys similar temperatures and weather conditions. The water here is wonderfully clear, reflecting the blue sky and white sand beneath the depths. Snorkeling and scuba diving are popular pursuits here given the clear water, bright-colored coral reefs and tropical fish that abound and this is arguably the nicest place to swim on the entire island. This is a new resort and development is underway in a very tasteful manner. This is a protected marine reserve and commercial fishing is forbidden here, keeping the water very clean and lovely for swimming.

Paragraph 2

T天涯海角
ianya Haijiao

Located at the foot of Xiama Hill in the town of Tianya, 24 km west of Sanya, Tianya Haijiao with its irresistible witchery, in recent years, attracts countless tourists all over the world. There are numerous rocks, with different size and shape, scatter along the silvery beach. Among them, these two, which are respectively engraved with Chinese characters "Tianya Haijiao" (end of the earth and corner of the sea) and "Nantian Yizhu" (the huge rock that emerges from the sea, making a "corner") are most famous. According to legend, two lovers form two hostile clans once escape here. They swore that they would never separate no matter where they

traveled and what happened. Constantly pursued by troops from both clans, they were forced to leap into the sea from this spot. People believe that this couple later changed to two huge rocks, which stand facing the sea. Moved by the loyal love between the two lovers, today, many couples come here to declare their love and promise that they would go to the "end of the earth" for one another.

Paragraph 3

五指山
Five Fingers Mountain

Five Fingers Mountain, known as the highest mountain in Hainan Province, is the symbol of Hainan and one of the famous mountains in China. It lies horizontally in the southwest part of Qiongzhong County. Thanks to prolonge natural erosion, its saw-like ridges rise high and low, hence the name Five Fingers Mountain. The second finger of the Wuzhi is the highest, with an elevation of 1 867 metres, 343 metres higher than the number one of the five mountains in China—Mount Tai. The third, fourth, and fifth fingers are connected each stands independently, forming an extraordinary scene. Walking into the primitive forest, the tourist finds the canopy shelter the sun, gigantic trees point sharply to the sky, steep slopes and vertical cliffs, which can make the tourist's heart throb with excitement. Looking from the top of the Five Fingers Mountain, the tourist feels that the cloud sea arises from bellow, just like having a space walk.

In a sunny day with a blue sky, the tourist can have a wonderful view of the Hainan Sea and the tiny little islands from this vantage point. In the early morning, the tourist can watch the sunrise with radiating rays of golden light; in the evening, the tourist can enjoy the sunset, as the sky and sea turn all red. There are a large quantity or precious animals, birds, and vegetation in the forest. Therefore this is an ideal place for vocation, adventure and scientific studies.

用英语说中国——旅游亮点
Introduce China in English—Scenic Spots

Paragraph 4

Sanya 三亚

Called the Hawaii of Asia, Sanya is a popular tourist destination located in the southern tip of the Chinese tropical island of Hainan. Located in Sanya, the Yalong Bay and the neighbouring Sanya Bay and Da Dong Hai Resort are regarded as the best beach in China. Enjoying the same latitude and similar weather conditions as Hawaii, the Sanya Beach in recent years has been the main attraction. The water is clear, reflecting the blue sky and white clouds in it. Playing in the water with the tropical fish swimming around, swimmers can fully relax themselves. In order to protect the marine resource and environment, commercial fishing is forbidden here. With a long coastline and a tropical temperature throughout the year, this is a perfect resort to relax - and enjoy the sun, sea, sand, coconut trees, diving etc. Yalong Bay Sea Shell Museum, covering an area of over 3 000 square meters, is located at Central Square of Yalong Bay National Resort. It is the first comprehensive sea shell museum in China, merging the shellfish and shell product display into an integral whole.

Paragraph 5

Luhuitou 鹿回头

Luhuitou Hill lies 5 kilometers south of Sanya city, on the side of Sanya Bay, with a deer-shaped peak extending to the sea. The hill leans against the sea in its three sides and is green all over the year. It is said that once upon a time, a young hunter of the Li nationality from Wuzhishan range (Five Fingers Mountain Range), after tramping over several hills and dales, chased a deer to the cliff by the seaside. The deer looked back and became a beautiful young girl of the Li nationality. Then they got married and lived a life of "men plough the fields and women weave" there. For multiplying generation by generation, a village of the Li nationality came into be-

ing. Since that time, the place has got its name of Luhuitou Byland. Now, Luhuitou Hill serves as a park, with a 12-meter- high deer statue stands on its top to reappear the myth. Occupying the top of the hill, you can easily have a bird's eye viewing of the beautiful landscape of Sanya city, especially at night.

海南椰雕

　　海南椰雕产生于唐代,是流行于海南岛的手工艺品,将椰壳雕刻日用品,如茶壶、套盒等。古代,人们用椰壳做成简单的容器。到了明清时期,其工艺日渐精细,有了装饰线条、浮雕、镶嵌、做片与彩画。这些艺术品可以用作装饰,椰壳片可以拼成各种艺术品。最出彩的是镶嵌银、锡或是铜,这些都曾是对清朝皇室的"海南贡品"。

encompass 围绕,包含	黄道婆遗址
sheer 全然的	Horse Saddle Ridge 马鞍岭
grotesque 奇形怪状的	Dong Po Study 东坡书院
square kilometers 平方公里	The Deer Looks Back 鹿回头
famous mountain on the sea 海上名山	Qiong Tai College 琼台书院
span 跨距,全长	Big East Sea 大东海
extend 延伸	Nanli Lake 南丽湖
loftiness 高;高尚;崇高;高傲	White Horse Well 白马井
abruptly 突然地,唐突地	Seven Fingers Ridge 七指岭
crest 冠;山顶	Underwater World 水下世界
Five Fingers Mountain 五指山	Heaven's Limit & Sea's Margin Scenic Spot 天涯海角风景区
Coconut forest 清澜椰林	
Remains of Mother Huang Dao	

9 港澳台地区
Hong Kong, Macao and Taiwan Province

Unit 1 香港特别行政区 Hong Kong SAR

Key Sentences 流畅精句

1. On July 1 of 1997 they withdrew from the island. The Chinese government resumed the exercise of the territorial sovereignty of Hong Kong. Hong Kong SAR was founded.

   1997年7月1日,中国政府对香港恢复行使主权,香港特别行政区正式成立。

2. The New Territories is located in the northern of Kowloon, connected with the Mainland.

   新界位于九龙半岛以北,与祖国大陆相连。

3. Hong Kong only has an area of 1 095 square kilometers.

   香港仅有1 095平方公里。

4. Hong Kong has three areas: Hong Kong Island, Kowloon, and New Territories.

   香港可以划为三部分:香港岛、九龙和新界。

5. Hong Kong adopted bauhinia as its emblem.

   香港以紫荆花为象征。

港澳台地区
Hong Kong, Macao and Taiwan Province

6. Both English and Chinese are official languages in Hong Kong.
   英语和汉语都是香港的官方语言。
7. Hong Kong is a shopping paradise, dietary world, leisure summer resort, and culture window.
   香港是购物天堂、饮食世界、休闲胜地和文化之窗。
8. Today Hong Kong's population is 6.5 million.
   如今香港人口为650万。
9. Hong Kong possesses the highest bronze statue of Buddha in the open air in the world.
   香港有世界上最高的露天铜佛。
10. The Chinese mainland is the biggest market for Hong Kong's imports and exports.
    中国内地是香港最大的进口和出口市场。
11. Hong Kong maintains one of the highest economic growth rates in the world.
    香港是世界上经济增长速度最快的地区之一。
12. Tourism has been a pillar of Hong Kong's economy for decades.
    数十年来,旅游业一直是香港经济的支柱。

Wonderful Paragraph 精彩片段

Paragraph 1

Victoria Peak 太平山

High above Hong Kong Island on the back of the Dragon, Victoria Peak is Hong Kong's premier visitor attraction, providing magnificent harbour and city views. Arriving late afternoon enables you to experience the dazzling panorama of Hong Kong Island, the harbour, Kowloon and the hills beyond. Later, you can thrill to the neon-dotted skyline by night. What's more, The Peak offers visitors a multitude of fantastic entertainment, dining

and shopping options.

Paragraph 2

凌霄阁 Peak Tower

The Peak Tram pulls into the Peak Tower, the icon of Hong Kong, on its last stop. Peak Tower sits at an elevation of over 396 meters (about 1299 feet) with a commanding view of the spectacular Victoria Harbor, Kowloon and the New Territories. Commissioned in 1993 and completed in May of 1997, the tower is a center of catering and amusement. The most spectacular attraction is the wonder hall, which is called "Believe it or not". It is the unique chain museum in the world, constructed by Robert L. Ripley in 1930. Inside the hall you see exhibits portraying the adventurous events experienced by Ripley. There are primitive forest, beauty taking sun bath, frenzied car, turning tunnel, shark aquarium, ultimate cruel torture, marvelous spectacles of human race and animals, complete works of tongue twister and mass media fun station etc.

Paragraph 3

浅水湾 Repulse Bay

Repulse Bay, located south of Stanley, is famous for its long, broad beach, its clean water, fresh sand, calm tide and gentle waves, and its popularity with locals and visitors, especially in summer. It is the most representative bay in Hong Kong, and it was named after a pirate ship that used to sail here in the 19th century.

With its lush green, sub-tropical backdrop and breathtaking views over sandy beaches, the area is an ideal place for a romantic dinner under the stars. Several open-air restaurants nearby specialize in the joys of wholesome barbecued food, including the freshest prawns, squid, fish and other seafood delicacies. All are cheery hives of activity every night of the week.

Repulse Bay also offers a good selection of shopping and entertain-